MANAGEMENT GUIDE
TO
COMPUTER SYSTEM SELECTION
AND USE

PRENTICE-HALL INTERNATIONAL, INC., *London*
PRENTICE-HALL OF AUSTRALIA, PTY. LTD., *Sydney*
PRENTICE-HALL OF CANADA, LTD., *Toronto*
PRENTICE-HALL OF INDIA PRIVATE LTD., *New Delhi*
PRENTICE-HALL OF JAPAN, INC., *Tokyo*

MANAGEMENT GUIDE

TO

COMPUTER SYSTEM SELECTION

AND USE

Jerome Kanter

DIRECTOR, PRODUCT MARKETING
HONEYWELL ELECTRONIC DATA PROCESSING
AND
LECTURER, NORTHEASTERN UNIVERSITY

Prentice-Hall, Inc., Englewood Cliffs, N.J.

© 1970 by Prentice-Hall, Inc.
Englewood Cliffs, N.J.

Current printing (last digit):

10 9 8 7 6 5 4 3 2 1

13-548537-1

Library of Congress Catalog Card Number 75-115129

Printed in the United States of America

To my mother with love and appreciation

PREFACE

The computer holds significant potential in almost every area of business and science. Engineers and scientists have fashioned a device that can gather, analyze, and disseminate data faster and more accurately than any other device so far produced. The computer has processing speeds of several million calculations per second. As with every technological development, the key to harnessing the potential can be expressed in a single word—management. Business managers with the wisdom and vision to understand today's business needs and requirements as well as tomorrow's must see how the computer can play a part in satisfying these needs.

The computer has been on the commercial scene about 20 years, and businessmen are becoming aware of its characteristics and capabilities. This book does not attempt to explain the basics of computers to managers—it is assumed that the manager has an over-all grasp and appreciation of what computers can do and the general types of tasks that they are capable of performing. Instead, it focuses on the role management must play throughout the entire computer selection cycle—beginning with the feasibility study, proceeding through the selection of the computer task force, the analysis of business problems, the study of a company's information flow, and the detailed systems study, and ending with the computer implementation plan. The book emphasizes that marrying a computer to a business operation begins with a thorough study of business operations, not with the computer. It develops a logical systems approach to gathering and analyzing the data necessary to reach a decision to acquire or not to acquire. Emphasis will be continually on management's role in this process.

The book is geared to the manager who: (1) is pondering the question of whether to install a computer or even to look into the matter, (2) wants a realistic look at the benefits and advantages of electronic data processing measured against the investment and commitment necessary to realize these benefits, and (3) is not directly responsible for Electronic Data Processing (EDP) but wants to understand the criteria for effective computer utilization and how he can prepare himself to partake more fully in the benefits afforded by modern computers. The book is also intended for educational institutions or training groups studying the management use of computers and the means to more properly plan and control the entry of the computer into business organizations.

The book is not a primer on what a computer is and how it is programmed. It focuses on management considerations in determining the feasibility, economics, and practicality of installing a computer. It proceeds from there to outline an approach to establishing priorities for computer application dependent on payoff considerations, to develop a plan for the systems study and systems design phases, and to explore methods of assessing the human resources and organizational environment necessary for successful introduction of EDP.

This book is written by a business manager who later entered the EDP field. The treatment is therefore from the viewpoint of a businessman looking at computers rather than from the viewpoint of a computer man looking at business. The book is written in the basic language of business rather than in the specialized language of computers. Thus, it is hoped the book makes a stand at attacking the imposing semantic barrier that exists between man and machine.

The treatment is practical and result-oriented. Frequent use is made of case studies and actual experiences of the author. Value judgments and opinions are made that may surprise and provoke, but lack of them, the author feels, would make for bland and unrewarding reading. The criteria for computer success will not be the degree of sophistication of a computer system, the esoteric appeal of the approach, what other companies are doing, or what has historically been the rule; rather the criteria will be how a computer can work for the businessman and the manager in improving performance and profitability.

A case study gives the thread of continuity throughout the book and serves as a frame of reference. The study is a composite of actual experiences and serves to keep the book at the practical level. Each chapter opens and closes with excerpts from the case study that are pertinent to the contents of the particular chapter.

I wish to make the following grateful acknowledgements:

To CLARENCE W. SPANGLE and members of management of the Honeywell Electronic Data Processing Division for their support and encouragement in undertaking this, my second effort.

To CHARLES C. CHRONIS of Honeywell for assistance in the development and validation of material in conjunction with computer courses we have jointly taught at Babson College, Northeastern University, and the Computer Institute for Management.

To MY WIFE CAROLYN who not only graciously tolerated an absentee husband, but also aided in the reading and evaluation of pertinent sections of the book.

To VERONICA CANNELL for her most capable, faithful, and dedicated effort in the editing, typing, and retyping of the manuscript.

Wellesley, Massachusetts   JEROME KANTER

CONTENTS

3   The Systems Study   46

*Delving into a thorough analysis of current
procedures and systems, Three B's quantifies
facts and figures to determine the business
and systems requirements of its operations.*

4   Systems Design   92

*Three B's begins to build a system that meets
its business objectives and takes advantage of
modern electronic data processing techniques.*

5   Computer System Justification   **136**

*Having decided that a computer can be of material
benefit, Three B's selects the equipment that best
meets its needs and then proceeds to justify the
investment.*

6   The Implementation Phase   **183**

*Three B's sets in motion the plan to install the
computer system it has selected.*

7   Maintenance and Modification   222

Having installed the computer, Three B's reviews and analyzes its operation to determine if the projected benefits have been attained, and if the system is functioning in an efficient and effective manner.

Index   255

THE COMPUTER

SYSTEM SELECTION CYCLE

The chapters that follow describe a company as it ponders whether a computer can help solve its current operational problems. This section discusses the steps that the company will go through in this quest. Figure 1 presents a schematic of the sequential phases of computer acquisition. The three major phases are: (1) Analysis, (2) Synthesis, and (3) Implementation. Analysis is defined as the separation of anything into its constituent parts or elements. This phase of the computer acquisition cycle is concerned with this initial step. Applied to computer acquisition, analysis involves the review and analysis of company operation and the division of the total operation into logical and workable units for measurement and evaluation to see if there are better ways of accomplishing the objectives of the business.

Synthesis, the opposite of analysis, begins to combine and build the parts or elements into a whole. The analysis stage dissects business operations to show up weaknesses and areas in need of improvement—particularly the area of information analysis and its effect on the control of operations. The synthesis phase combines these elements in such a way as to improve the original operation.

The implementation phase is the proof of the pudding. Here, the synthesis (or improved solution) is actually designed, programmed, and put into operation. The conclusion of this phase is the maintenance and modification of operational applications to ensure that they remain free of errors and discrepancies.

A further breakdown of the computer selection cycle indicates that the analysis phase consists of the feasibility study and systems study subphases. The feasibility study begins with the establishment of objectives including the time and cost of the study, selection of the people who will conduct the study, and the general manner in which the study will be conducted. The feasibility study is directed to the question: "Does a computer offer sufficient benefits to a company to warrant further investigation?" An effective systems study requires a considerable investment in time and money and should be undertaken only if a preliminary study indicates that a computer presents a feasible solution to problems.

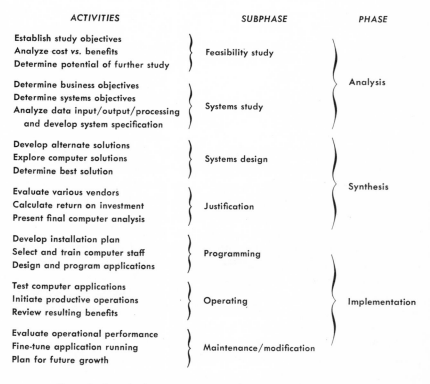

ACTIVITIES	SUBPHASE	PHASE
Establish study objectives Analyze cost vs. benefits Determine potential of further study	Feasibility study	Analysis
Determine business objectives Determine systems objectives Analyze data input/output/processing and develop system specification	Systems study	
Develop alternate solutions Explore computer solutions Determine best solution	Systems design	Synthesis
Evaluate various vendors Calculate return on investment Present final computer analysis	Justification	
Develop installation plan Select and train computer staff Design and program applications	Programming	Implementation
Test computer applications Initiate productive operations Review resulting benefits	Operating	
Evaluate operational performance Fine-tune application running Plan for future growth	Maintenance/modification	

Figure 1   Steps in the computer system selection and implementation cycle.

It may be that further systems study will indicate that a computer is not justified, but a company should be reasonably sure that it is before embarking on a comprehensive systems study.

The systems study begins with an analysis of over-all business objectives. Normally, this starts with very broad statements, such as: "The objectives of a business are to take raw materials into a plant, combine them in such a way as to turn out a finished product that will be purchased by the buying public—and accomplish all this on a profitable basis."

The systems study then will focus on the information and control system, which enables a company to better plan and schedule operations to produce the product at the lowest possible cost and still satisfy customer demand. The total information system will be broken down into progressively smaller and smaller units of study until the focus is on meaningful and manageable subsystems. The input, output, and processing steps of these subsystems will be carefully analyzed to form the foundation for the synthesis phase of the computer selection cycle.

The synthesis phase consists of the systems design and justification subphases. The systems study answers the question of *what* is being done and compares it to what should be done. Systems design is concerned with *how* it is being done and compares that with how it should be done. In systems design, the detail produced during the systems study is used to develop alternate solutions that will better achieve the defined business and systems objectives. The systems design subphase usually concludes with the development of specifications describing how a company expects an electric data processing system to improve its operations. The company is now ready to submit these specifications to computer manufacturers for their evaluations and bids.

The justification subphase evaluates the responses and offerings of vendors to the systems specifications submitted to them. There are various methods of competitive comparison that eventually result in the selection of a single vendor or in some cases multiple vendors. Knowing the cost of the computer system, the company next proceeds to justify the cost by measuring it against the expected benefits. The various methods of cost justification usually include some type of return on investment analysis. After the justification process, the final presentation is prepared and presented to those responsible for making the computer decision. The selected vendor is then told of the decision, but the order is normally not signed until an equipment delivery date is determined.

The implementation phase includes developing the installation plan, which outlines the resources necessary to prepare for the computer installation. The installation plan and schedule determine the delivery date of the computer. The implementation phase includes the programming, operating, and maintenance/modification subphases. The implementation staff, after selection and training, transforms the systems design specification into progressively greater and greater detail, thus preparing the system for computer processing.

The resultant programs are tested and finally put into productive operation. The productive programs are then reviewed to determine if they meet the systems objectives and, therefore, the business objectives. The resultant improvements and benefits are measured against those that were projected.

The implementation phase does not end at this point, but includes the important maintenance/modification subphase. The over-all operational performance must be evaluated as a preliminary step to fine-tuning the running applications. It is inevitable that operational errors and program discrepancies will occur with time—a plan must be instituted for their resolution and correction. With the fine-tuning accomplished, both short- and long-range plans for future growth are refined.

In reality, the phases of analysis, synthesis, and implementation are never-ending cycles. As soon as initial computer applications are put into productive operation, additional ones are tackled. The operational applications must be periodically reviewed and updated to run more efficiently and to adapt to changing business conditions and needs. As more applications are put on the computer, it is not too long before the company reaches the capacity of its current computer and the entire computer selection cycle must be reinstituted. This continued and seemingly never-ending cycle may appear a bit frustrating, but it can be one of the most rewarding activities in which a company is involved.

In closing this section, the reader must face up to the truth so aptly expressed by an anonymous early 20th Century businessman: "The only way to prevent systems analysis is never to let it begin."

1

THREE B'S, INC.

INTRODUCTION

Surveys of prominent companies using computers show that there are about as many companies whose expectations of computer-related benefits exceeded actual results as there are companies whose computer programs lived up to expectations. Woven through the personal experiences of managers involved in installing computers are common problems and common approaches. Some of these approaches have been uniformly unsuccessful whereas other approaches consistently have been responsible for the success of computer installations. Managers who have been responsible for computer decisions in the past are prone to employ the frequently-heard business cliché: "If only I had it to do all over again."

This book affords the author (who has used that cliché several times before in his career) an opportunity to discuss what he would do differently. It will help managers who have yet to acquire their first computer and thus yet to make their first mistake. Notwithstanding a normal learning curve that must be reinforced by personal error, the thesis of this book is that a management-oriented discussion of the computer selection cycle based on a realistic case study can serve to improve the manager's batting average.

The company selected for study is called Three B's, Inc. The reader may well find he is going over familiar terrain in reviewing the business environment in which Three B's operates. Indeed, it would be surprising if certain of Three B's' problems are not universal in nature. Three B's is a small manufacturer of bicycles, successfully competing in the market but facing operational and growth problems that threaten its success.

It is important to have a good grasp of Three B's' operations because the chapters that ensue will follow the normal sequence of events as Three B's analyzes its needs, selects a feasibility study team, conducts a feasibility systems study, evaluates competitive computer vendors, makes its computer decision, and installs its computer. The purpose of the case study is to establish a model or framework to make more meaningful the discussion of systems principles that are discussed in each chapter.

THREE B'S, INC.

Bob Perry reported for his first day's work as staff assistant to Warren Coolidge, vice-president in charge of production at Three B's, Inc. Coolidge had hired Perry as a special staff assistant to assume general responsibility for all production and inventory control activities in the company. Perry understood that Coolidge expected him to improve the production organization's performance in meeting customer demand while maintaining a more balanced inventory position. He was also to concern himself with rising production costs. One of the first things Perry did upon joining Three B's was to review the over-all company background and organization.

COMPANY BACKGROUND

The principal products of Three B's are bicycles of all types and sizes ranging from the basic single-speed model to the Italian style ten-speed racing bike. They also manufacture motor bikes and other power-assisted bikes as well as tricycles, scooters, and kiddie cars.

The past year marked the tenth year of business operation for Three B's. The company was founded by the Barrett brothers and is still operated as a tightly-controlled family organization. Bill Barrett is president and chief executive officer and his older brother Sam is chairman of the board. Several of the Barretts' sons and sons-in-law hold positions with the company. Sales, less than a million dollars in the first year, have risen substantially each year to the point where the sales volume for the previous year was $14 million. The Barrett brothers expect sales to continue to grow in the future. They feel that they produce the highest quality bicycle on the market and that their reputation is second to none. Of concern to the Barretts is the fact that although sales have been rising, profit margins, in their opinion, are not rising proportionately.

The Three B's line is handled by company salesmen and jobbers throughout the country. All bicycles are manufactured in the main plant in Cleveland, Ohio, and are shipped directly from there. Salesmen take orders from large department stores and bicycle shops as well as from smaller outlets, and mail the orders to Cleveland where they are processed and filled. Figure 1.1 presents a profit and loss statement for the previous year and a balance sheet as of year-end. Cost of sales comprises 35% labor, 50% materials, and 15% expenses.

COMPANY ORGANIZATION

There were no organization charts at Three B's as the Barretts did not believe in them. However, Perry sketched his own rough chart noting some of the key people (see Figure 1.2). Warren Coolidge, vice-

Sales		$14,469*
Variable costs	$8,202	
Fixed costs	$4,102	
Administration costs	$ 723	
Cost of sales		$13,027
Net profit before taxes		$ 1,442
Federal income tax		$ 692
Net profit after taxes		$ 750

Balance Sheet

Assets			Liabilities		
Cash	$ 935		Accounts payable	$1,586	
Accounts receivable	$1,447		Accrued expenses	$ 600	
Inventory	$4,823		Short term debt	$ 125	
Other current assets	$ 585		Other current liabilities	$ 150	
Total current assets		$ 7,790	Total current liabilities		$ 2,461
Plant		$ 2,042	Stockholders equity		$ 5,432
Equipment		$ 2,120	Retained income		$ 4,016
Other fixed assets		$ 317	Other liabilities		$ 360
Total assets		$12,269	Total liabilities		$12,269

*The last three zeroes have been omitted.

Figure 1.1   Profit and loss statement.

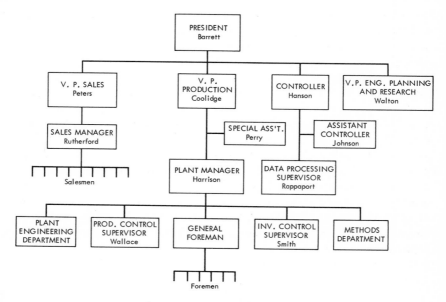

Figure 1.2 Company Organization.

president in charge of production, and Paul Peters, vice-president in charge of sales, are the senior officers of the company and have considerable influence in the decision-making process within Three B's. The controller, Harry Hanson, has been with Three B's since its inception and is a brother-in-law of Bill Barrett. Hanson is 62 years old, and expects to retire in a year or two. His assistant, Dexter Johnson, is a recent graduate of a prominent business school and joined Three B's a year ago as the result of an accidental meeting with Bill Barrett on a flight from Cleveland to Los Angeles. Barrett considers his company's data processing operations extremely backward and was most interested in Johnson's EDP background. Johnson was a data processing specialist for a manufacturing company and also served as a systems manager and salesman for a large computer manufacturer.

The plant manager is Burt Harrison who is the man that really keeps Three B's' production lines running. Harrison has 25 years of varied production experience, starting as a milling machine operator and working his way to night foreman, general foreman, and finally plant manager. He is considered a rough customer to deal with, but he has a reputation for getting the job done. He is adamant in his feelings toward computers and so-called sophisticated systems approaches. Although he complains about the inaccurate production and inventory records, he is very skeptical about introducing a computer into his operations. He has friends in other plants in the city who say that their computer installations have failed. Harrison always refers to this when the word *computer* comes up at weekly staff meetings. He believes that the best system is the simple system. When it comes to computers, Harrison defiantly proclaims: "My theme is the KISS theory—Keep It Simple, Stupid."

Perry began to gather statistical information concerning the finished products, assemblies, and piece parts manufactured and assembled by Three B's. He discovered that there are approximately 200 finished goods items of which 150 are active items that are produced on a regular basis and carried in stock. There are approximately 5,000 assemblies and piece parts supporting the 200 finished goods items. There is an average of six parts per assembly. On the sales side, Three B's receives about 160 sales orders per day; the typical order containing six items. Despite the fact that a good amount of Three B's' business is in the southern and western part of the country, there is a strong seasonal influence on sales. Of the 5,000 piece parts, approximately two thirds are inventoried. Purchase orders average 50 per day, with a typical purchase order containing four items. There are approximately 35 machine centers, divided about evenly between fabrication and assembly operations. Because most of the products are produced on a repetitive basis, large production runs are the rule.

DATA PROCESSING BACKGROUND

The data processing department reports directly to Harry Hanson, controller of the company. It consists of a large punched card installation with equipment cost of approximately $3,000 per month. The data processing staff includes a data processing supervisor, Dennis Rappaport, and a staff of five people who handle operations and programming. In addition, there are three keypunch operators assigned to the data processing department. Recently, Hanson and Rappaport had a lengthy discussion with Bill Barrett in which the latter was quite critical of their operation. Barrett had just returned from an executive session on computers and was impressed by the strides that the EDP industry was making; at the same time, he was rather disappointed at his company's use of data processing. His general feelings were that with Three B's' rapid growth, it was time to take another look at where the company was headed in the area of information processing, to develop a long-range plan for some type of management information system, and to explore the use of on-line, real-time techniques.

Hanson had conducted a computer feasibility study two years previously. The conclusion was that Three B's should first get its punched card installation running efficiently before considering a computer. Hanson believed that the computer had not lived up to the promises of the industry spokesmen. Rappaport did the majority of the fact finding for the feasibility study.

COMPANY INTERVIEWS

During his first month of employment with Three B's, Perry spent a good deal of time with the sales manager, the inventory control supervisor, and the production control supervisor.

SALES DEPARTMENT

He started with the sales manager, Bill Rutherford. In reviewing the sales picture, Perry discovered that two weeks prior to the beginning of each month, Rutherford would project the expected sales activity for the coming month. He based this primarily on previous months' sales, his own ten years' experience with Three B's, and his monthly meetings with key company salesmen. The sales manager was also responsible for a six-month forecast twice a year.

Order turnaround time was approximately 30 days. In other words, a salesman mailing an order to Cleveland could expect his customer to receive the goods 30 days from the time he mailed the order. In many cases, this caused a good deal of customer dissatisfaction as certain customers needed merchandise more quickly than 30 days after placing an order. This was particularly true in those areas that had a short spring selling season. The salesman had to explain that this was the best he could do.

On rush orders, salesmen were bothered by the fact that although the inventory records showed certain bicycles were in stock, when they placed the order they were informed that they actually were not in stock. The salesman would then have to relate this back to his customer. More and more, salesmen were beginning to hear the remark: "If you didn't make the best bike on the market, we'd certainly place our business elsewhere." Rutherford was deeply concerned because two other major bicycle manufacturers were improving their bikes and the quality edge that Three B's experienced was narrowing.

INVENTORY CONTROL

The inventory control supervisor, Jay Smith, was continually besieged by the production people who asserted that they had to shut down production lines due to unavailability of particular parts and assemblies. At the same time, the controller was pointing out the increasing amount of capital that Three B's had tied up in inventory. One of his basic concerns was the lack of a system that could take the sales manager's forecast and rapidly obtain the necessary piece parts and assemblies to produce enough bicycles to meet it.

About 60% of piece parts and assemblies used in production were purchased. The remainder was fabricated from base metal stock. Smith indicated that his major problems were connected with purchased parts and assemblies. The number of parts had risen substantially with the addition of bike styles and new product lines. He could obtain certain parts with short lead time, but others came from plants that had a bad reputation for meeting delivery schedules. Unfortunately, these were the only plants producing the quality of parts that Three B's demanded. Smith also knew his inventory records were unreliable. In some cases, production lines were shut down for lack of parts when the parts actually were available in another part of the plant but were not recorded as such. Some departments had built up their own staging areas where they maintained a day or two's supply of piece parts and assemblies in order to ensure a full day's production run.

The inventory control department kept a record of price breaks for each of the vendors. When a particular part or assembly hit a reorder point (the reorder point was a month's projected usage plus an additional half month's buffer stock for items ordered from the "unreliable" vendors), the inventory clerk handling that item would initiate a purchase requisition. It usually took two to three days from the time a purchase requisition was prepared to when the purchase order would be written. The order quantity was based on the price breaks. The quantity ordered was at the price break point where the quantity ordered would not exceed eight weeks' usage. Usage figures were maintained on Cardex files in the inventory control office. The files were posted from the weekly inventory reports issued by the data processing department. Smith knew these usage figures were historical and did not reflect changes in buying habits or seasonal factors. He had no way of obtaining a product explosion of piece parts and assemblies based on current sales trends.

PRODUCTION CONTROL

J. B. Wallace, production control supervisor, indicated that his main problem was the constantly changing order requirements. He placed little faith in the sales manager's forecast and knew from experience that he must adjust it himself in order to anticipate the changes that inevitably occurred during the month. He realized that an important company asset was its highly skilled labor force, which was one of the key reasons for the high-quality bicycle produced by Three B's. A prime consideration from the president on down was to level out production so that there would be minimal fluctuation in the labor force. "Accomplishing this, while keeping costs down and inventory balanced, was all there was to do," the production control supervisor facetiously stated. Wallace felt that he was doing a good job, considering the rapid growth of operations over the previous five years. He was gravely concerned over the effect further expansion would have on production operations.

Wallace continued to elaborate on the problems as he saw them. He stated that Three B's was not the small company it had been five years ago, but in many ways it still acted like it. The production control supervisor was of the opinion that the company was breaking apart at the seams. Labor costs were rising and this was directly related to the scheduling and inventory problems. Production lines had to be shut down and skilled labor idled while dispatchers searched for parts. The workers in some cases were redeployed but the work then was below their skill level. Not only did this result in higher labor costs but the company ran the risk of a morale problem if it continued to operate in this manner.

Wallace related the decision rules he used to schedule production:

> My primary consideration is keeping a level work force. This puts a greater burden on the availability of piece parts and assemblies. I always shoot for long production runs to minimize set-up costs. We have outside storage facilities that I can use for temporary overstocks. If I had a forecast I could rely on, I could do a better scheduling job. Some of our unskilled help is part time so we can call on them as needed. This gives me a way to increase or decrease production at relatively short notice; however, even in this situation, I'm beginning to hear about it from the union steward. The key to our problem is getting a more accurate long range forecast to work from—then I can level off production while keeping costs down. For example, we've incurred major overtime last month because of several urgent rush orders from our two largest customers.

At a recent meeting attended by Warren Coolidge, Paul Peters, Harry Hanson, and Bob Perry, Bill Barrett indicated that the time had come to take some action to resolve the major problems of the company and to improve the profit picture. Barrett thought the answer might be an improved information processing system that could utilize an automated sales forecasting system as a basis of better balancing inventory, improving production control, and reducing production costs. He specifically stated that Perry should consult with Dexter Johnson to plan the next steps.

SUMMARY

The reader should now have a general knowledge of the Three B's company, its type of business, its management, and its problems. Three B's started as a closely held family operation some ten years ago, but has had exceptional growth. Its profit margins are good and one must conclude that it has been successful. It produces a high quality product that is well received by the market. However, its growth has been so rapid that it is beginning to encounter growing pains. On the sales side, a 30-day cycle time has become the rule and this is not popular with Three B's' customers. Other departments within the company are looking for a more accurate sales forecast on which to base production and inventory levels.

On the production side, the factory seems to be flying by the seat of its pants. The production control supervisor adjusts the forecast as he sees fit, tries to anticipate material needs, and attempts (often unsuccessfully) to keep the highly skilled labor force working on jobs that are consistent with their skill level. The inventory control supervisor is having a difficult time juggling inventory and in many cases is not doing a good job because expensive machinery must be shut down due to lack of material. Some operating departments store their own inventory in hidden staging areas to keep the production line running on a full shift basis.

It seems that Three B's may be reaching a crucial crossroads in its development. Possibly the company is reaching a stage where it may begin to lose its competitive edge because of sales and production inefficiencies. The number of saleable items and the resultant assemblies and piece parts comprising the end items have grown to a point where planning and control are becoming increasingly important—no longer is Three B's the family-run bicycle plant around the corner.

The management of the company still rests very strongly in the hands of its founder and president, Bill Barrett. Barrett thinks the answer to many of Three B's' problems may be more advanced electronic data processing equipment to control the paper work and thereby improve the control of operations. He has hired Dexter Johnson, a young man experienced in EDP, to take a look at this situation. Likewise, Bob Perry has been brought in to analyze and recommend changes to the production and inventory control operations, which seem to be the crux of Three B's' problems. Attitudes towards computers vary quite a bit among the management team from Burt Harrison's skepticism to Bill Barrett's enthusiasm.

Thus the stage is set for a discussion of the steps Three B's will be taking as regards the study, analysis, and decision on whether a computer is the answer to the problems it is encountering.

As stated at the outset, it is hoped that the reader finds some common ground in reading about Three B's—if not with the type of operation and problems, then with the people and their attitudes in facing these problems. The chapters that follow delve deeper into the activities outlined in the Preface, which are the steps that Three B's must undertake to answer the basic question: "EDP or not EDP?"

SOURCE MATERIAL AND SUPPLEMENTARY READING

The Three B's case is not based on any particular company; it is a composite of several companies that I have either been associated with or have aided as a consultant. For other case studies on EDP, see:

Data Processing, XII (1967). Published by Data Processing Management Association. (1967).

Dearden, J. and F. W. McFarlan, *Management Information Systems: Texts and Cases*. Homeward, Ill.: Richard D. Irwin, 1966.

International Case Clearing House, Published Index. Harvard University Graduate Business School, Boston, Mass.

Kanter, J., *The Computer and the Executive*. Englewood Cliffs, N. J.: Prentice-Hall, Inc., 1967. 134 pp. (Chapter 4 describes one company's development of an integrated management information and control system.)

Optner, S. L., *Systems Analysis for Business Management* (2nd ed.). Englewood Cliffs, N. J.: Prentice-Hall, Inc., 1968. (Includes 9 case studies.)

2

THE FEASIBILITY STUDY

The president of Three B's, Bill Barrett, thinks that a computer might help his company resolve some of its problems. He has developed this idea from a number of sources. First, he recently attended an executive seminar where advanced management information systems and mathematical decision theory were discussed. He was quite impressed with the things modern computers are capable of doing. Next, he was playing golf with a business associate who is president of a company about the same size as Three B's. His colleague indicated that after a slow and somewhat discouraging start, his company's EDP program is beginning to pay off. Finally, Barrett made a brief personal study of his own data processing operation and decided that it is considerably behind the times.

Barrett appoints Dexter Johnson, assistant controller, and Bob Perry, special assistant to the vice-president of production, to form a two-man computer feasibility team. He gives them free reign to explore and analyze all areas of the business in order to determine the impact a computer will have on the Three B's company. He tells them he would like a report in a month to answer the impact question and to determine what further steps are necessary.

INTRODUCTION

Referring to Figure 1, this chapter explores the feasibility subphase within the analysis phase. It is during this phase that management will determine whether a computer is a feasible investment for the company. Techniques for quickly assessing computer potential will be presented. These include the correlation of annual sales volume and computer expenditure, and the relation of various activity indices, such as number of sales orders or purchase requisitions, to computer feasibility. Then the methodology of a successful feasibility study will be thoroughly discussed, including the development of over-all study considerations, the selection and training of the study team, and various project control techniques to assist in formulating a realistic schedule for the study effort. The variety and types of computer costs will be viewed in light of the kinds of benefits afforded by a computer. The benefits and costs will be categorized and placed in the context of a return on investment analysis. The discussion will focus on the question: "The computer represents an investment to a company; what are the tangible and intangible benefits that justify this investment?"

The chapter concludes with the presentation of the feasibility study conclusions to management, paving the way for entry into the other phases and subphases of the computer system selection and implementation cycle.

THRESHOLD OF COMPUTER ENTRY

It is human nature to look for a shortcut or at least to minimize the time and effort in answering a complex question like computer feasibility. The first logical issue that arises in pursuing the computer question is whether a company is large enough to afford such a device. Various rules of thumb and various sets of statistics can assist in the quest. Several approaches will be studied but a word of caution must precede the discussion. It is true that exceptions prove the rule, and in establishing size qualifiers for entry into electronic data processing, there are many exceptions. Many small companies that do not satisfy the threshold criteria to be discussed have found significant benefit and payoff from EDP. It may be that these companies just have not bothered to look at the statistics. Nonetheless, it is beneficial to view the various yardsticks and at least determine the probabilities of a company needing a computer.

SALES VOLUME AND COMPUTER EXPENDITURE

Surveys made of computer installations have brought out the correlation of sales volume and expenditure for electronic data processing. One such survey of manufacturing companies found that EDP expenditures average $5,600 per year for every $1 million of sales. For example, a company with $20 million of sales would expend $112,000 per year on its computer program. The survey further showed that the EDP expenditures were allocated as follows:

1. 38% equipment rental,
2. 33% operating costs, and
3. 29% systems and programming costs.

Operating costs include computer supplies such as punched cards, and magnetic tape as well as the salaries of personnel responsible for operating the equipment. The systems and programming costs are the salaries of the systems analysts and programmers working in the EDP department.

By simple calculation, a company could multiply its sales volume by $5,600, determine the savings and benefits afforded by the computer, and ascertain if the benefits and savings divided by the dollar computer investment produced a satisfactory rate of return.

The analysis would appear as follows:

$$\frac{\text{Savings} + \text{Benefits}}{\text{Investment}} = \underline{\quad} \%$$

It will be brought out later in the chapter that the computer investment is in reality a combination of one-time costs and recurring costs. The former are represented in the denominator of the formula and the latter would serve to offset a portion of the savings and benefits in the numerator of the formula.

Obviously it is not quite so simple, but the computer cost figures from the survey represent a starting point. Several considerations must be kept in mind. First, the survey from which the $5,600 yardstick was developed was based on manufacturing companies and was heavily weighted by medium to large companies—$50 million sales volume and up. A pertinent question is whether the $5,600 figure holds true for smaller companies. This is a difficult question to answer.

One might surmise that the smaller company requires less computer investment in relation to sales because a small company's operations are less complex and its data volumes are a great deal smaller. Another reason is that the organizational structure is more straightforward, permitting rapid decision making and implementation. Although this is true to a certain extent, several considerations work against the small company. The breakdown of computer costs into the three elements outlined previously facilitates a clearer analysis of the matter. It is common to focus almost entirely on computer equipment cost when discussing the subject of EDP expenditure although in reality the equipment cost comprises less than 40% of the total cost.

The cost of implementation (the 29% portion of total cost) is often more a function of the nature of the application rather than of the volume. For example, the decision rules in an inventory control application (forecasting demand, calculating reorder points, and producing reorder quantities) are roughly the same whether there are 4,000 or 40,000 items being controlled or whether there are 10,000 or 100,000 transactions processed per week. The systems and programming effort to develop the computer programs is not proportionate to the volume of inventory items and transactions. Therefore, it may well be that systems and programming costs are higher per million dollars of sales.

On the equipment cost side, it is true that the implementation of the lower volume applications will require less computer time and computer processing power. However, industry experts state that the pricing structure in the industry is such that computing power increases roughly as the square of the rental price. This is to say that an $8,000 per month computer offers four times the power of a $4,000 per month computer ($8^2 = 64, 4^2 = 16$; 64 divided by 16 is 4).

There is truth in this statement but the author feels this is more apparent in scientific-oriented computer applications, which rely heavily on internal computer processing power, as opposed to business applications, where input and output requirements are predominant. A countervailing factor is that in an attempt to develop a broader customer base at the very lucrative lower end of the market, computer manufacturers have passed along many big system features with relatively low price tags attached to them.

The 33% operating cost element is better correlated to dollar sales volume than are the other two elements. This is due to the fact that supplies, forms, and operating personnel are a function of volume. The previous discussion would seem to indicate that EDP costs per million dollars of sales may indeed be higher for the smaller company than for the larger one. A survey made of manufacturing companies of under $20 million sales supports this contention. It shows that the EDP expenditures for surveyed companies (the average sales volume was $12 million), was $8,000 per $1 million sales, or 43% higher than for the larger companies. It is interesting to note that 80% of the companies surveyed indicated they had received a satisfactory return on their computer investment.

In summary, statistics indicate that smaller companies normally pay more for data processing per sales dollar than the larger companies pay, but this has not been a deterrent to their successfully utilizing EDP.

MINIMUM COST OF EDP

An additional element in calculating whether a company can afford a computer is the minimum cost of data processing. What is the lowest price of a general purpose computer that has the necessary peripheral gear and options to accomplish a complete business application like payroll or inventory control? Ruling out special purpose computers and small scientific computers, the minimum figure is about $1,200 per month. Based on the allocation of computer costs of 38% hardware, 33% operating expenses, and 29% systems and programming costs, total EDP costs would amount to $3,158 per month or $38,000 per year. Working backward from the yardstick of $8,000 EDP costs per $1 million sales for smaller companies, the company with $5 million sales might well take a look at computer feasibility.

These yardsticks must be reviewed each year because computer costs are continually being reduced, a rather rare phenomenon in an economy where prices of most products and services are on the upgrade. For the most part, the reduction in computer costs is in the hardware rental portion—the 38% part of total EDP cost. Because the prime element in the other 62% is salaries, this portion has not reacted in the same manner as hardware costs. The salaries, particularly of systems and programming personnel, have risen steadily for the past ten years. The shortage of qualified computer people has pushed up salary scales. Offsetting the wage escalation has been the increase in systems and programming productivity brought about by the software aids developed by computer manufacturers, software firms, and independent systems concerns. The higher salaries have been about equalized by the increase in productivity brought on by improvement in systems techniques embedded in the various software developments. Because of this, it must be realized that a 30% reduction in computer rental lowers total EDP cost only 11.4% (30% $\times$ 38% = 11.4%).

Determining the cost of something before getting an idea of what it is going to accomplish may appear to be placing the cart before the horse. However, it is felt that there is benefit in deriving a "ball park" estimate of cost. This sets the general feasibility study framework and affords a base for analyzing the business improvements and operational benefits that must be realized in order to justify the expenditures for EDP. The $5,600 EDP expenditure per $1 million sales for medium to large companies and the $8,000 figure for smaller companies are obviously no more than generalizations or rules of thumb. Realizing this, the author feels they represent reasonable guidelines to answer the question often raised by management: "Approximately what is an EDP operation going to cost?"

ACTIVITY INDICES

Realizing the risk in placing too heavy a dependence on sales volume as an index of computer potential, a company will find an analysis of activity indices to be a useful supplement. Electronic data processing is beneficial when there is need to repetitively process a large volume of transactions against some type of master file and produce meaningful management reports in a prescribed time frame. A $20 million a year manufacturer who operates exclusively on a job shop basis and produces large durable items may have less computer justification than a $5 million nondurables manufacturer who produces low cost items on a repetitive basis and sells from inventory. This is because the job shop manufacturer does not have the volume of repetitive transactions referred to.

Studies of companies have uncovered specific activity indices that give a quantitative measurement of computer potential. These indices are: (1) sales orders, (2) purchase orders, (3) time cards, (4) inventory items, and (5) work centers. The first three indices represent basic source documents, which initiate a large proportion of the paperwork flow and activity within a manufacturing company. The sales order initiates the shipment of finished product to customers, the establishment of an account receivable, and the eventual customer payment. The purchase order initiates the flow of raw materials and piece parts into the factory so that the necessary materials are available to maintain a manufacturing schedule that meets customer demand. The time card is the basis of calculating the factory payroll and the issuance of various labor cost summaries. The importance of the purchase order and time card as source documents becomes apparent when one realizes that these two documents initiate the major portion of a company's expenditures.

Whereas the first three activity indices are measurements of transaction volume, the other two indices are a measure of manufacturing complexity. The more complex the product being produced, the more inventory items and the more production centers there are. A production center is defined as a complex of similar machine types that are geared to a specific operation, for example a drill press center.

The activity threshold established for each of the indices is shown in Figure 2.1.

Computer Index	Activity Threshold
Sales orders	75 per day
Purchase orders	40 per day
Time cards	200 per week
Inventory items	2,000
Work centers	30

Figure 2.1

A company need not reach all the activity thresholds in order to prove computer potential. Indeed, it would be rare if this were so because there is not a direct correlation among the indices. For example, a company buys large quantities of finished parts and assembles them for mass distribution. The company has a small number of work centers and a relatively small number of inventory items. However, it has a large number of sales orders and purchase orders. Figure 2.2 indicates relative computer potential based on the activity thresholds.

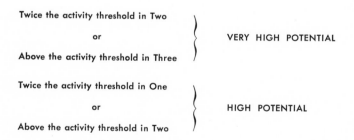

Figure 2.2

Two techniques for quickly answering the feasibility question have been presented. They are, to be sure, quick approaches that can normally be accomplished in a few days of fact finding. This two-day approach may be compared to lengthy feasibility studies taking upwards of six months. It is obvious that the "instant" feasibility study may be helpful in enabling a company to get a general idea of its size and volume as related to other companies that have installed computers. However, one must search a good deal deeper. Though the average expenditures and activity indices were based on actual survey, the degree of success and the actual benefits afforded by a computer must be viewed in light of a company's own operating characteristics. Although it is true that companies are similar in operation, they certainly are not identical. The quick approach may be viewed as a prefeasibility study indicating whether an in-depth computer feasibility study is in order. It is only after a company analyzes its own problems, business objectives, long- and short-range plans, information network, and personnel resources that it can determine whether a computer is a feasible investment.

ESTABLISHING OVER-ALL STUDY CONSIDERATIONS

Conducting the feasibility study is not the job of the perennial special projects man or the man who happens to be available. If this is the case, then it might be best to forego the feasibility study for the present. A feasibility study can be looked upon as another project similar to many that the company has undertaken in prior years or it can be viewed as an opportunity to review the entire organizational structure of the company, beginning with the basic business objectives, proceeding through an analysis of the physical operations of the business, and concluding with the information flow that parallels and controls the physical operations. More often than not, a well-directed computer feasibility study uncovers the root of major company problems.

Top management should participate in setting the ground rules for the feasibility study, beginning with the establishment of basic objectives. The study can be viewed from a very narrow or a very broad perspective. The narrow perspective will focus the study on the current methods of handling information to ascertain if these methods can be speeded up, reduced in cost, or streamlined in any way. This is the cost-cutting point of view whose main purpose is to improve the current method of processing data, primarily by doing it more cheaply. Although there is much to be said about doing something cheaply, in reality it is a conservative approach and fails to recognize that an information system can do far more than cut information processing costs.

The other perspective of a feasibility study is the profit-making point of view. Management recognizes several serious or potentially serious problem areas, the solutions of which are vital to the continued success of the enterprise. The problems are information control problems. Because the computer's prime purpose is to control information, the feasibility study is viewed as a vital reevaluation of business operations.

It may be, for example, that a retailer is experiencing a serious shrink problem. Shrink is defined as the difference between the dollar value of inventory entering the store (at retail) and the dollar value (at retail) leaving the store. One would assume that the two figures would be the same and that the difference would be explained only by pilferage. However, the method of control is often such that what is considered shrink is in reality erroneous record keeping. Either receipts are recorded in error or the clerk is miskeying the cash register. The subject of shrink is a mysterious one that continues to plague the retailing trade. If a computer can help answer this perplexing question, it will have resolved a major business problem.

There are similar instances in other industries where a broadly based computer feasibility study can play a most significant role. Thus it seems prudent for management to define the scope of the feasibility study, determining whether it will be primarily a cost cutting one, primarily a profit making one, or a combination of both. In many instances, it will be the last. At this point, a brief aside is in order. Despite the far reaching effects a computer can have on a company's operation, it should be viewed in perspective. In the case of the shrink problem just described, a good deal of management discussion, analysis, and judgment must be brought to bear on the problem. This is a necessary prerequisite to developing an automated systems solution. Although it has been stated many times before, it still bears repeating that the computer is the tool and not the thinker. Even though the computer is a quite powerful tool, possibly the most powerful one of our century, it nevertheless requires a program to operate it.

The framework of the study should not be that of a solution looking for a problem. The feasibility study team should not be predisposed to the conclusion that the company needs a computer. It is true that in quite a few instances, many if not all of the benefits obtained from a computer system might well be obtained without the computer itself. The computer feasibility study might bring out that more can be gained by cleaning up and improving the current information system than by converting to EDP or that cleaning up should at least be done first.

In this case, the computer serves as the catalyst for the much needed system reevaluation. I was associated with a computer effort in which the clerical staff was allowed to dwindle by attrition in anticipation of computer installation. Subsequent financial and computer staffing problems caused a cancellation of the computer order, yet the clerical effort proceeded as before with 20% less staff. The computer had acted as a catalyst in bringing to light inefficiencies in paperwork processing.

Management should set the priorities for the feasibility study. This normally will involve trade offs between the time, people, and resources available for the study. However, it is best to establish the original study framework independent of the trade offs that may be necessary after later review. There usually are one or two areas of a business that are the sources of a large percentage of the company's problems, the solution of which seems directly related to better control of information. It may be the shrink problem or it may be an inventory problem, a transportation problem or a sales problem. Management must determine the most crucial trouble spots and establish the relative priority of each. The comparative time and effort to study each area then can be viewed in relation to their potential benefits to business operations. The establishment of priorities also will help in determining who will conduct the feasibility study. It may be that management will assign to the study team an individual knowledgeable in one or more of the high priority areas.

Although a case has been made for the profit-making study framework, it is possible that the crucial high priority problem area is rising administrative costs. This is particularly true in the insurance and financial industries where the main product is service and where administrative cost is the major controllable expense. In this instance, a cost-cutting framework for the study may well be in order. However, even in this instance, management must not overlook potential profit-making areas that may be hidden in the administrative area. In attempting to reduce order billing costs, it may be possible to improve customer service and also to improve cash flow by improved analysis of accounts receivable.

PROJECT MANAGEMENT

Management also should establish time and cost parameters of the study. Feasibility studies, if not properly controlled, can get out of hand and can run a good deal longer than necessary. There are many stories cynically implying that the nature of feasibility teams is that they have more fun looking for something than finding it. The facetious definition of long-range planning—losing sight of the forest *and* the trees—is also appropriate in certain ventures that I have experienced. Although management must be cautious not to apply overly restrictive time barriers for the study, it is felt that the feasibility phase must be bounded by a time frame. The study team should feel that it can ask for an extension, if necessary, but should work under the pressure of meeting a deadline. Periodic status reports can indicate to management if the study group is working under undue time constraints.

Though broad in scope, the feasibility study is a discrete project and, as such, should be controlled by some type of project management technique. Whether the technique be a simple time based event (Gantt) chart or a more sophisticated PERT system, the need for control is present. Because PERT (*Program Evaluation and Review Technique*) will be utilized in simplified form at various intervals throughout the book, a brief description of it is in order.

PERT is in widespread use today, principally because of its sponsorship by the U.S. Department of Defense. Most companies that have used PERT are convinced that it is a most practical and useful tool. However, because of its popularity, tongue in cheek tales are related on the subject. The following is an example:

> When the Pharaohs of Egypt were building their pyramids, operating management was already on the scene and firmly entrenched. In fact, although it is not generally known, a worker on one such project, having just pulled a block of stone seven miles across the desert in the wrong direction, suggested a better system. He called it PERT—Pyramid Erection and Routing Technique. It is recorded that his supervisor had him flogged to death on the spot.

What is a reasonable time frame for a feasibility study? Obviously, this depends on the scope of the study and the qualifications of the people comprising the study group. A general guideline is that the feasibility study should take between three and four months if at least one member of the team is working full time. Although this may seem like a considerable period of time, the question of whether a company needs a computer cannot be a snap decision. The same 20th Century businessman quoted earlier was heard to proclaim: "The manager who makes a snap decision on computer feasibility may have time to repent in leisure."

A prerequisite to using PERT is dividing the over-all project into its basic components. For example, if the over-all project is hanging a picture, the basic components or activities of the project might be: (1) procure hammer, (2) procure nails, (3) position picture, (4) hammer nails, and so on. The PERT system organizes these project components into a meaningful network showing the appropriate relationship of one to another.

This network of activity relationships is probably the most familiar aspect of PERT. The PERT network is a diagram representing the plan for achieving some goal. It has two basic components: events and activities. An event is a point in time in which something is completed or at which some new situation arises: for example, an event might be the completion of a study or the delivery of a computer. An activity, on the other hand, is the effort applied to produce an event: for example, it might be the work of the study group or the manufacture and shipment of the computer. By showing the events necessary to complete a project and the various activities leading up to each event, the PERT network portrays the over-all schedule of a project. The PERT network, by depicting the interrelation of events, highlights the events that must be completed before other activities can be initiated. Thus, the PERT network serves two important purposes. First, it outlines an entire project; second, it establishes a schedule for that project.

An example of a simple PERT network to depict the project of hanging a picture is shown in Figure 2.3.

Figure 2.4 is a general PERT network outlining the feasibility study. It indicates the starting point at time *D* (decision to conduct a feasibility study). The various activities and the estimated time each will take in relation to the starting point are indicated. As can be seen, the general management guidelines for the study will be established and reviewed (Event 5) one month from the start date (time periods are in months and fraction of months). The presentation to management (Event 14) will be completed in four months.

The computer is a most revolutionary piece of equipment that in many ways is unlike any device that has preceded it. A thorough analysis and evaluation is required to answer the feasibility question. It is very doubtful that just having a feel for the situation is going to be of much value. A solid analysis of business and information processing is a necessary prerequisite to a sound decision—and this usually takes from three to four months.

SELECTING THE FEASIBILITY STUDY TEAM

There are several key issues to be considered in selecting the people who will conduct the feasibility study. One consideration at the outset is that

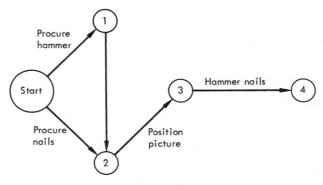

Figure 2.3

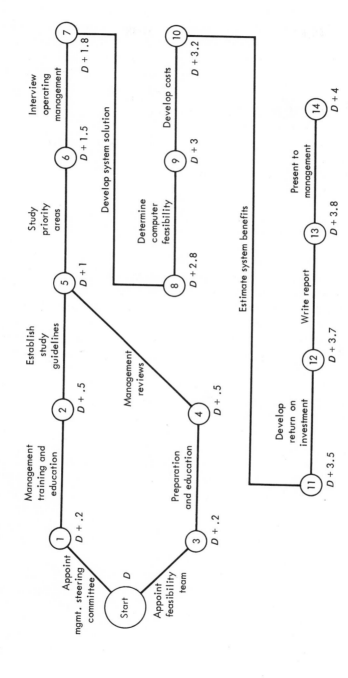

Figure 2.4 PERT chart of feasibility study.

the capability required during the feasibility phase may not be the same as that required during the systems study and systems design study. It may be that the same individual(s) does not have both the over-all business perspective required in the earlier stages and the technical abilities required in the later stages of systems analysis. The following five questions are pertinent in selecting the feasibility team:

1. Should the study team be comprised of a single individual or several individuals?
2. Should the group be assigned on a full time or part time basis?
3. What are the capabilities required of the study team?
4. To whom should the group report?
5. Should outside resources be used?

INDIVIDUAL OR GROUP

The ideal composition of the feasibility group is a team of experts representing each functional operating area of the business. Because this often is impractical, the next best choice might be a representative of an operating department (sales, production, or engineering) and a representative of the systems or data processing operation. Because of its broad nature, the feasibility study seems a natural for a committee or task force investigation. In appointing a task force, the path of least resistance is not to appoint a leader but to allow the committee to operate on its own natural momentum. This will not offend those who are not selected as the leader. However, if the decision is to have a multidisciplined task force, it is most important to appoint a forceful and capable leader. A study that encompasses an entire organization and cuts across departmental lines can get off the track unless it is firmly directed. A qualified group leader must be able to see when a particular arm of the study is headed toward a cul de sac or, at least, when it appears to be heading toward a point of diminishing returns. He must have the authority to steer the study back on course. It is not the purpose of this section to explore the study of group dynamics. The message is simply that there is direct correlation between the increased complexity of a project and the need for firm direction.

In many cases the availability of key individuals will dictate that the feasibility team is in effect a one-man unit. This, of course, puts great weight on the selection of the right man. If the individual selected has the necessary technical aptitude as well as the general business perspective, it is possible to obtain good results in a shorter time period than is possible with a group. However, in the majority of instances, because of the scope of the analysis and the need to exchange and debate various ideas, it is unlikely that a single individual can do justice to the feasibility study. A general rule in answering the question of individual or group is that the latter is more desirable, and the more operating areas potentially affected by the computer that are represented in the group, the better will be the results.

FULL OR PART TIME

Another question in selecting the feasibility team is whether the members should be full time, part time, or some combination thereof. In considering this question along with the former question, a compromise solution is to have a multidisciplined feasibility study team but have the members participate on a part time basis. Although this sometimes works better than having one man on a full time basis, it usually is far from completely satisfactory. Assume the assistant to the production control supervisor is appointed as a part time member of the feasibility study team. It is a fact of business life that the shorter term problems facing an operating person take precedence. When it is a question of the prime job versus the secondary job (the secondary job being the feasibility study), the prime job will win.

Another problem of a part time group is that particular study team designees will have a high absentee rate from their feasibility duties, thus placing the burden on one or two of the members. When the absentees are important to the group, this can seriously diminish the effectiveness of the study. At best, the part time approach will add weeks and even months to the feasibility study schedule—at worst, the entire study effort can disintegrate before a decision is reached.

Another factor weighing against a part time team is the nature of the study itself. The feasibility study requires an exacting, analytical look at operations. It often happens that a crucial stage in the analysis is reached when, because of an operating crisis, the prime job beckons. It is difficult to interrupt the analysis, resolve the crisis, and then pick up the feasibility study where it was left. Human psychology does not allow full dedication to several important projects at the same time.

A compromise to the full time/part time dilemma is to have a full time group with access to part time *ad hoc* groups from the business areas under study. The feasibility team calls on the *ad hoc* groups for specific questions and to test out preliminary findings and conclusions. This is often a very desirable compromise. The full time members give stability and continuity to the efforts whereas the *ad hoc* members offer their experience and knowledge in specific operating areas.

REQUIRED CAPABILITIES

The ideal members of the study team have: (1) several years' experience in systems in general and computer systems in particular, (2) several years' experience in two or more key operating areas of the business, and (3) the necessary personal capabilities. The personal capabilities are logical reasoning power, imagination, creativity, and a solid business perspective. In reality, a company usually has to compromise on the best two out of three of these qualifications. A ranking as to the relative importance of these qualifications would be in the reverse order in which they are mentioned. This may seem surprising, as one might surmise that systems skills are more vital than general business experience. However, it has been found that if one possesses the personal qualities mentioned, it is possible to bridge the systems gap.

A well-planned computer systems orientation program can give the generalist the background he needs to conduct the feasibility study. Two to four weeks usually is required and the training can be obtained from the growing offerings of various educational and commercial firms throughout the country. The investment of two to four weeks in systems training is considerably less than the investment to train the systems man in the operations of a business. It should be emphasized that the training should be general EDP systems training and should not delve into detailed areas such as computer programming. Although it is desirable to have a general understanding of programming in order to estimate the time and cost necessary to prepare applications for the computer, a technical programming knowledge is not necessary at the feasibility study stage.

It is prudent at this time to arrange for several introductory EDP courses for various members of the operating management. Although it may seem premature at this early stage, a sound computer indoctrination at all levels of management can prove a most beneficial investment. Such a program can establish the foundation for management involvement in the computer program and can help build the psychological climate that is so vital to any forthcoming change.

REPORTING STRUCTURE

This question is a most significant one. The reporting structure of the feasibility group can have a material influence on the scope and significance of the study. If the group reports to the controller's department, it might mean that the focus of the study becomes slanted toward the financial and accounting application areas. Likewise, if the study group reports to one of the major operating departments, for example, marketing or production, the focus of the study might well be geared in that direction. This is not necessarily to say that a feasibility study cannot be under the egis of the controller or one of the operating department heads and still be successful. Rather, it might be better placed under an independent body to rule out the question of study bias. Such an arrangement might result in the establishment of a steering committee or a review board comprised of the department heads of the groups expected to feel the impact of the computer installation. The feasibility study team would report to this committee during the study effort. Although they would report to their original department heads on an administrative basis, they would be functionally responsible to the steering committee for the feasibility study project.

In some cases it may be appropriate for the feasibility group to report directly to the president, the executive vice-president, or the general manager. This removes any doubt that the scope of the study is to be broad in nature. It also ensures that the departments whose activities will be analyzed during the study will be cooperative and willing to contribute the necessary time in answering questions posed by the feasibility group.

The trend appears to favor the emergence of the TCE or *Top Computer Executive*. This is particularly true in large companies and is also beginning to appear in the smaller ones. The TCE reports to a high company official and is not under the control of either the controller or an operating department. A correlation has been found between the relative success of a computer installation and the adoption of the TCE concept. Because of this, it may make sense to adopt the TCE concept from the outset even though this places greater weight on selecting the right man for the position. The goal should be to elevate the EDP functions and to select the type of person who is a respected member of the company's management team. Selecting a TCE who does not have the qualifications for the job can backfire and produce the reverse effect —instead of elevating the EDP function, the other department heads feel their stature has been lowered.

USE OF OUTSIDE RESOURCES

The question of using outside resources is another tough one to answer because the answer depends upon a company's assessment of its own capabilities and resources. The general rule can be made that where the required talents are available, it is better to avoid outside assistance until later in the computer selection cycle. Outside resources in the form of consultants and computer manufacturers' representatives have a vital role to play, but too early a reliance on either may cause a company to reduce its own involvement. Because the feasibility study holds so much potential for the company and may indicate a plan of action that will radically affect business operations, the company must not delegate this responsibility.

Although consultants can materially assist once they are brought in, the tendency is to become completely dependent on them. A company must develop its own expertise and capability to evaluate EDP potential. The initial feasibility study is just one event in a long string of activities that are related to an EDP program. Certainly if the company has no one who is qualified or is currently available to conduct the study, it must face the trade off of delaying the study versus relying completely on outside help. In such a situation, it may be that the consultant gets the nod.

Because consultants charge for their services, there is a strong tendency to examine an alternate source of outside assistance—the computer manufacturer who does not charge for his services. (This is not true in all cases since some manufacturers recently announced that they will charge for these services.) In most cases, this is not a sound approach. The manufacturer has an important role to play but that role usually is further along in the selection process. The computer manufacturer's representative does not want to sell equipment to companies that cannot afford or are ill-prepared for a computer as this will result in a dissatisfied customer and a negative reference point. Even so, the representative's personal zeal and enthusiasm for computers may tend to unfairly bias the situation. The efforts of the manufacturer can be brought to bear after the feasibility study has been concluded and the company has determined on its own that a computer seems to be a reasonable approach in resolving its problems.

There is also the question of the halo effect caused by the establishment of an early relationship with a particular vendor. One may begin to feel comfortable with the vendor he is working with to a point where it can prove detrimental. This is so if the vendor turns out not to have the system that is most suitable for the company's operation. An individual may feel that he can work with a person and still remain independent in his thought processes, but it is human nature to follow the path of least resistance—and that path may not be best for his company.

Assistance from a computer manufacturer(s) in conducting the feasibility study can be utilized effectively under certain conditions. If the company has its own expertise to conduct the study but requires the answers to specific hardware and software questions, then it may be able to get the information directly from the computer manufacturer instead of hiring a consultant. In this instance, the company is not asking general feasibility assistance but assistance of a specific nature.

In summary, the significance of a feasibility study to the long-range business plan of a company makes it too important a task to delegate to outside sources. The company must face up to this task itself. The answer to the feasibility question must be the company's own answer. In addition to the impact of the decision itself, an invaluable by-product will be the development of the expertise to undertake the additional tasks necessary to study more fully the computer question.

WHERE TO START THE FEASIBILITY STUDY

Up to this point, the discussion has focused on over-all feasibility considerations, the general scope of the study, priority of study areas, time frame, and the pertinent elements in selecting the feasibility staff. We turn now to the study itself and the pressing question of where to begin.

PROBLEM AREAS

Previous discussion has indicated possible beginning points. For example, an appropriate point might be the problem areas that initiated the study. More often than not, the impetus for the study is a particular operating situation that is affecting costs and company profits. For example, it is apparent that the Three B's company has some major problem areas (e.g., inventory and production control), which if not improved are going to seriously impede operations in the near future. A starting point, in this case, is the study of the current systems, analyzing where they fail to meet business objectives. In Three B's' situation, it is a case of establishing priorities among the problem areas whether the starting point be inventory control, production control, or possibly order processing.

There is a countertheory stating that the study should not begin with an analysis of current methods and current problems, this being too narrow a viewpoint. The proponents of this theory argue that bounding the problem at too early a stage limits the degree of innovation that can be brought to bear on the situation. They say that the study should begin with an analysis of the basic business objectives and competitive economic climate in which the company operates, working from there to the more specific information systems that support and control the various operating areas. The argument is: "Why study the various methods by which an order can be processed more expeditiously through a warehouse when in reality what is needed is an additional warehouse or possibly a consolidation of several warehouses?" Too narrow a study scope may cause the company to lose sight of the forest for the trees.

Although one can make a good case for this theory, it is felt that structuring a computer feasibility study along these lines is creating too broad a scope. If a company feels that additional warehouses or additional product lines are needed, these should be made part of a special study and should not be included as part of the computer study. Therefore, it is felt that the foundation of the study should emanate from a thorough analysis of the key problem areas and the existing methods of information handling. Bounding the problem to this extent should not be construed as reducing the desirability of designing new information systems that differ quite radically from those currently in operation.

There may appear to be a contradiction between the starting point suggested here and that suggested in the subsequent chapter. Chapter 3 indicates that the starting point of the systems study should be a broader over-all analysis of business operations. The reason for the difference is timing. The feasibility study is in reality a mini systems study to determine whether it is desirable to undertake the larger and more detailed second stage. Though the feasibility study should be consistent with over-all business objectives, it should focus quickly on specific systems. This is necessary in order to determine in a reasonable time frame the over-all feasibility of a computer and the desirability of proceeding further in the computer selection cycle.

LOOKING FOR PRIME COMPUTER APPLICATIONS

The activity indices mentioned earlier in this chapter give a good starting point for seeking out application areas that have the potential for computerization. Generally speaking, computers can be of benefit when several of the following elements are present:

1. *High volume of transactions*

   For example, sales orders, inventory issues, receipts, purchase orders.

2. *Repetitive type of transactions*

   Not only does there exist high volume but a repetition of the same type of transactions.

3. *Common source documents*

   Information from the same source document is used for several

purposes. As an example, a sales order forms the basis of shipping the item and a basis of paying sales commissions.

4. *Mathematical processing*

A considerable amount of mathematical computation is required.
For example, a sales forecast is determined by statistically analyzing past demand, calculating a trend, and projecting that trend
into subsequent time intervals.

5. *Demand for quick turn-around time*

For example, a daily inventory stock status report or a sales
commission statement is required the day after the work week
ends.

Another approach is to review those application areas that historically have been the ones most commonly tackled by computer users.
Figure 2.5 presents such a list. The list should be used only as a guide,
because relative popularity of an application area is certainly not the
sole criterion for computerization. Applications have been computerized
in relation to their simplicity and often not in relation to their potential
benefit to a company.

ESTIMATING COMPUTER COSTS AND BENEFITS

The solution of the simple return on investment formula, shown on
page 17, is germane in answering the feasibility question. A closer look
at the costs and benefits associated with a computer program is now in
order.

COMPUTER COSTS

Computer costs can be segregated into two major categories, recurring and one-time or nonrecurring. It was stated that of the recurring
costs, 38% is hardware rental, 29% is systems and programming cost,
and 33% is operating cost.

Looking at the hardware cost, the majority of companies rent computers as opposed to purchase. Although the percentage of purchases
has been accelerating, the ratio of rental to purchase is still about 70/30.
The trend is expected to favor purchases as the continued stability of the
industry lessens the fear of rapid obsolescence. If a company rents, there
is in reality no hardware investment because it pays for the machine in
monthly installments. A rule of thumb is that the purchase price of a
computer is found by multiplying the rental price by a factor of from
45 to 50. On the surface, this would indicate a four-year payback

period; however, ownership includes payments for maintenance (included in the rental price) and taxes and insurance on the computer.

Estimated hardware costs reflected in the feasibility study should be realistic. A study team is prone to underestimate the computing and data storage requirements as well as the necessary ancillary equipment (key

Accounting

1. Payroll checks, payroll registers, deduction registers, and a variety of payroll reports
2. Customer billing
3. Accounts receivable and cash payments
4. Accounts payable
5. Expense reporting and analysis
6. General ledger accounting
7. Standard cost accounting and variance analysis
8. Expense analysis
9. Fixed asset accounting

Sales

1. Sales forecasting
2. Sales analysis by product, customer, geography, salesman
3. Mailing lists
4. Open order analysis and expediting

Inventory Control

1. Stock status reporting
2. Maximum/minimum control system
3. Recorder point/economic order quantity control system
4. Inventory usage and obsolescence analysis
5. Purchase order writing
6. Vendor analysis

Production Control

1. Maintaining bills of material
2. Factory labor loading
3. Factory machine loading
4. Dispatching
5. Production line balancing
6. Work in process control
7. Quality control

Engineering

1. Work measurement
2. Establishing labor standards
3. Project management
4. Design automation
5. Numerical control

Figure 2.5   Computer applications.

punches, verifiers, and so on) needed to effectively implement the computer system. More often than not the total hardware cost is considerably higher at time of installation than was estimated during the feasibility study. A realistic estimate will result in a more meaningful analysis.

Programming and systems salaries constitute another major cost element. It may seem logical to assume that a good portion of this cost is nonrecurring. The reasoning is that once the basic applications are operable, the staff can be reduced to a small maintenance and trouble-shooting force. It is true that a major investment will be made before the computer is installed and this portion of the cost should be treated as a nonrecurring one. However, as has been stated, there is a continued demand for new applications as well as improvements in the existing ones. If the computer installation is successful in realizing the projected benefits, the benefits afforded by computerizing other applications often can far overshadow the original ones.

In addition, extending the scope of existing applications can begin to aid the management decision-making process and have greater impact on company profits. More often than not, systems and programming costs will increase rather than decrease with time—they definitely fall into the recurring cost category. If a company wishes to evolve a computer program over a larger period of time, it can often do so with a smaller staff; conversely, benefits will be accruing in a more evolutionary manner. However, management normally is not content with a lengthy development cycle, thus ruling out the evolutionary approach. As with hardware costs, it is common to underestimate the systems and programming costs necessary to get the job done in a reasonable time frame. Again, it is important to be realistic in the estimation of systems and programming costs.

Operating costs include the salaries of operators charged with running the equipment as well as the cost of supplies such as forms, punched cards, paper tape, magnetic tape, magnetic disk packs, and printer ribbons. Also included in this category are the power and air conditioning necessary to operate the equipment. The computer supplies business is growing and lucrative. It is reasonable to assume that a computer installation will continue to require a considerable expenditure in this cost category. Though magnetic tape and disks are long life items, still they should be categorized as recurring costs because a company regularly adds to its library of tapes and disks.

Nonrecurring costs include the investment in preparing the computer facility, the initial systems effort preceding the installation of the computer, the cost of converting the company's existing data files onto the media required by the computer system, and the costs of parallel running of systems as the computer system is introduced. Figure 2.6 indicates some representative figures for nonrecurring computer costs.

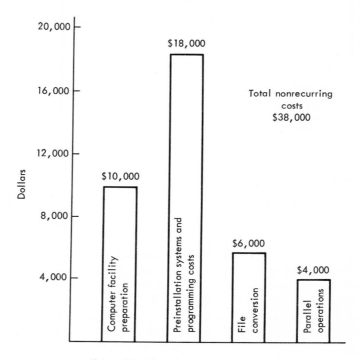

Figure 2.6　Nonrecurring computer costs.

COMPUTER BENEFITS

Turning now to the type of benefits that can be expected from a computer program, we can distinguish two general categories—tangible and intangible. A tangible benefit is one that can be accurately measured and can be directly related to the introduction of a computer system. An example is a clerical cost reduction where work formerly accomplished by clerical people now is handled by the computer. An example of an intangible benefit is an improvement in customer service brought on by a more responsive order processing system. Although it often is clear that the improvement is a result of the computer, it is difficult to place a monetary value on the effect this has on over-all company profitability. There are degrees of tangibility in computer benefits. Certainly the benefit of improved company image as a result of the computer installation is less tangible a factor than the benefit of improved customer service, although both benefits fall into the intangible category.

It is interesting to note the major benefit areas experienced by companies that have installed computers. In order of significance they are as follows:

1. Ability to obtain reports and information heretofore unavailable.
2. Availability of reports and information on a more timely basis.
3. Improvement in a basic operating area of a business.
4. Increased ability to perform computations that were not practical before.
5. Reduction in clerical cost.
6. Maintenance of competitive position.
7. Aid in management decision making.
8. Intangibles such as customer image, leadership in the industry and community, increased customer morale, and management confidence.

It is significant to note that clerical cost reduction falls well down the list as a principal benefit. Most companies first entering data processing have a tendency to overemphasize this element and later discover that benefits have come in those areas listed in the first four categories.

In assembling the final feasibility study, the time dimension of when the benefits will occur is important. If the study encompasses the entire information system of a company, it seems clear that such a development will take a rather lengthy period of time to implement. Some type of phase-in plan must be instituted, which means that the benefits will come gradually and not all will be apparent during the first year of installation. The feasibility study return on investment analysis should reflect this fact.

Placing a dollar value on anticipated computer benefits is a difficult task. An example in a specific area may serve to illustrate the type of analysis that can be used for this purpose. Many companies have inventory problems—certainly Three B's does—resulting in a major overstocking of certain items and understocking of others. The key consideration in inventory control is maintaining a balanced inventory that provides the required level of customer service. How much reduction, if any, can be accomplished by automating the inventory control operation? Most business managers would say "Plenty," but this is hardly a quantified statement of fact.

One might look at other companies with similar operations that have computer-based inventory control systems to determine what reductions they have obtained. Another way is to use a computer to analyze past history of demand and prior levels of inventory. This necessarily will have to be on a service bureau machine or at some other facility if the company is conducting its initial feasibility study. Through a process called simulation, the computer can indicate what levels of inventory would have been required using mathematical inventory decision rules to meet the desired customer service level. Comparing these simulated levels with actual levels gives a company a good idea of potential inventory reductions.

Although the simulation procedure described gives a solid indication of what is possible, it still may not be completely convincing. Another approach is to work backwards, utilizing a break-even analysis. After accumulating the projected computer costs, a calculation of the amount of inventory reduction necessary to cover these costs can be ascertained. Maintaining inventory results in carrying costs such as taxes, insurance, investment on the capital, spoilage, obsolescence, and space. These costs usually amount to between 15 and 20% of the inventory value. If the total computer costs (rental, operating, and systems costs) are $60,000 per year, it can be calculated that an inventory reduction of $400,000 is necessary to offset these costs (15% $\times$ $400,000 = $60,000). Management now can focus on the question of how likely is it that an automatic inventory control system can reduce inventory to that extent. This type of break-even approach can be used in assessing computer benefits in other operating areas as well.

REPORT OF THE FEASIBILITY STUDY TEAM

Figure 2.7 portrays a summation of the salient cost figures that form the foundation of the feasibility study report. It separates costs into recurring and nonrecurring and benefits into tangible and intangible, and it combines these figures into a *Return On Investment* (ROI) calculation. Note that only tangible benefits are used in this example. Each figure must be backed up by a thorough in-depth analysis and must be a logical outgrowth of the facts uncovered during the feasibility study. Management may want to rework the ROI based on its judgment of whether particular costs or benefits are stated accurately. The report should allow for easy entry of judgmental factors in the analysis. It may be desirable to present alternative ROIs based on different conclusions in key areas. For example, an ROI based on reducing inventory levels 20% may be presented as well as an ROI based on a 10% reduction.

Part of the report should state a tentative timetable for proceeding further into the computer selection process. This is pertinent, of course, only if the feasibility study indicates there is potential for further study.

Figure 2.8 represents such a timetable in simplified PERT format. The *D* indicates the point in time that management reaches an affirmative decision on feasibility and authorizes the study team to proceed further. The training and organization necessary to move ahead is esti-

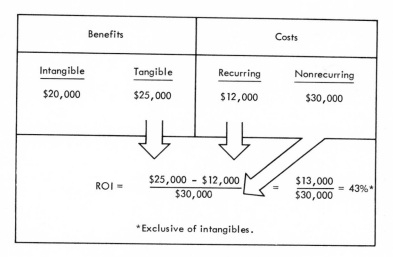

Benefits		Costs	
Intangible	Tangible	Recurring	Nonrecurring
$20,000	$25,000	$12,000	$30,000

$$ROI = \frac{\$25,000 - \$12,000}{\$30,000} = \frac{\$13,000}{\$30,000} = 43\%*$$

*Exclusive of intangibles.

Figure 2.7　Return on investment analysis.

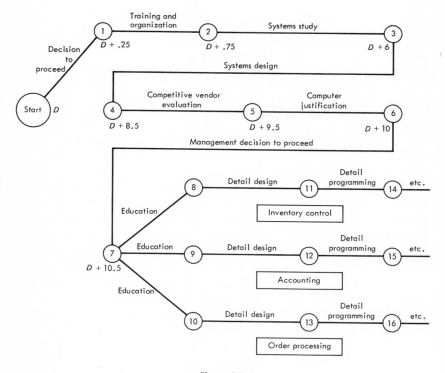

Figure 2.8

mated to take half a month and is designated by $D + .75$. The PERT network indicates that there will be three implementation teams tackling in parallel:

1. the inventory control applications,
2. the accounting applications, and
3. the order processing applications.

The company will be ready to commence work on these applications ten and a half months from the time the feasibility decision is reached.

SUMMARY

At this point, the feasibility question has been answered and management has the facts to determine: (1) that there is feasibility in pursuing the computer question further, (2) that a computer is not feasible at the current time, or (3) that the findings are inconclusive and further study is needed. At this stage, it is important to keep the momentum going and to organize the staff that is necessary to continue the computer selection cycle into the systems study area. It should be kept in mind that the feasibility study has not assured the company that it should have a computer. Rather, it has indicated that the idea is feasible and further study is warranted. However, it is safe to state that if the feasibility question is answered in the affirmative, the odds are high that a computer eventually will be installed.

THREE B'S' APPROACH TO THE FEASIBILITY STUDY

The feasibility study at Three B's has been dictated from the top. To conduct the study, Bill Barrett has appointed two seemingly bright young men who have recently joined the company. The study has top-level direction. It seems clear that Barrett wants a fresh look at the situation, for he has bypassed the original study team that was organized under direction of the controller and data processing supervisor. Barrett has made a wise move in selecting a representative of the production department and a representative of the controller's department. The production department has a good number of problems that seem receptive to computer solution and the controller's department has the systems know-how. A team leader was not designated but Dexter Johnson became the directing force because of his personality and EDP background. Although Johnson worked under the administrative direction of the controller, it was obvious that Barrett himself had direct influence over the conduct of the study. This proved to be very advantageous in resolving interdepartment conflicts.

As it turned out, Bob Perry could spend only part time on the study and Dexter Johnson was withdrawn at intervals to undertake important financial analyses for the controller. Both Johnson and Perry felt that they lost time readjusting their thinking back to the feasibility study each time they were pulled off for a week or two. This served to extend the study time frame from the one month that Barrett directed at the outset to six months. The delay was not caused completely by the part time nature of the study participants but also by the fact that Barrett underestimated the over-all effort required. He set the original scope of the study very broadly by indicating that he wanted to develop a management information system to resolve Three B's' operating problems. One month is scant time to consider the feasibility question with this broad a study framework.

The initial threshold analysis indicated that the company had a large enough sales volume to support a computer. Three B's also is above the threshold point based on activity indices. After exploring the over-all information systems, the study focused on the sales order processing and inventory control areas. Johnson and Perry realized that these areas represented key problems at Three B's. In addition, they were the necessary vanguard for solving production control problems and other problems at Three B's.

Johnson encountered an impasse in his relationship with Dennis Rappaport. It was important to tap the knowledge that Rappaport had of existing operations but Johnson had difficulty in doing so. There was a natural hostility because Johnson was new and had been selected over Rappaport, the conductor of the previous study. Recognizing that Rappaport was crucial in the fact finding, it probably was a mistake not to make him a member of the study team. Lack of the EDP supervisor's whole-hearted cooperation proved to be one of the key factors in extending the time frame of the study.

Study objectives centered on reducing the 30-day order cycle and on providing an inventory system that could achieve a better balance of inventory. An objective was also to reduce the dollar investment in inventory, which everyone seemed to agree was excessive. Inventory turn was three times, a very low figure for the type of business in which Three B's is engaged.

In the study of the order processing area, the sales department played a key role as did the production people and particularly the inventory control supervisor in the inventory area. Although Burt Harrison, plant manager, was basically skeptical about computers, the presi-

dent's backing of the program created the impetus for full cooperation with the study team. During the feasibility study, Johnson, with the help of a data processing education institute, conducted a series of EDP indoctrination courses for management. These sessions were given on company time one afternoon a week for four weeks. They were well received by management and Johnson noted that the sessions precipitated frequent visits by the managers to his office to ask questions concerning the computer.

A final report, written and oral, was prepared and presented to the executive committee. The cost figures indicated that the monthly expenses would amount initially to $8,000 per month, consisting of $3,500 computer rental, $2,400 for systems and programming salaries (two systems men and a programmer), and $2,100 for two operators and supplies. Nonrecurring costs were estimated at $25,000. Projected benefits included a savings of $4,000 consisting of punched card equipment and clerical services that would be replaced by the computer. An improved order processing system was projected to cut the order turn-around time from 30 days to ten. This was considered an intangible benefit but statements of salesmen indicated that they could increase sales substantially (particularly repeat orders) if this were accomplished. The key benefit area was a forecasted 10% reduction in inventory. This would amount to a direct annual savings of

$$\$72,000 \ [10\% \ \times \ \$4,820,000 \ = \ \$482,000 \times 15\% \ = \ \$72,000].$$

This annual savings would more than offset the added computer costs of $48,000 [$8,000 — $4,000 = $4,000 per month] and pay for the nonrecurring costs in about a year. The improved production efficiency resulting from a better balance of inventory was another positive intangible benefit.

It did not take long for the executive committee to approve the feasibility study recommendation. The committee agreed with the report that a computer appeared to present a most feasible approach to solving many of Three B's' problems. A PERT chart mapped out the steps that the company should take in furthering and extending the study. The outcome of the feasibility study was "go" and the company made plans to move into the systems study phase of the computer selection cycle.

SOURCE MATERIAL AND SUPPLEMENTARY READING

Blanton, Traut and Associates, *Computers and Small Manufacturers.* Boston, Mass.: Purnell Co. Inc., 1967. 159 pp. (The section in this chapter on Activity Indices is based partly on this article, using my own extrapolation.)

Datamation. (The June 1967 edition is devoted to Building Blocks for Small Scale EDP.)

Dean, N. J., "The Computer Comes of Age," *Harvard Business Review* (January/February, 1968).

Dean, N. J. and J. W. Taylor, "Managing to Manage the Computer," *Harvard Business Review* (September/October, 1963). (The section in this chapter on Sales Volume and Computer Expenditure is drawn from the Dean and the Dean and Taylor articles. Also, the reference to the TCE, Top Computer Executive, is found in the article by Dean.)

Lock, D. L., *Project Management*. London, England: The Gower Press, 1968. 210 pp.

Sanders, D. H., *Introducing Computers to Small Business*. Park Ridge, Ill.: Data Processing Management Association, 1966. 197 pp.

Stilian, G. N., *Pert, A New Management Planning & Control Technique*. New York: American Management Association, 1962. 192 pp.

Wiest, J. D. and F. K. Levy, *Management Guide to Pert & CPM*. Englewood Cliffs, N. J.: Prentice-Hall, Inc., 1969, 192 pp.

3

THE SYSTEMS STUDY

Three B's has completed its feasibility study, concluding that a computer can help to resolve many of its problems. The justification is based primarily on reducing inventory and improving the order processing cycle time. In conducting the analysis, the study team uncovered a significant amount of information concerning the manner in which paperwork is processed within Three B's. Although the team members reviewed the existing data processing structure within the company and predicated improvements, they did not delve into the detailed analysis of input and output volumes, peaking considerations, file storage requirements, and the like. The detailed, step by step system and subsystem analyses are necessary prerequisites for developing a computer solution to Three B's' problems. The next phase in their quest for a computer is to gather, structure, and analyze the detailed data—to launch an in-depth systems study.

After the feasibility presentation, Mr. Barrett indicates that he wants Dexter Johnson to assume full time responsibility for the systems study. He states that because the feasibility study took longer than ex-pected, he would like Johnson to select two people within the company to work with him on a full time basis in order to expedite the work. He tells Johnson to select the people who, in his opinion, are best qualified to do the job and to disregard the hardship it may have on their respective departments. Barrett asks for full cooperation from management, particularly from production vice-president Warren Coolidge and sales vice-president Paul Peters, as it would appear that their areas would be most affected initially.

Johnson selects Bill Osbourne, a young inventory control clerk, and Harry Farnum, a punched card operator from the data processing department, to work with him. Despite the president's support, Johnson was forced to compromise on his staff. His first two selections were turned down. The department managers indicated that the transfer of these men would be extremely damaging to their operation at the time but that they would consider it again in three months. Realizing the urgency of the project, Johnson settled for Osbourne and Farnum. Johnson and his young team are now ready to tackle the complex systems study phase.

INTRODUCTION

The previous chapter described the feasibility phase of the computer selection cycle. Now, it is necessary to analyze existing operations in greater depth to see more specifically how a computer can assist a company and pave the way for the comparative evaluations of competitive computer systems. Many companies bypass the systems study phase and move directly into the computer selection process. This, of course, speeds up the decision but actually gains nothing in the long run. There is no way around actually doing the systems work. If it is not done before computer selection, then it most certainly must be done afterwards. Because the systems study must be accomplished, it is better to do it before the computer selection, as it forms the basis for a sounder and far more comprehensive computer decision.

During the systems study, it is important to steer away from premature computer solutions; in fact, it is desirable not even to consider specific hardware or computer approaches at this time. Systems work begins with a study of user requirements and the needs of the particular enterprise. A predisposition to one type of computer approach can undesirably bias the study effort.

Figure 1 indicates the two general subphases of the major phase of analysis. Chapter 2 describes the feasibility study. This chapter is concerned with the systems study, attacking the three basic issues of:

1. determination of business objectives,
2. determination of systems objectives, and
3. analysis, in specific detail, of the data input, output, processing requirements, and development of the system specification.

There often is an overlap in the activities performed within the feasibility study and the systems study subphases. Depending upon the length and scope of the feasibility study, that phase might well have answered, or at least partially answered, some of the questions that are encountered during the systems study. The purpose of the systems study is to add more depth to the feasibility study, to either prove or disprove the findings, and to pave the way for the entry of the computer if it still appears to be warranted.

THE SYSTEMS STUDY PHASE

Figure 3.1 presents a more detailed schematic of the systems study phase. The starting point is the market place in which the company competes. Although it is not the responsibility of the systems study group to develop the over-all business objectives from the nature of the market place, the group must be aware of the developments and the policies at this level. The fact that the systems study begins at such a high level may seem presumptuous, but it is essential if the resultant systems study is geared to improving company operations. Certainly it is possible to undertake systems development at the lower levels without considering basic business objectives; however, surveys and studies point out clearly the inadequate results obtained by companies that follow this type of approach.

Definitions of the terms *business objectives, external* and *internal strategies*, and *business system objectives* are in order at this time.

BUSINESS OBJECTIVES

Business objectives state the reason the company is in business. A direct parallel is the job description of an individual, which explains the purpose and nature of his job and the objectives he is to accomplish. For a business, the broadest category usually is to maximize revenue, keep costs down, improve profit, and increase rate of return on investment. These goals usually are quantified by specific dollar figures. Institutions such as hospitals, schools and colleges, and nonprofit and not for profit companies have different goals in some areas; but it generally is true that on the broadest plane, each enterprise has objectives of this

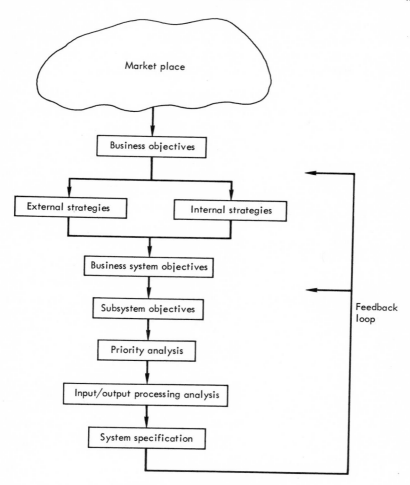

Figure 3.1 The system study phase.

nature. The establishment of these objectives is contingent upon the market place in which a company conducts its business. Thus, the profit objectives of a company like Three B's that sells bicycles are different from an insurance company, a bank, or a brokerage house.

BUSINESS STRATEGIES

Of more significance to the systems study group are the specific external and internal business strategies evolving from the business objectives.

External strategies are related to the marketing function and state the way the company plans to attain the necessary sales revenue from the market place in which it competes. The external marketing strategies usually revolve around the answers to three basic questions:

1. With whom do I want to do business?
2. What should I sell them?
3. Why should they buy from me?

The answers to these questions will lead to strategies like extending the geographical boundaries of the marketing area, concentrating a homogeneous product line in a specific marketing area, expanding product offerings to provide a full line, expanding sales 15% per year, and so on. These external objectives have considerable influence on the systems study group.

The scope of the systems study should not be confined to systems analysis but should also be directed at systems planning. There is an important distinction between the two terms. For example, an important parameter in defining systems requirements is the volume of transactions that must be handled by an information system. Knowing that a company plans to increase sales 15% per year has a major impact on systems design. This is particularly true in the sales area for, as illustrated in the preceding chapter, the sales order is a significant source document that initiates activity throughout the system. In fact, the sales order has a snowballing effect on other information systems. Determining growth requirements and providing a system that is consistent with a company's current and future business strategies are examples of systems planning. Top level systems work includes a strong planning ingredient.

Internal strategies concern those functions related to turning out the product or service offered to the market. These strategies are built around the central focus of providing the product and/or service that meets the external marketing strategies and yet utilizes the company's resources in such a way as to minimize the costs, thus attaining the company's profit and return on investment goals. These internal strategies affect the basic production, purchasing, inventory, quality control, accounting, personnel, and engineering and research functions of a company. There usually are specific internal strategies that have great bearing on the systems study group. A strategy might be to level production because of the scarcity of skilled labor or to achieve a 98% quality control standard because of the costly impact of product failure to a customer. Another internal strategy might be to institute a standard cost program to control production costs and establish a better basis for pricing. The systems study must be aware of these internal strategies, the probabilities of each occurring, and their expected time frame.

The combination of the external and internal strategies is the necessary "front end" of establishing business system objectives. It is true that systems objectives can be established independently of this type of analysis, and many reasons can be presented for so doing. For example, it is apparent that some companies have ill-defined or undefined over-all strategies. The decision then becomes one of waiting until the strategies are determined or of assisting in the establishment of the strategies before embarking on the systems study. This is a trade off that a company must face realizing that a system that is inconsistent with over-all company objectives can prove quite detrimental. It is possible to assume on one's own what strategies the company should have and to build a system from there, but this can be risky. This is one of the underlying and hidden reasons that a systems study takes so long; often it is not the fault of the systems study team but the result of management's inability to agree on basic business strategies. Systems people, in their zeal to begin, may tend to avoid the major overriding issues in an effort to bypass what they consider top management red tape. The systems group can take this attitude, but in many cases it is like building a house on quicksand. It is better to face the issues, convince management that it must reach decisions, and begin the systems study on solid ground.

BUSINESS SYSTEM OBJECTIVES

Refer again to Figure 3.1. The next term requiring a definition is *business system objectives*. A business system is defined as the paperwork complex that parallels the physical operations of a company. A business system is not the physical operation itself, although the two go hand in hand. For example, a Three B's bicycle is produced by fabricating and assembling various raw materials, piece parts, and assemblies at various work centers. The physical process of bringing together the necessary materials and machines to produce the bicycle is an example of a physical operating system. On the other hand, the process that produces a production schedule telling the foreman what materials and what machines are required to produce a specified number of bicycles by a specified time is defined as a business system. It is the paperwork system that controls the operating system. An example of an operational system change would be realigning work centers for increased productivity. Although business system studies can point out possibilities and advantages of such changes, this is not the function of a business system in the sense that it is being used here. A business system focuses on the paperwork control of an existing operation. It is important to understand this distinction. A study aimed at increasing factory productivity by changing the plant layout should be the subject of a separate effort and should not be related to the business system study. A word of caution is in order at this point. It is an ideal situation when the business and operational systems can be viewed independently. In practice, they are closely tied together, and it is difficult to change one without affecting the other. However, in systems design, it is important to attempt to maintain the separation and to approach the ideal situation.

In the broad sense, a business system is the information network that controls the entire operation of a company, integrating into one entity the functions of sales, finance, production, and engineering. An example of a business system objective in the broadest sense is the development of a system that does that—integrates the paperwork network of the entire company. In the narrower sense, a business system objective can be the development of an order processing subsystem that can process an order in ten days in lieu of the 30 days it currently takes.

SUBSYSTEM OBJECTIVES

In analyzing a company's operations, it will be obvious that the over-all business system can be broken down into a hierarchy of subsystems, and the subsystems in turn into other subsystems. The starting point of the systems study should be analysis of the hierarchy that exists within the company being studied. This will enable a clearer definition and statement of system and subsystem objectives. The latter part of this chapter presents an approach for developing the system and subsystem hierarchies.

PRIORITY ANALYSIS

After the definition of the system and subsystem objectives, it becomes apparent that the achievement of the entire range of objectives is a gargantuan task and that some type of phasing or priority analysis must be undertaken. The feasibility study should have established some framework for determining priorities. The systems study by now should enable the systems group to present various alternatives to management for its evaluation. The establishment of priorities is a management, and not a systems, prerogative.

INPUT/OUTPUT PROCESSING ANALYSIS

Once study priorities have been established, detailed data comprising the input, output, and processing requirements of each subsystem are gathered, categorized, and analyzed. These steps should be undertaken only after the preceding ones, listed in Figure 3.1. Oftentimes systems work is begun with the input/output/processing detail, omitting the important homework that must precede this analysis. Significant and costly backtracking is the result of such an oversight.

SYSTEM SPECIFICATION

The final result or output of the systems study is a system specification. This should reflect the specific requirements of the system in significant enough detail to enable computer vendors or the company's own internal group (or a combination of both) to propose a computer that will meet the specifications. System specs should be developed along the same lines as engineering specs for a specific piece of equipment. The clearer and less ambiguous the spec, the more realistic the proposed computer solution will be. If, for example, the spec omits a requirement to handle a volume up to 20% greater by the time the system is installed, the computer configuration will be underbid, posing a serious problem at time of installation. The method by which the spec is developed is discussed later in the chapter. Because the system spec is so important, it is significant at this point to take a look at its ingredients.

For illustrative purposes, the order processing system, one of the subsystems in which Three B's management is interested, is described. The level of detail is intentionally sparse in order to facilitate understanding. The components of a system spec are as follows:

1. Systems description
2. Systems objectives
3. General flow chart
4. Input/output requirements
5. File considerations
6. Volumes and other specific details
7. Complementary subsystems
8. Cost and other ground rules

The addendum to this chapter presents a synopsis of the type of information found in each of the eight sections of the system specification. The reader may wish to refer to the addendum while reading the following description. The systems description (Section 1) is a written narrative of either the current system, the new system, or both. It usually is advisable to develop a good degree of detail on the existing system because the phase-in plan is based on where the company stands at the time the new system is implemented. It also is important because the cost considerations may dictate the maintenance of portions of the old system. For example, there may be a cost limitation on input equipment, and if the company has a purchased paper tape input system, it may be mandatory to keep the old input devices even though new techniques may be more efficient. In this instance, the old system is described in very brief terms.

The systems objectives (Section 2) are extremely important because they form the *raison d'être* for the systems study. As has been stated, objectives can take the form of rather modest streamlining of existing data processing methods, eliminating duplication, cumbersome operations, unnecessary time delays, and so on, or the objectives can envision a five-year master plan to develop a total management information system.

The general flow chart (Section 3) illustrates in symbolic form the written systems narrative of Section 1. It is easier to follow than the written word and begins to shape the system for eventual computer solution. The flow chart described in the addendum is an extremely simplified one and shows only the most general functions carried out by the system. Subsequent flow charts pinpoint specific areas in progressively greater detail to the point where there is a full understanding of each step in the operation.

Input/output requirements (Section 4) move into the more specialized areas of the systems study. The output is particularly important because this is how management and operating personnel view the system. Two examples of the reports emanating from the sales order processing system are presented. These are the ones that enable the company to reach the systems objectives listed previously.

Once the output requirements are established, the systems study works backwards to determine the input necessary to produce the output. For example, it is essential to know the item ordered and the quantity before the order can be extended and priced. This data comes from the individual salesman or sales office. The maximum size of the alphanumeric characters in each field is listed.

File considerations (Section 5) describe the amount of storage required to maintain the necessary fixed information required by the system. By adding up the number of alphanumeric characters in the customer file and inventory file and multiplying by the number of customers and number of inventory items, the file storage capacity required of the computer system can be determined. Also, by superimposing the time requirements on the various files, the response capabilities of the file storage media can be ascertained. For example, if a salesman must know immediately if an item is in stock, the inventory file must be located in immediate access storage.

Volumes and other specifics (Section 6) are important to determine the input and output speeds required of the system. The basic input and output documents were described in Section 4. These now must be viewed in light of the volume considerations listed in this section. For example, the daily average input load to the system can be calculated by multiplying the number of orders per day by the number of alphanumeric characters per order. The system also must be designed to handle peak input loads.

Unless the system is an isolated one, which is rare, it is necessary to know the complementary systems (Section 7) that either feed the system or are fed by it. The system may be designed to run by itself, but the necessary flexibility must be established to enable the order processing system to tie into other systems that are added at a later date.

Finally, cost and other ground rules (Section 8) must be stated, as they are significant parameters that bound the system. It may be that the company does not wish to state definite cost ground rules lest it unnecessarily limit the scope of the systems solution. In this event, this section can be omitted. However, particular cost parameters may be most significant. For example, it may be that the company owns several bookkeeping machines and wants to make use of them until they are fully depreciated. Although the economic validity of the company's depreciation practices may be challenged, if this is a company policy, the systems study must be consistent with it.

This then represents the contents of a system specification. Figure 3.1 indicates a feedback loop implying that the systems study group should continually reevaluate its work against the original business objectives and business system objectives that were established. The business world is a dynamic one and it is important that the resultant system reflect the current business environment. The systems group should be placed organizationally, so that it is immediately aware of any changes or shifts in the policies of top management that bear on the systems study. Constant tuning of the systems study with the business and business system objectives is extremely important.

KEY MANAGEMENT CONSIDERATIONS AT THE OUTSET

With the preceding discussion in mind, it should be clear that several important considerations must be explored in order to set the framework of the systems study. These are management considerations.

SYSTEMS ANALYSIS OR SYSTEMS PLANNING

The subject of systems analysis or systems planning was touched upon briefly but it is an important consideration that deserves further discussion. In the preceding chapter the distinction was made between a cost cutting system scope and a profit making approach. If, indeed, the focus of the study is to clean up existing methods with a view toward reducing costs, then it probably is sufficient to confine the system study to analysis. Assuming that the existing systems are consistent with established business objectives and strategies, as long as the current systems approaches are not altered or changed, then the new system will remain in tune with business objectives.

However, if the scope of the systems study is a profit making one, the systems study will no doubt alter the concepts employed by the existing system. Changes in inventory control techniques, labor reporting, and costing systems will occur. These can have a significant impact on the over-all business objectives. For example, it would seem obvious that a system aimed at improving customer service while increasing inventory would not be suitable to a company with a capital shortage. Therefore, a profit making system study framework calls for systems planning. Systems planning takes into account the current and future goals of the company. Because the information system parallels the actual physical operation, the two must go hand in hand. The patterns and policies employed in the physical operation are most relevant to the information system. For example, is the company rapidly growing and changing so that one of the key system parameters is the degree of flexibility built into the system? The resolution of the issue might be to make the system as flexible as possible. However, it should be kept in mind that a system must be optimized around certain key factors. The optimization point should occur at the most probable position of the company projected out to a reasonable future date. Deviating from the optimum point will cause either higher costs or less efficiency in the system. The point is that you pay a price to incorporate system flexibility at the design level. It may be worth the price, but it may not be if the company never requires the flexibility. There is a host of system trade offs that must be analyzed and made prior to the systems study. These trade offs are the key systems planning functions.

The following is an example of a systems trade off. A planning consideration is whether the system should be designed to evolve into a total or integrated data processing system; that is where initial subsystems are computerized, built, and designed so that they are able to interface (without major rework) with other subsystems developed at a later stage. Again, the answer to the question obviously may seem affirmative. However, the trade off that must be made is that an integrated system will cost more at the outset because more initial planning and analysis are required. This means that either a later completion date must be tolerated or that manpower must be allocated to the systems study effort.

Another cost trade off often is a larger computer configuration at the outset than would be otherwise required. It is like building a house—if you expect to make major additions at a later stage, you usually install a larger furnace. Although the modularity of modern computer systems minimizes this factor, it still exists to some degree. Thus, a trade off decision must be made. It is simply: "Do I pay a little more now to get a little more later?" I believe that in most cases the answer should be yes, for the true value of a computerized information system is in having the systems planning and business planning proceed simultaneously and the information system an integral and vital part of business operations. The one proviso is that the company have the required systems and management talent to devote to the systems study.

LEVEL OF MANAGEMENT INVOLVEMENT

The actual level of management involvement depends a good deal on the company's viewpoint to the previous discussion. It is possible for the systems staff to conduct the study almost completely by itself, gaining operating management involvement only on a limited scale. This can be called the closed shop approach versus the open shop approach where operating management and operating personnel participate in the systems study to a great degree. There are pros and cons to each approach.

It is fairly obvious that the study can be completed more quickly if the closed shop is used. The systems people utilize existing records and procedure write-ups to analyze the present system. Operating management and operating personnel are asked only to verify or refute what is already gathered by the systems personnel. If the systems personnel are skilled enough and if clear and concise written procedures are available, then this type of approach can get results. However, more often than not the existing documentation will be found lacking and active participation from management and operating personnel is a necessity. It is obvious that this approach will take longer but the benefits will be worth the time. For one thing, operating personnel and operating management are the people who will have to institute the system once it is implemented. Therefore, it seems prudent to begin paving the way for their use of the system and for their participation. This will begin to develop the necessary personal involvement and the required working psychology to effect a new system introduction.

For the most part the systems objectives should be determined by operating management. Systems people might disagree and point out that operating management and operating personnel, when interviewed, usually do not know what type of system is required or what type of report they really need. Although this may be true to some degree, it is operating management that has the final responsibility and control over how the department is run. Even if a system is instituted in a department without the concurrence of the department's management, the system can prove ineffectual. I recall a system that resulted in the issuance of an inventory status report that had anything and everything a buyer or inventory control supervisor would need. When an audit was made of the use of the system, it was found that the buyers were taking the figures from the computerized report and posting them to their manual Cardex file. Obviously there was something lacking in the area of management and operating personnel involvement.

Without fairly extensive operating management involvement, serious oversights and mistakes can be made during the systems study. For example, in a simple automated payroll application, the new system may do away with the traditional time card as the source document. The employee reports his hours worked through a data collection device that is connected directly to the computer. What may be overlooked is that the foreman may have been using the time cards to control overtime and to gain a weekly indication of the cost of particular jobs. It still is feasible to develop a system that does away with the time card; however, the system must ensure that there is some type of report at the end of the week that goes back to the manager to give him the same type of control (as a minimum) that he had before.

This is but one example of a host of things that may be forgotten in a systems study unless operating management and operating personnel are consulted. It illustrates the case of an informal use of a system that is not recorded in the written procedures. Talking with operating personnel may serve to uncover situations in real life that are not evident by outward appearance. In-depth interviewing and discussion begin to bring out a common phenomenon in many companies that might be called the *systems osmosis syndrome*. This is the phenomenon whereby a system grows up by osmosis through the many years it has been in operation. It is a composite of individual pieces, each of which is known intimately by a particular individual. However, that individual does not have the slightest idea of how the other pieces are handled. In many cases, there are unnecessary duplications and redundancies. It probably is true that at one time someone knew the entire operation. However, because of employee turnover, hosts of minor changes and refurbishments, and the lack of an over-all evaluation, the system has evolved into an unintegrated hodgepodge. The conclusion is that even though it may take a little longer and may add time to the systems study phase, it is very desirable to include operating personnel and to utilize the open shop approach. Figure 3.2 shows a company letter that may be used to initiate involvement on the part of operating management and operating personnel—involvement that is so necessary in attaining the desired results from a systems study.

```
TO        All Operating Personnel, Three B's, Inc.
FROM      W. W. Barrett, President
SUBJECT   Systems Study

We are in the process of evaluating our
current information processing system with
the thought that possibly an electronic
data processing system might improve
certain areas of it. This approach will be
a continuing long range program that could
extend over several years. The study is
being conducted by the systems study group
under the leadership of Dexter Johnson.
Members of Dexter's department will be
calling upon you to discuss your
department's operation and your role in
existing systems. It is extremely
important to gain your input to ensure that
an accurate assessment of system needs is
made. Your experience will be invaluable to
the systems study; we solicit your
cooperation as well as your participation.

Because most of you are unfamiliar with the
computer and electronic data processing,
you may wish to learn some basic computer
fundamentals. This will place all of us in
a better position to see what these
types of systems can do for the company. We
plan to hold periodic sessions to update
your knowledge of the uses of computers in
a variety of ways. There will be afternoon
```

orientation courses held once a week for
two-hour periods. In addition, you are
welcome to take, at company expense,
various courses offered by outside
agencies. (You should check with your
supervisor.) Dexter Johnson will also hold
informal discussion groups with individual
departments.

The important thing is that the development
of a successful automated data processing
system can be accomplished only with your
assistance. Despite the wondrous things
that computer systems are accomplishing
today, we fully recognize that machines
work while people think—we need your
thinking power.

(signed)
W. W. Barrett

WWB/c

Figure 3.2

STUDY TEAM SELECTION AND TRAINING

The previous chapter discussed the type of personnel required for the
feasibility phase. For the most part, the same type of talent and capability is required in the systems study phase; however, there are several
differences that must be considered.

First, the systems study phase necessitates a closer look at existing
systems and a more in-depth analysis of the strengths, weaknesses, and
areas of improvement. It requires personnel well versed in systems

technology and experienced in the analysis and development of successful computerized approaches to information processing. This type of person may be difficult to find within one's own organization, especially if the company is not as yet using electronic data processing equipment. It also may prove difficult to find such an individual from the outside. Competent systems personnel are in short supply. In addition, computer personnel tend to prefer working with larger companies that have more advanced EDP systems and are working on more sophisticated applications. Nonetheless, it is possible to attract an experienced individual who sees a challenge in having the opportunity to start at the ground level and to play a significant role in directly influencing the systems growth within a company. Because a company may not have had a senior systems man on its staff, it must be prepared to pay a higher salary than it may have considered previously. Probably there is not an equivalent job category within the company. It is far better to establish a new category than to try to slot the job in an existing salary range that may be far too low to attract the senior systems talent needed to accomplish the job.

Second, because the systems study, particularly if the scope is broad, will affect the basic operating areas of a company, it is prudent to have a qualified representative of an operating department as a member of the study team. This was true in the feasibility study and is even more significant in the systems study phase. The individual will no doubt have to undergo some systems and EDP training but his knowledge of the operating area will be invaluable. If an operations manager can be found who has the necessary systems background, it may be desirable to put him in over-all charge of the systems study. It is important to select an individual who can deal comfortably with top management, and the operating manager usually has this ability. However, because the systems study involves heavy reliance on systems methodology, it is rare to find an operating manager who has the necessary systems background.

The president's letter and the discussion thus far bring out very strongly the need for a training program at all levels. The education program should have commenced during the feasibility study; it must really get into high gear now. The company must give more than lip service to this important area; it must see that a comprehensive training plan is established. The personnel department should play a part in setting up the mechanics of how this is to be accomplished. Mechanics include considerations such as time and location, method (seminars, home study, and so on), training staff (internal, external, college), and the like. Figure 3.3 presents a checklist of possible training sessions for various levels of management and operating personnel.

	Intro to EDP	Mgt. intro to EDP	EDP project control	New concepts in EDP	Systems design (basic)	Systems design (advanced)	Conversion planning	Programming (basic)	Programming (advanced)	Physical operation
Top management		X	X	X						
Operating management		X	X	X	X					
Operating personnel	X			X	X		X			
Systems analysts	X		X	X	X	X	X	X		
Programmers	X			X	X			X	X	X

Figure 3.3 Training program.

This is only a guide, as it is obvious that some tailoring must be made according to the particular situation; for example, the management of these departments that are scheduled for immediate systems activity would want to undergo more extensive training than management who will not be directly affected. The timing of the training at the various levels is also a very important dimension.

THE SYSTEMS STUDY SCHEDULE

The PERT chart in the previous chapter indicated a time period for the systems study. Figure 3.4 describes the activities to be performed in more detail and is based on the systems study steps discussed previously in the chapter. The time for the study obviously is a function of many things; among them are: (1) the scope of the study, (2) the quantity and quality of the systems team, (3) the level of operating management involvement, (4) current systems status, and (5) top management pressure. The schedule presented in Figure 3.4 indicates a week's lapse between the conclusion and presentation of the feasibility study and the decision to proceed. Procrastination at this point can of course slow down the schedule. It is most important to avoid this and to maintain the momentum developed during the feasibility study. Another two weeks is allocated to selection, organization, and training of the systems team. This can be shortened if the systems study group is the same as the feasibility study group or it can be materially prolonged if additional qualified personnel must be hired. Once the study team is hired and trained, the schedule shows the study to be completed six months from the end of the feasibility study. This assumes that no major obstacles or deterrents are encountered.

A major element in determination of the schedule is the number of subsystems selected for detailed study (beginning after Event 6). If the over-all business system is studied first, it is possible to accomplish the subsystem studies in parallel. Therefore, the progress here depends upon the number of systems analysts available. The time frame illustrated is predicated on the availability of two analysts, each studying one subsystem.

It is important to view the systems study with perspective. Systems people often attack the job with a high degree of undue optimism. A common expression heard in the systems ranks is: "I know it took the XYZ Company ten months to conduct its systems study, but with our staff we can do it in half the time with half the people." Confidence and optimism are desirable traits, but the systems people should bear in mind that the job is big and some of the major considerations may

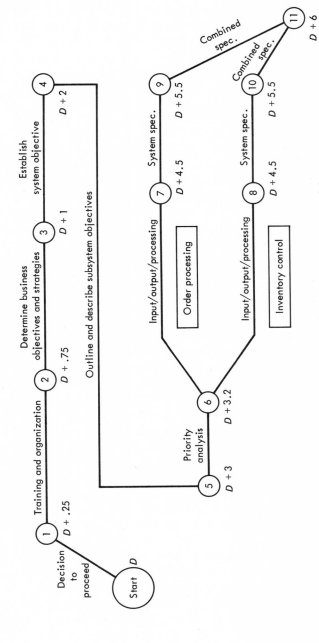

Figure 3.4 Systems study schedule (numbers represent months).

not be under their specific control. Such a consideration is gaining management agreement on a new systems concept—for example, introducing a sales forecasting system as a basis of establishing sales quotas. The details of the new quota system must be resolved before systems work can commence.

On the other hand, a company should not devote an inordinate amount of time to the study (indeed a PERT chart with time restraints is strongly urged). Systems perspective and balance are necessary to keep a systems study on solid ground—to avoid digging too deeply into systems minutiae and reaching a point of diminishing returns. Because of the complexity of certain systems, inexperienced systems people are susceptible to overworking a particular area. This points out once again the importance of having an experienced systems analyst either as head of or a prime member of the systems study group.

SYSTEMS STUDY METHODOLOGY

The steps of the systems study have been described. They include the determination of basic business objectives and strategies, the development of business system and subsystem objectives, and the establishment of priorities. Then the detailed input/output/processing analysis takes place, resulting in the final system specification. The contents of a typical system specification have been illustrated. This section explores the methodology or techniques for accomplishing it.

A brief disclaimer is in order at this point. The systems function has not as yet become a recognized profession. There is no question that it takes a high degree of technical competence and native intelligence to conduct successful systems analysis. However, there is no generally accepted body of systems knowledge or discipline as there is, for example, in accounting or in the legal profession. There is something called the systems approach, which will become better defined as the electronic data processing industry matures, but there is no universally adopted set of courses within a business school leading to a degree in information technology or systems management.

With this in mind, a framework or methodology for conducting the systems study will be constructed. A company's information process may be viewed as a series of blocks, each one fitting into a larger one (much like the blocks a youngster plays with, fitting smaller ones into larger ones until there is but one entity). The entity represents the total company and each succeeding smaller block becomes an individual subsystem of the total entity.

Systems analysis does not begin with the small blocks or subsystems;

it begins with the big block or entity. This is most significant. An analogy might be drawn between systems analysis and a final examination that has but one long problem. The more successful student approaches the problem by reading it in its entirety, seeing where each section, each paragraph, and each sentence fit into the total meaning. He then analyzes the total problem and plans an approach or solution that ties in all aspects of the problem. The problem is divided into its component parts and solutions are developed that attack these individual parts in a mutually consistent manner. It is possible to tackle the individual parts one by one but not to really resolve the major or composite problem.

Systems analysis can begin with individual parts or subsystems, and often it is easier to take this route. However, the results will usually be similar to those achieved by the student who begins to fashion his solution by analyzing and resolving the problem a section at a time. It is unnecessary to belabor the point. The systems study framework that analyzes the total problem first is called the total systems approach (or sometimes integrated data processing). What it says simply is that before embarking on a subsystem analysis, it is essential to take a look at the total system to see that each subsystem is consistent with the other subsystems. This will preclude painting yourself into a corner and reaching a stage where one subsystem has no way of communication with another subsystem that is desired at a later time. The situation then becomes one of redoing the original subsystem or living with unnecessary duplication.

An approach to analyzing a system regardless of its nature is the use of the systems module. A computer system has *input devices* that are capable of accepting transactions in the form of punched cards, paper tape, or optically scanned documents. It transforms this physical input media into electronic pulses that the computer's processing unit can understand and manipulate. The input data is then processed (sorted, rearranged, and calculated) and converted back into pulses that drive the printers, visual displays, and other output devices of the computer system. The three basic components of the computer system are shown in Figure 3.5.

The output has been placed on the left because unlike most processes, which start from the beginning or from what goes into a system,

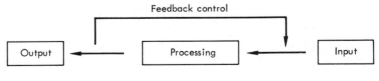

Figure 3.5

systems analysis begins at the end—with the output. The printed report is the final result of the processing and the reason for the system's existence. Systems studies therefore first determine the output requirements and then work backward to establish the input requirements. As with the process illustrated in Figure 3.1, there is a feedback loop or control mechanism that ensures that the processing or transformation of the input into output has followed the proper procedures—that it has been consistent with established policies and with predetermined decision rules. The feedback of an out-of-control condition in a computer system is triggered either by the stoppage of the machine itself or by the display of an appropriate error message. If both of these mechanisms fail, the feedback comes from the receiver of the output. If the output is a payroll check, the employee will indicate an underpayment or if the output is an invoice, the customer will state that he has been overcharged. (It should be readily ascertained that this type of feedback works far better in the case of underpayments and overcharges than in the reverse situations.)

As mentioned earlier in the chapter, the systems study is concerned with the information system, not with the physical operating system. However, it also has been mentioned that because the information system is based on the operating system, knowledge of the latter is essential. Using the systems module described in Figure 3.5 the physical and information systems within a company can be described. The broadest systems module is the over-all physical operation of the business, which can be viewed in Figure 3.6.

This is an oversimplified schematic of the physical operation of a manufacturing company. It represents the entity (the largest box in the children's building block analogy) and it is obvious that there are many smaller and more detailed subsystem modules underlying the entity. Layers and layers of underlying detail can be analyzed to elaborate on the sales function on the left, which controls the flow of finished goods to the consumer, or the purchasing function on the right, which controls the flow of the raw material from the supplier into the factory.

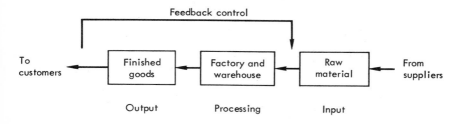

Figure 3.6

Likewise, the factory and warehouse function in the center, which transforms the raw material into finished goods, can be illustrated by a series of progressively more detailed subsystem modules. It is interesting to note that the systems module for the company is very similar to the computer systems module described in Figure 3.5.

Analysis of the systems module in Figure 3.6 can help focus in on the key over-all company business objectives. In its broadest sense, the business objective is to effect the physical transformation of raw material into finished goods to meet customer demand and at the same time maintain production costs at a point where a satisfactory profit is attained. Questions such as "What are the objectives concerning level of customer service?" and "What are the products needed to compete successfully?" are issues pertinent to business objectives that affect the marketing functions on the left. Questions such as "How can quality of product be improved?" or "How can production variances be decreased?" are issues pertinent to business objectives that affect the production functions in the center. Questions such as "How can I maintain competent sources of supply and reduce the cost of goods purchased?" are significant to the procurement function on the right.

A business information system can be built around the company's physical systems module. If the information system covers the entire physical process from raw material to finished goods, then every subsystem will be included and a total system will be the result. Thus the use of the physical systems module will facilitate the total systems approach.

THE TOTAL SYSTEMS APPROACH

Figure 3.7 begins to depict a total information system built on the basic physical systems module (the shaded boxes) just described.

The unshaded boxes represent information subsystems that control different aspects of the physical process. The subsystems are interrelated as the output of one becomes the input of another. In some instances, key source documents such as a customer order or inventory receipt are indicated. The result of this analysis will enable the systems analyst to identify the major subsystems within the company, to comprehend the interdependence of the subsystems, and to begin a more detailed study of selected subsystems.

Figure 3.7 concentrates on the left hand side of the physical systems module, the activity that is concerned with delivering the finished goods to the customer. It has been stated: "Nothing happens until someone sells something." This certainly is true, and the order emanating

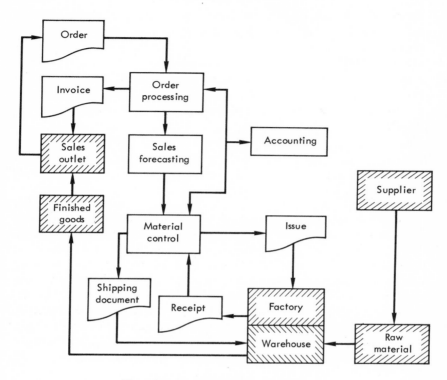

Figure 3.7 Total systems approach—Part I.

from the sales outlet is a most important source document. The order enters the first of the information subsystems—order processing. From there, the connecting arrow indicates that the order is screened within the material control subsystem. If the item is in inventory, a shipping document is sent to the warehouse and the ordered product is shipped to the customer. At the same time, the order processing subsystem issues an invoice to the customer, billing him for the product. The order processing subsystem is connected to the accounting subsystem, indicating that accounts receivable activity must be initiated with eventual cash receipt and reconciliation.

Historical data from the order processing subsystem updates the sales forecasting subsystem. This subsystem, in turn, periodically issues sales forecasts and revises inventory control parameters, such as economic order quantity and reorder points, as a basis for controlling inventories. Thus, the combination of the order processing and the forecasting subsystems determines product requirements.

Material control is concerned with raw material and in-process inventory as well as finished goods. Issues and receipts are shown entering and leaving the subsystem and serve to update inventory. The receipt will be an acknowledgement of raw material coming from the supplier into the warehouse. Issues indicate finished goods leaving the warehouse or the recording of in-process items moving from one stage of production to another.

At this juncture, the following information subsystems have been defined:

1. Order processing
2. Sales forecasting
3. Material control
4. Accounting

These subsystems are associated with controlling the flow of finished goods to the eventual consumer. Each one is a systems module in itself, having input, output, and processing. The feedback loop actually is present but is not shown. For example, the input to the order processing subsystem is the order whereas the output is a link to the material control subsystem (the two-way arrow indicates this is a feedback link because the order processing system must know if there is finished goods stock on hand to fill the order). Another output of order processing is information on sales movement to facilitate sales forecasting. The processing within order processing involves the calculations necessary to extend the order and to calculate shipping charges, discounts, allowances, and the like, resulting in output in the form of a sales invoice going back to the customer. There may be more than one input or output in each subsystem but the basic systems module still exists in each instance.

Figure 3.8 adds three additional subsystems to the over-all framework: requirements generation, production scheduling and production control. These cover the central portion of the physical systems module —that portion geared to transforming the raw material into finished goods.

The requirements generation subsystem takes finished goods requirements (sales forecast plus sales orders minus finished goods in inventory) from the material control subsystem and determines the requirements for subassemblies, piece parts, and raw material by multiplying the number of finished goods items by the components that constitute each end item. The total for each subunit then is measured against inventory records to produce net requirements.

This netting process is direct input into the production scheduling subsystem. The routing data indicates the sequence in which the subunits are combined to form the end item. Thus with the what and how described, a production schedule can be produced.

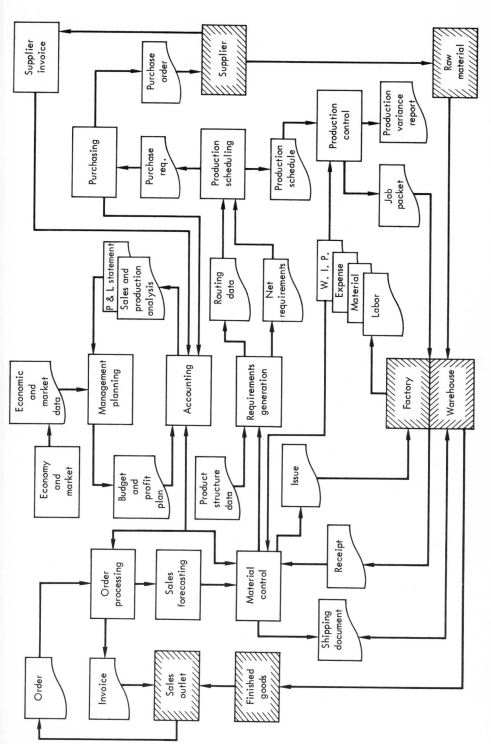

Figure 3.8 Total systems approach—Part II.

The production control subsystem then deals with the day-to-day implementation of the production plan by issuing job packets to the factory, accepting feedback of jobs completed (including labor, material, expense, and work-in-process data), and producing a variety of production variance reports. Inventory records also are updated, based on the feedback and reports from the production floor.

Figure 3.9 adds the purchasing subsystem covering the right hand portion of the physical systems module, that portion involved in obtaining the necessary raw material and other semifinished material from outside suppliers. The production scheduling subsystem determines whether an item is made or purchased. If purchased, a requisition enters the purchasing subsystem where a purchase order is written and sent to the supplier. The supplier ships the requested material to the warehouse where receipts are prepared to update the inventory records. At the same time as the vendor ships the goods, he sends an invoice, which enters the accounting subsystem and serves as input into the accounts payable process.

The final subsystem—management planning—enables management to receive internal statistics from the accounting system and external statistics concerning the market place and economy and to produce planning yardsticks, such as budgets and profit plans. This completes the cycle and serves as a measuring stick for over-all company operations. The use of special operations research techniques, such as simulation and linear programming, also are considered part of the management planning subsystem.

The schedule just mentioned is a framework of nine interlocking subsystems, that together make up a total system for a manufacturing company. The total system was built on a physical systems module and each subsystem in itself is an input/output/processing systems module. In addition to the input/output/processing elements, a fourth element must be added in the case of the subsystem modules—the *data base*. The mortar that holds the total system together is what is called a data base. A data base holds all relevent information about a company's operation in one readily accessible file.

The file is arranged so that duplication and redundancy are avoided. Information concerning ongoing activities is captured once, validated, and entered into the proper location in the data base. Normally the data base is subdivided into the major information subsets that are needed to run a business. These subsets are: (1) customer and sales file, (2) vendor file, (3) personnel file, (4) product information file, (5) inventory file, (6) work status file, and (7) general ledger accounting file. Different departments use information from the same file. The key element in a data base concept is that each department utilizes the same

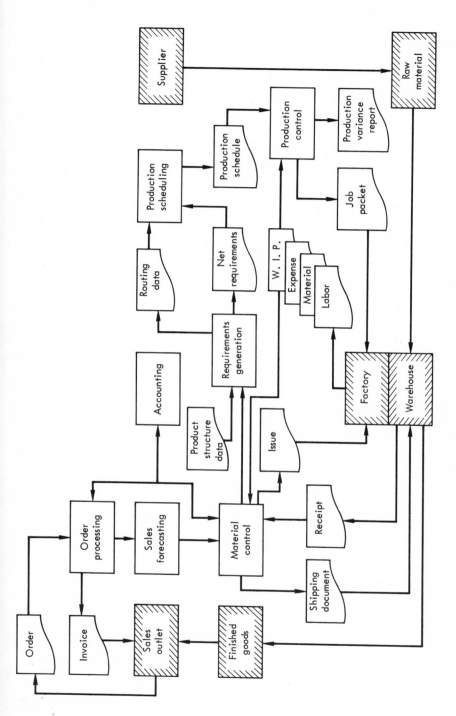

Figure 3.9 Total systems approach—Part III.

73

data base in satisfying its information needs. Duplicate files or subsets of the data base are avoided.

It should be evident that a data base can be overlaid on the total system that has been constructed. For example, the customer and sales file is a source of data for the order processing, sales forecasting, material control, and accounting subsystems. The supplier or vendor file is source of data primarily for the purchasing and accounting subsystems. The product information file and inventory file are sources of data for almost every subsystem in the framework.

This discussion of integrated or total systems, interlocking subsystems and data bases serves to set the stage for proper analysis of business objectives and strategies, system and subsystem objectives, and priority analysis. It is apparent that each of the nine subsystems can be broken down further into additional subsystems and these subsystems into other subsystems. One may begin to look at the systems study with a bit of dismay after viewing the task with the total systems perspective. The job is immense; can a total systems objective ever be accomplished? The answer probably is that it cannot, but this is not to say that the total system is not a good goal to shoot at. The other alternative is to attack each subsystem on its own and forget about its place in the total conglomerate. Realizing that a fully integrated system is probably unattainable, the systems study uses the total system as a framework or roadmap. It reminds the study group to avoid redundancy and duplication of effort whenever possible and to remember the basic commonality of inputs and outputs and the interlocking of subsystems in a total system.

Having described the total system, we can determine the areas to investigate by a priority analysis. This will be based on factors such as resources allocated to systems development, potential financial benefits, impact of the company's various problem areas, previous experience and involvement in electronic data processing, and the time frame in which results are desired. It takes time to study the over-all company operations and to analyze operations from such a global view. However, it is felt that the potential benefits are well worth the efforts. Even though the study group now begins to tackle subsystems one at a time, it has an over-all plan of what the company's information system can look like in the future. It could take as long as five years to computerize all of the nine subsystems described in Figure 3.9. However, there is now a potential of getting there; without a framework or plan, the potential of getting there is nil.

The total system described is geared to a manufacturing company like Three B's. However, the concept has equal validity in other industries. Figure 3.10 illustrates a total systems framework for an insurance company. The same concepts of system and subsystem input/output/processing modules apply in this insurance example.

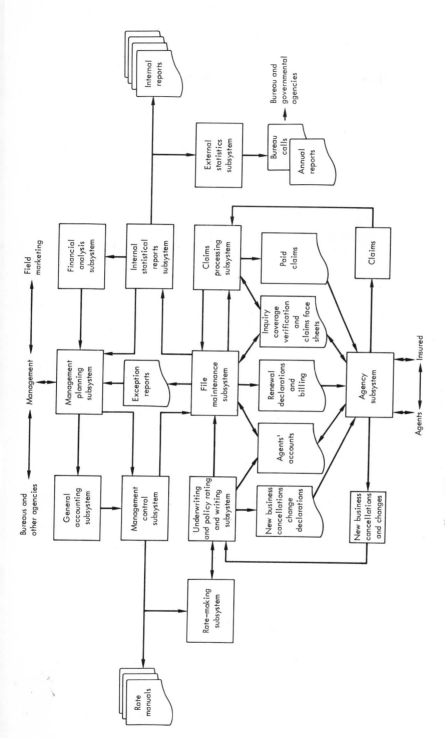

Figure 3.10 Integrated management information and control for fire and casualty insurance.

PRODUCING A SYSTEM SPECIFICATION

This section describes a system methodology for taking an individual subsystem and developing the necessary input/output processing and data base information in order to produce a system specification. The data matrix (Figure 3.11) is an approach or framework for developing the information required for the system spec. It is a simple method of gathering and summarizing information in an orderly fashion to facilitate analysis and the formulation of an eventual data processing system. The data matrix illustrates that the starting point is at the bottom of the chart, the users' section. This section of the matrix lists the people and departments who will be using the reports emanating from the information system. As indicated earlier, system designs begin with output so the flow, illustrated by the arrows, follows a clockwise rather than a counter-clockwise path.

The left hand portion of the matrix indicates the reports or output needed by the users to effectively control their respective operations. Managers act on information and normally the information is provided through the media of written reports. The source of information for these reports is the data base or master files of the company (top of the matrix). The data base is in turn fed by input from source documents (e.g., sales order or inventory receipt) listed in the right hand portion of the matrix.

Although the system design proceeds clockwise, the resulting system will reverse the process; that is, the input (business transactions) will be processed (note the processing block) into the data base and from there processed again into the final reports required by the users. Note that this then evolves into the familiar input/output/processing systems module.

The following simple example illustrates how the data matrix is used. One of the sales manager's requirements is a sales forecast. Start at the sales manager's block (see Figure 3.11) and follow the arrows. A circle is placed under the sales forecast report. Move upward from the sales forecast report. The sales history portion of the data base is needed to provide the information for the forecast. A circle, therefore, is placed on the coordinates connecting the sales history file to the sales forecast report. Following the systems flow, sales history information emanates from customer orders; therefore, a circle is placed on the coordinates connecting the customer order with the sales history file. Customer order input is the responsibility of the order processing system, which is under the direction of the controller's department. Therefore, a circle is placed on the coordinates connecting the controller with the customer order input.

Another prime user need is an inventory control report that indicates the current status of inventory and triggers purchase requisitions when an item slips to a predetermined reorder point. This is required by the sales manager and the controller as well as the production manager, as indicated by the dots placed in the respective columns. Move upward in the matrix. Data on sales history is required (inventory control is based on a sales forecast using past demand as an index) as well as data on each inventory item being controlled. The dot and the circle, both on the sales history line, indicate that two output reports and two different subsystems (forecasting and inventory control) use the same data base information. Follow the inventory column across. Dots are placed in the coordinates connecting inventory and customer order, inventory control parameters (elements such as lead time to order items and price of each item) and receipt. The controller is responsible for providing the input concerning the inventory control parameters whereas

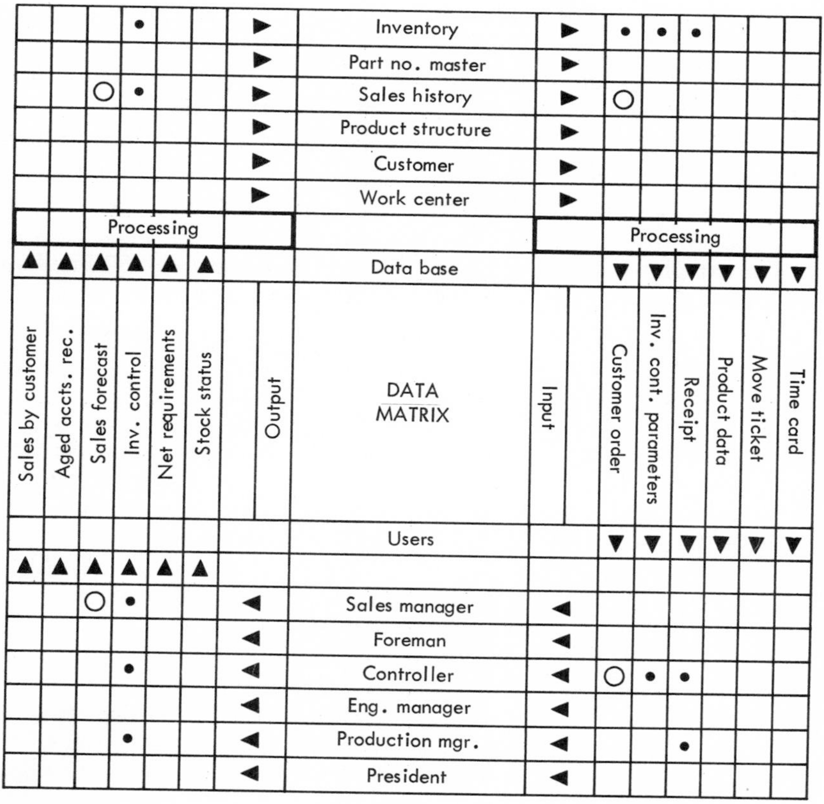

Figure 3.11 Data matrix.

both the controller and the production manager are responsible for the input of receipt information. In a like manner, all the user's needs can be charted to illustrate the commonality of reports, data base, and input requirements. The concepts of the total information system and the central data base are accentuated further by this type of analysis.

The data matrix technique can be used to analyze individual subsystems in far greater detail than has been illustrated. The input/output and data base requirements can be developed for each of the individual subsystems to be studied. Figure 3.12 illustrates a second level of detail of such an analysis for the order processing subsystem. Finer and finer cuts eventually will provide the basis for developing a complete system specification.

The completion of the data matrix leads directly to the development of a system specification for each of the subsystems under study.

TOP MANAGEMENT PHILOSOPHY IN A SUCCESSFUL SYSTEMS STUDY

As has been stated repeatedly, management philosophy, particularly that of top management, can set the stage for either the ultimate success or failure of a systems study. More significant than the particular system methodology used is the attitude management has toward the systems study and toward the whole concept of electronic data processing to the company.

The experience of a small integrated steel producer (with $20 million sales) illustrates a management philosophy that has been successful. It is significant that the following quotes were written by the president himself in describing his company's approach to EDP.

> Several years ago, we came to the conclusion that any company big enough to afford a computer that does not have one either functioning or in its planning for the immediate future is not going to grow in the competitive business world of today. Everything we've learned during our first year as a computer user has served to reinforce that conviction.
>
> If we were willing to spend the money, we could manually prepare most of the reports our computer is giving us today.
>
> Five years from now this will not be true. We will then have a management information system pervading all phases of our corporate activity, and we will be achieving the growth and earnings objectives we have set for ourselves, which we could not hope to achieve without the computer.

Subsystem name	Activity name	Output	Data base		Input
			File name	Data element	
Order processing	Edit, credit check, and book	Open-order file, unaccepted orders.	Customer master	•Cust # •Cust name •Cust addr. •Credit code	Customer orders
	Check inventory avail., price and print acknowl-edgement	Customer acknowledge-ments	Part number and inv. master	•P/N •Avail. bal. •Description •Qty. reserved •List price •Xfer price •Discount code	Open-order file
			Customer master	•Cust # •Cust name (Bill to) •Cust addr. (Bill to) •Cust name (Ship to) •Cust addr. (Ship to) •Date last trans.	
	Print product shippers and invoices	Picking lists, packing lists, invoices	Part number and invoice master	•P/N •Desc •Loc code •Pieces/pkg •Package type •Package # •List price •Xfer price •Discount code	Open-order file (ack. date)
			Customer master	•Cust # •Cust name (Bill to) •Cust addr. (Bill to) •Cust name (Ship to) •Cust addr. (Ship to) •Tax code •Ins. limit •Ship. inst. •Hold code	

Figure 3.12   Information requirements—order processing subsystem.

A small company dedicated to growth thus can utilize the benefits of a computer more fully and in a shorter period of time than a large complex corporation. The complete management information system we are installing here, for example, will be accomplished in five years or less.

A key consideration brought out by this statement is the importance of an information system that can grow along with the company. Note the use of the concept of management information system and the suggestion that it may take as long as five years to accomplish.

To ensure that the computer has no adverse effect on the company and to hasten its full utilization, it is necessary to properly indoctrinate all of the management group to its use. The procedure is the same as the indoctrination program after the purchase of a new piece of sophisticated machinery. You have a training program for those who are to be involved with it. The only difference is that in this case the computer is a tool that is used by the whole management group, not by just a handful of operating people, so the whole management group is included in the educational programs.

Prior to the installation of the computer we began our indoctrination program with a three-day seminar at Cornell University for our whole management group to discuss what we hoped to accomplish with our new computer. We then formed a committee of operating people who analyzed every piece of paper in use in the entire corporation. After the committee completed its work, we held a second seminar to talk about what we had accomplished in the course of that year—but no longer were we talking about just a computer. We were talking now about our business, its progress, and its goals. At this second seminar, we introduced the management information system concept, explaining that such a system had always existed, but in a very crude form. All of those pieces of paper we had worked with every day were part of this system; for that matter, information written on a paper napkin would be part of it.

The company decided it was important to indoctrinate the entire management group. A committee of operating people was formed. The statement is made that after a while, the management group was not talking just about a computer; the members were talking about the business, its progress, and its goals. This is an extremely vital part of systems analysis, as stressed throughout the chapter.

We try to manage this business by objectives. In order for us to do this, management people must make commitments on how they are going to operate each unit of the company. The computer is beginning to play a big part in helping them to set these goals and to reach them.

For example, one new plant manager faced with setting his standards for the year was able to make a massive analysis of past operations to secure some particular data he felt he needed that would have been impossible to get with our old tab equipment. Furthermore, with some corrections and revisions, this same system is helping him now to attain his objectives by supplying him with a weekly status report. Soon he may be able to have updated information on a daily basis as part of our complete management information system.

In another instance, the sales department was able to use a very detailed sales analysis of past performance provided by the computer to predict what they will sell to each customer this year, not just in dollar volume, but by product, broken down by specific chemistry and size. This in turn permitted our manufacturing people and purchasing people, who formerly had to base their cost objectives on groups of products, to determine more accurately the specific alloys they will require and the amount of material they will have to produce in various sizes, and therefore to forecast more accurately what the cost of sales will be. The more accurately you can predict, the more effectively your costs can be reduced.

Because we do measure management people by their performance relative to the objectives they themselves have set, they also determine what information they want and what the computer can do to help them. Manufacturing applications, for example, are developed by manufacturing people assisted by the people in the computer department—and not the other way around.

Again these are examples showing that the computer is becoming woven into the basic fabric of the company's operation. The computer is helping refine the company's objectives, set goals, and assist in reaching those goals. Another key statement is that manufacturing applications are developed by manufacturing people. This is extremely important to successful use of the computer and is an example of management involvement at the operating level.

I do not know what possibilities we will uncover in the future, when more data becomes available. We are contemplating a complete random access system, with terminals in all of our operating departments. I foresee people, for example, in order processing, production scheduling, or sales, with a computer inquiry station at their desks being able to to press a button when a customer calls and have instantly displayed all information needed to give an immediate answer to questions about delivery, pricing, and so on.

I can envision a computer-controlled continuous steelmaking

process in which a scrapped automobile will go in at one end of a plant and a finished steel product will come out the other end. It is possible that this kind of thinking eventually will cause a complete revision of the operating systems we have now.

As my function is more planning and looking to the future, I do not need information in the detail or with the frequency that people involved in making our day to day decisions do. But I would like to have on my desk each morning a summary report of corporate activities up through the day before—cash balance, accounts receivable, accounts payable, shipments, production, and the like —for each segment of the business. This can not happen for a long time, of course, but eventually it will be possible.

The president and the company have a planned and organized approach to EDP. The president can see the possibilities of tomorrow but fully realizes that it will be a while yet. The important thing is that without a plan and without management involvement, it can never happen at all.

SUMMARY

The steps in the systems study were illustrated in Figure 3.1. Systems analysis begins by reviewing the over-all business objectives of a company and the external and internal strategies employed to meet those objectives. This is necessary in order to ensure that the resultant business system is in tune with the over-all business objectives. At this point the basic business system objectives are determined, filtering the basic over-all goals into progressively increasing layers of detail to arrive eventually at a system specification for those portions of the business system that are to be computerized.

Management considerations at the outset of the study were mentioned and included a discussion of the distinction between systems analysis and systems planning, the level of management involvement, study team selection and training, and the systems study schedule. The discussion then settled on a methodology to evolve the system specification from the basic business objectives. The systems module was described as a simple method of viewing a system, whether it be a physical operating system or an information system. Using the systems module, a technique was developed for analyzing the total or integrated systems complex of a company. The significance of the *central data base* to an integrated system was stressed. This led to a natural build-up of individual subsystems comprising the total entity. Then the data matrix was illustrated as a method for gathering and organizing the necessary input/output/processing and data base requirements in order to develop a system specification. Finally, the experience of a steel company was presented in order to gain the perspective of top management toward a computer installation.

THREE B'S' APPROACH TO THE SYSTEMS STUDY

Based on the discussion of the systems study phase in this chapter, the approach used by Three B's now can be evaluated. Bill Barrett, the president, still is personally involved in the computer study—it is obvious that he is bent on maintaining the momentum established during the feasibility phase. His personal philosophy might sound similar to that espoused by the steel company president. However, there is danger that he may not be bringing the rest of his management team along. Dexter Johnson has not been able to build his team with the strength he needs. For various reasons, Paul Peters of the sales department and Warren Coolidge of production have not been able to supply the personnel requested by Johnson. From previous background, it may be assumed that plant manager Burt Harrison may have had something to do with this.

The proper management philosophy outside of Barrett himself may not be present—in fact, the others may resent somewhat the boss's pushing of the project. It is likely that further discussion, possibly a computer seminar or workshop, is necessary to gain a better understanding of the potential of a computer program to Three B's.

The systems study group headed by Johnson (who now had been assigned full time) and including Bill Osbourne, an inventory clerk, and Harry Farnum, a punched card operator, proceeded from the findings of the feasibility study. The feasibility study had lagged beyond its scheduled completion date and had taken six months. Johnson now tries to increase the tempo in an attempt to make up for the previous delay. Osbourne is assigned the inventory system whereas Farnum studies the order processing system. Johnson attempts to work with Farnum and Osbourne, who are inexperienced in systems analysis. Each has a tendency to get bogged down in a morass of detail. Johnson has all he can do to keep them above water and properly directed toward the goal of producing a system specification in their respective areas.

Four months after the study is begun, Johnson holds a review session in which Farnum and Osbourne present their findings to Peters, Coolidge, and their respective staffs. The meeting is little short of a disaster. Peters and Coolidge bring out the point that the studies have been proceeding independently when in fact they should have dovetailed closely. (Johnson sees that there are obvious inconsistencies.) Both Peters and Coolidge indicate that this is the first time either was aware of what was really happening. They cast doubts on whether the systems so far conceived can have a material effect on resolving the major sales and inventory problems they are experiencing.

Although a considerable disappointment to Johnson, this result was not totally unexpected. He questions his own handling of the situation. In his effort to make up for previous delays, he had accepted without great rebuttal the selection of Osbourne and Farnum though he knew that the background of both left much to be desired. He attacked the subsystems in question straight off, without taking an adequate look at the over-all business and systems objectives of Three B's. Furthermore, Farnum and Osbourne had no EDP training other than a three-day systems indoctrination course. Probably the most damaging element was the fact that although Johnson was purportedly assigned full time, he was called off the project by Harry Hanson to oversee an audit being made by the Internal Revenue Service. Although this was not a full time assignment, it detracted from his role as head of the systems study.

Johnson decided that radical surgery was needed at this juncture. He told Barrett of the situation and suggested a meeting of top management to discuss the problem. The meeting was held and Johnson laid out a plan of attack. He took the major share of blame for the lack of real progress to date and asked for management's cooperation in resolving the matter. Johnson indicated that he personally was reworking the systems study done by Farnum and Osbourne. This was being accomplished in the light of a major reevaluation of the original business and systems goals and the coordination of the sales and inventory systems into an integrated approach. He apologized for Farnum and Osbourne, indicating that they had been thrown into the systems study too quickly but that both had learned a great deal and were at a point now where they could make a major contribution. Johnson asked for more assistance and participation on the part of management and promised more frequent updating sessions on the progress of the systems group.

Following this plan, the systems study was brought to a successful completion. However, the entire study had taken eight months and not the six that the schedule called for. The scope of the study had been broadened over the original plan and Johnson believed he had a more comprehensive grasp of Three B's' problems and the knowledge of how a computerized information processing system can help. The system specification was reviewed thoroughly by management with consensus that major progress had been made; management had become part of the EDP program and felt good about it. Johnson, Farnum, and Osbourne were working as a team and the latter two had reached a satisfactory level of systems competence. They now turned their attention to the next phase of the job—the synthesis phase where the system spec would be subjected to alternate computerized solutions. Three B's was getting closer to making its computer decision. It had taken longer than estimated, but the company was learning some interesting and valuable things about its business and gaining more perspective on the role of a computer system in its operations.

ADDENDUM: SYSTEM SPECIFICATION

ORDER PROCESSING SUBSYSTEM—THREE B'S, INC.

SECTION 1—SYSTEMS DESCRIPTION

Three B's' line of bicycles is handled by 200 salesmen and jobbers throughout the country. The geographical distribution and sales volume are described in Section 6. Orders are placed by the salesmen by telephone to the sales administration office in Cleveland. The calls then are backed up by a written order form submitted by the salesman himself or by a sales office, if there are enough salesmen in an area to justify an administrative staff. When the order form is officially received, a credit check is made and then a punched card is produced. This card provides input to the billing system where the individual items are extended, costs and weights are calculated, and the various discounts and allowances are figured. This card also is used by the inventory system to deplete finished goods if the item is in stock or to trigger make orders if the item is not in inventory. When the entire order is assembled, an invoice is issued to the individual customer as a basis of setting up an accounts receivable record.

SECTION 2—SYSTEMS OBJECTIVES

The previous narrative has described the existing system of order processing. The following are the objectives of the new system:

1. Reduce order cycle time from current 30-day average.
2. Reduce out of stock condition.
3. Improve accuracy of inventory records.
4. Allow for a 20% transaction increase.
5. Facilitate adding new items and removing others.
6. Improve order expediting.
7. Set automatic notation of appropriate substitutions if out of stock.
8. Reduce ratio of cost to order processed.

SECTION 3—GENERAL FLOW CHART

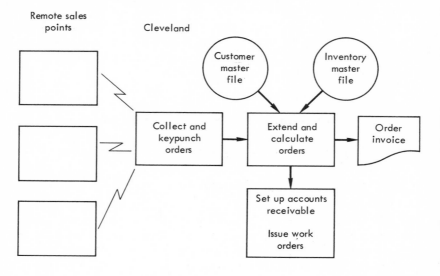

SECTION 4—INPUT/OUTPUT REQUIREMENTS

Figure 3.13 describes two basic output forms emanating from the system—the inventory action report and the billing form. These documents describe the required output for the new system. It is felt these reports will give management the proper control over the order processing cycle. In addition, they present useful statistics currently not available, such as percentage gross margin on each order, reorder points, and economic order quantities. These figures form the basis for periodic inventory and sales analysis reports.

Basic order processing input is submitted by the salesman or sales office and includes the following:

Field name	Numeric	Alpha
Store number	7	
Item code	5	
Quantity	6	
Item description		20
Store name		20
Store address		30
Current month/day/year	6	
Desired delivery date	6	
Requested terms	10	
Shipping instructions		20
Insurance instructions		25
Total	40	115

INVENTORY ACTION REPORT

INVENTORY ACTION REPORT							Date ____	INVENTORY ACTION REPORT					Date ____	
Item no.	Description	On hand	On order	Total available	Projected demand	Reorder point	Economic order quantity	Item no.	On hand	This order	Amount short	% available	Action code	Substitute item no.

BILLING FORM

Store address	Store copy							Store #	Order #	Date ____
Item description	Item retail	Unit retail	Item number	Quantity	Discount unit and allowance cost	% gross margin				

Figure 3.13

SECTION 5—FILE CONSIDERATIONS

The two major files required are as follows:

Customer file			Inventory file		
Field name	*Numeric*	*Alpha*	*Field name*	*Numeric*	*Alpha*
Store code	7		Item code	5	
Store name		20	Item description		20
Address		30	Size		4
Credit terms	10		Color		4
Discount	6		Unit price	6	
Allowance	6		Quantity price	6	
Region and area code	5		Weight	7	
Open order	8		Gross margin	7	
Open balance	8		Economic order qty.	8	
Maximum credit	8		Reorder point	6	
Order number(s)	50		Substitute code	2	
Customer class	2		Cost	7	
Annual purchases	8		Tax	7	
Date(s) promised	50		Insurance	7	
Overdue status	6		Average sales	8	
Salesman	6		Historical sales	12	
Total	**180**	**50**		**88**	**28**

SECTION 6—VOLUMES AND OTHER SPECIFICS:

1. Average of 160 orders received per day.
2. Average order 6 items.
3. 125 company salesmen.
4. 75 jobbers.
5. Two thirds of the orders taken in the spring and in the fall.
6. Eight sales regions; southwest and west are largest.
7. Teletype network between Cleveland and Los Angeles, and between Cleveland and Atlanta.
8. 200 finished goods items; 150 carried in stock.
9. Average of 20 orders per day expedited.

SECTION 7—COMPLEMENTARY SUBSYSTEMS

The sales order processing system is very closely related to the inventory control, accounts receivable, sales analysis, and sales forecasting

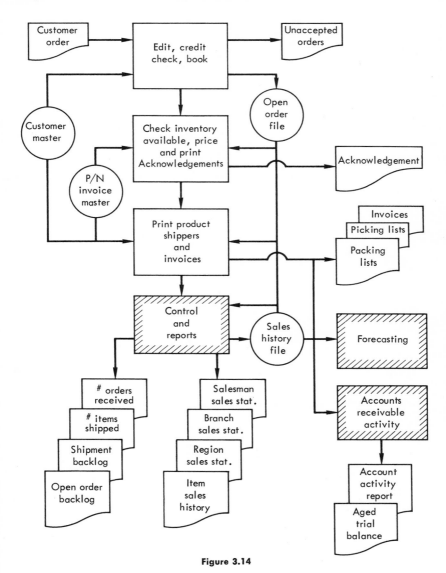

Figure 3.14

subsystems. A prime consideration is to build an open ended order processing system that can logically lead into subsequent implementation of
the other systems. Figure 3.14 illustrates in flow chart form the tie-in
of the sales order processing system to these other subsystems (shaded
boxes).

SECTION 8—COST AND OTHER GROUND RULES

The system proposed should be able to handle comfortably a 20% increase in the current transaction volume over the next two years and a 50% increase over the next five years. The hardware cost to accomplish the job (bearing in mind that the sales order processing and complementary subsystems comprise about 30% of the total data processing work load) should not exceed the current hardware cost plus 50%. The teletype network should be maintained, as it serves functions other than supplying order processing input. It is greatly desired that the total data processing job be able to be completed within one machine shift.

SOURCE MATERIAL AND SUPPLEMENTARY READING

Anthony, R. N., *Planning and Control Systems. A Framework for Analysis.* Division of Research, Graduate School of Business Administration, Harvard University, 1965.

Blumenthal, S. C., *Management Information Systems.* Englewood Cliffs, N. J.: Prentice-Hall, Inc., 1969. 274 pp.

Churchill, N. C., J. H. Kempster and M. Uretsky, *Computer Based Information Systems for Management—A survey.* New York: National Association for Accountants, 1968.

Datamation. (The March 1968 issue is devoted to the subject of information storage and retrieval.)

Deardon, J., *Computer in Business Management.* Homewood, Ill.: Dow Jones–Irwin, Inc., 1966. 300 pp.

Enger, N. L., *Putting MIS To Work.* New York: American Management Association, 1969. 255 pp.

Factor: Integrated Management Information and Control System For Manufacturing. Honeywell, Inc., 1967. (The section in this chapter on the total systems approach is based on this document. I had responsibility for the development of the factor system.)

Hanold, T., "A President's view of MIS," *Datamation* (November, 1968).

Harvard Business Review, Special reprint series on Management Information (14 articles). Boston, Mass.

"Managing the Systems Effort," *EDP Analyzer* (July, 1968).

Plossl, G. W. and O. W. Wight, *Production and Inventory Control.* Englewood Cliffs, N. J.: Prentice-Hall, Inc., 1967.

Robbin, D. A. Jr., "A Small Company Turns to the Computer," *Management Thinking* (October, 1968). Published by Harvard Business School Association, Boston, Mass. (The quotes in this chapter under the Reading of Top Management Philosophy in a Successful Systems Study are from this article.)

4

SYSTEMS DESIGN

Three B's has completed its systems study and Dexter Johnson believes he has a good grasp on the information processing requirements of the company. His job now is to design a systems solution that meets the systems specifications developed during the systems study phase. Realizing that management is becoming slightly impatient at the continued delays and departures from the original schedule, Johnson wants to move quickly through the design job.

Johnson has what he considers good specs on the over-all total systems approach desired by Three B's in the long run as well as individual and detailed specs on order processing, inventory control, and those applications currently being performed on punched card equipment. With this in hand, Johnson submits the specs to three computer vendors. He limits the selection to the three vendors who have been calling upon him (his current supplier of punched card equipment plus two others). He issues a covering letter to each as follows:

```
TO          Computer Vendors
FROM        D. T. Johnson
SUBJECT     Request for Computer Proposal
```

Attached are systems specifications for
the major applications of the Three B's
company. You have been selected as a
computer vendor to bid on these
specifications. In order to be considered
for the eventual contract, you must submit
your proposal in writing no later than four
weeks from the date of this letter.

Three B's desires a computer system to
handle the specified applications within
one shift of computer operation, leaving
the second shift for growth. As mentioned
in the over-all specification, an
open-ended and flexible approach is desired
—an approach that will allow Three B's
to move toward an integrated data
processing system in three to five years.
A suggested phasing plan with required
hardware, software, and personnel resources
at each phase is considered optional in
your response.

A listing of current data processing costs
is included in an addendum. A cost goal is
to spend no more than 30% above what is
currently being expended. It is assumed
that the major portion of our existing
hardware will be replaced. The replacement
plan, including a time table, should be
defined clearly.

Alternate hardware configurations may be submitted but your reply should state which alternative in your judgment is best suited to handle Three B's' requirements. Price and delivery times should be indicated, as well as a complete statement of generalized and specialized systems support offered by your company. At the vendor's option, an over-all implementation schedule with necessary manpower can be presented.

It should be kept in mind that Three B's desires a system that can satisfy current demands while leaving ample growth potential. We do not want to pay any more than we have to; however, we desire a realistic appraisal of hardware needs. The system must have the power and capacity to do the job. It should be obvious that we will not be content with doing the traditional data processing tasks but must be able to tackle the key money-making applications described in the specifications.

My staff and I will be available to answer questions or elaborate on any area that requires it. Feel free to call upon us, as we realize the importance of your having the necessary data upon which to base your proposal. In addition to your written proposal, you are invited to present the salient features of your recommendations to Three B's' management in a two-hour session, which will be scheduled after submission of the proposals.

We would appreciate an immediate reply as to
your intention to bid on our specifications.
                     Sincerely yours,

                     (signed)
                     Dexter T. Johnson
                     Director, Data Processing
/c

*While the vendor's proposals were being prepared, Johnson and his
team decided to tackle the systems design job themselves so as to be
ready to evaluate the responses. The use of consultants was discussed
but ruled out at this time. Rather than have a consultant develop an
independent systems design, it was decided that consultants might well
be brought in to evaluate the various vendor proposals after they had
been submitted.*

INTRODUCTION

Look back at Figure 1. The analysis phase of the computer system
selection cycle has been completed, leading now into the synthesis phase.
During the analysis phase, the total data processing system needs were
reviewed and broken down into individual subunits or subsystems. This
has involved a continual process of dissecting existing information systems into their simplest components and putting them under the scrutiny
of the microscope. After the analysis of the relationships of each part
with the other and the viewing of these in light of over-all company
information needs, detailed systems specifications were developed. The
job of the synthesis phase is to put the pieces together again—retaining
what can be salvaged and replacing what can not—into a new system
that satisfies the stated specifications. Thus, the task must now become
solution-oriented. The goal is to design a system that accomplishes the
applications at hand but does so in the fastest, most efficient, and most
economical manner.

The approach is to develop as many alternate solutions as possible
within the time restraints and then to test each against the computer configuration necessary for its solution. This step can be done independently
of computer manufacturers if the company has sufficient computer expertise; it can be done by the various competing vendors or it can be

done concurrently with the vendor's evaluation. Another approach is to have an outside consultant make the evaluation. The important prerequisite to any of the approaches is to have solid systems specifications in hand.

No mention has been made to this point of particular computer or particular hardware characteristics. It would have been premature to do so. The data requirements, the input and output needs, and the flow of information processing steps have been analyzed and categorized thoroughly. Now is the time to impose a hardware or computer solution, and to discuss elements such as file storage media, input devices, printing facilities, computer capacity, and processing speeds. These must be combined in such a way as to provide an optimum solution consistent with the time frame allocated to the job and the personnel resources available to accomplish it.

The systems design phase is normally the prerogative of the systems group. Management has been vitally interested in reviewing and helping develop the what of the system. The how is now left to the systems designers. If the specifications are clear, management is willing to delegate the design to the people who specialize in this type of analysis—the systems professionals. However, it is assumed that the designers must be guided and restrained by cost and investment parameters. Normally trade off points are reached as the systems design proceeds. For example, it may develop that a particular systems requirement necessitates a special device that is extremely expensive and is not required by any other part of the system. At this point, it may be practical to either modify the systems specs or at least reevaluate the specific requirement in light of the cost to meet it. Management should be involved in these trade off decisions. The decisions reached and the reasons for them should be well documented, because the issues have a tendency to crop up again later in the design or after the system is in operation. A historical record of these decisions and the rationale for them will save a good deal of rework at later stages.

THE BASIC SYSTEMS DESIGN PROCESS

The systems design process can be viewed in terms of the basic systems module described in the previous chapter. The purpose of the design is to satisfy the systems requirements in the most efficient manner and at the lowest possible cost. In order to do so, one must consider what is fixed about a system, what is variable, and how the fixed and variable elements can be combined in such a way as to produce the optimum redesigned system (see Figure 4.1). In practice, various iterations are

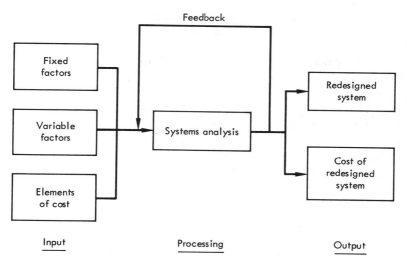

Figure 4.1

made as different combinations of fixed and variable elements are evaluated and compared until the best design is developed.

The terms *fixed* and *variable* warrant clearer definitions. The fixed elements are those that cannot be changed and must be adhered to in designing the new system. For example, a company may have an existing paper tape transmission system that it wants to maintain as part of any new approach. A variable factor is one that can be changed to arrive at a new design such as whether a report is printed and sent to a manager or is available upon request by means of a cathode ray tube in the manager's office. Either the printed report or visual display may satisfy the information needs of the manager, but one method may do so more efficiently and effectively. Obviously, cost also plays a part in this decision. One may argue that fixed factors are arbitrary in nature, as it is obvious that anything can be changed if there is good reason to do so. However, in a practical sense, these fixed elements exist. For example, it may be possible to obtain a new building to house the proposed computer center but the chances of this occurring make it advisable to consider the requirement to locate the computer in existing facilities as a fixed element.

Thus, the fixed and variable elements along with the costs associated with each are blended into a systems design. Figure 4.1 shows a feedback loop indicating that the process is repeated until the best system is found. It can be stated realistically that the final redesigned system is not necessarily the optimum. It is true that there always will be room for an imaginative mind to improve the final system even further. However, it is unwise to pursue systems design to a point of diminishing returns for the efforts that are expended.

Figure 4.2 describes a basic computer system as consisting of input devices (punched card readers, paper tape readers, and so on), a processing unit that has the ability to perform arithmetic operations on the incoming data by use of a stored program (sequence of step by step instructions), storage units that hold fixed information (data base) such as records of inventory items or policy holders, and output devices (printers, cathode ray tube displays, and so on). The job of system design is based on the buildup and composite needs of each subsystem to arrive at the required computer input, processing, storage, and output devices to accomplish the job.

SEQUENTIAL OR DIRECT ACCESS

The following systems design discussion focuses attention on the crucial decisions the systems analyst must face in developing a system in the changing EDP environment.

An analogy can illustrate the difference between the sequential and direct access approaches to systems design. This is an extremely important underpinning of the entire system. In a business environment, most line personnel operate in a sequential manner whereas line management operates in a direct access manner. Let us look at the line foreman and the production personnel who report to him. The production person works on a particular job; in fact, his work is normally specialized to the extent that he may work on repetitively producing a specific part one after the other. Thus, his job is sequential in nature. The foreman waits until he can schedule a full lot of an item and then makes the assignment to accomplish the job. If the part is complex enough and the lot size large enough, the production worker may perform only a defined

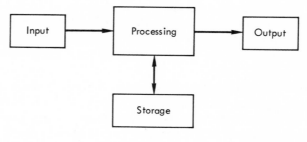

Figure 4.2

machine operation, passing along the part to another work center and worker for accomplishing a subsequent operation. This is an example of the batch sequential type of operation—the job is accomplished by a series of sequential steps and is done in batches (many items are produced at once).

In direct contrast is the job of the production line foreman. His working day is filled with a host of problems to solve, decisions to make, and actions to perform, all coming at him in a random and interspersed manner. Machine A is down and he must tell the workmen what to do until the machine is fixed. A minute later, Machine Center C reports that it is running low on raw material and so the foreman must expedite the delivery of material to the area. Almost concurrently comes a call from the cost accountant telling him that the production cost variances are up 6% over last week and the general foreman wants an immediate explanation. These situations represent problems that must be resolved, one at a time, as they occur. They cannot be batched and neatly sequenced, as with the work of the production line people. The foreman might find it advantageous to be able to batch his problems into categories so that he could devote, for example, the first hour of the day to machine failures, the second to inventory problems, the third to efficiency reports, and so on. He could no doubt fulfill his over-all job responsibility far more expeditiously; however, the current way of doing business does not allow it. Although the batch sequential mode is the way in which most businesses would like to operate, the direct access mode is indeed the way businesses do operate. This fact will be most significant in our discussion of sequential and direct access information systems.

This procedure is similar to a data processing system's handling of information needs and points out an important distinction between sequential and direct access systems.

SEQUENTIAL SYSTEMS

Figure 4.3 illustrates a schematic of a typical data processing application following the input, processing, storage, output framework. The sequential storage medium for computer systems is magnetic tape similar to recording tape that can be played on a home recorder.

Data is stored in the form of magnetic spots in tracks along the tape and can be sensed and interpreted by a computer. It is an efficient storage medium when you wish to extract data from the tape in a sequential manner. However, you run into the same problem that you do on a home tape recorder when you wish to start with a message that is

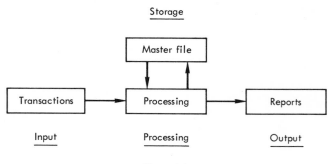

Figure 4.3

half way down the tape—you have to pass half the tape to get to the message you want. This is not very efficient, particularly when a magnetic tape is 2,400 feet long and can take four minutes to pass. If there is a transaction that calls for an item at the end of the tape followed by a transaction at the beginning of the tape, it is desirable to wait and process the second transaction first. Obviously, a situation where you cannot wait to batch before processing is not conducive to sequential handling. A portion of the order processing application can illustrate the manner in which a sequentially-oriented business system operates. The parallel between the batch-oriented production job should be evident.

Figure 4.4 illustrates the five sequential steps necessary to produce a customer invoice from an incoming order. The first step involves transforming the pertinent information on incoming orders into machine readable form. The information can come via a telephone call, a written order form mailed into the office by the customer, or a form filled out by the salesman after a sales call. The information is key punched into cards, which are then edited, checked, and written onto magnetic tape. Other input media such as mark sensed cards, punched paper tape, or optically read font can be used. In addition, the input can come directly from a remote site by means of a communications line, thus bypassing the first step in the sequence. This possibility will be discussed when communications-oriented systems are discussed.

The orders are received randomly from individual customers and each order may have several items. The system must have the ability to see if there is sufficient inventory on hand to fill the order and then to extend the quantity ordered by the price of the item.

A master inventory file is sequenced by a predetermined item number. In order to find and extend each item, the orders must be sequenced in the same manner as the inventory file. Thus, Step 2 in the system is to sort the orders into individual item sequence; however, each item

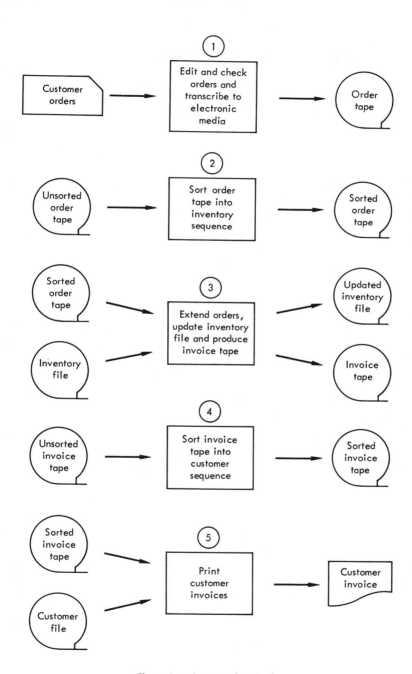

Figure 4.4 Sequential methods.

still must carry the customer identification so that it can be reassembled later with the customer order.

Step 3 involves passing the order file against the inventory file until a match occurs. Then the inventory file is reduced by the amount of the order and the necessary cost data is used to price and extend the individual items. Step 4 re-sorts the extended inventory tape (now called the invoice tape because it is the basis for invoicing customers) back into customer sequence. The items ordered are once again associated with the particular customer who ordered them. Step 5 involves the passing of the invoice tape against a master customer file. This file has the information required to write an invoice such as the customer's address, credit terms, allowances, special deals, and the like. The final result of all this processing is a printed customer invoice.

This is a simplified example of a sequentially oriented batch type systems design. This type of design would not be practical for handling one order at a time—its efficiency comes from handling a large number of orders in a batch. In fact, the larger the batch, the more efficient is this type of systems approach. Because it is comprised of five separate computer runs or operations, the set-up time would begin to equal or exceed the productive running time as the number of batches per day builds up.

A consideration in evaluating the merits of sequential systems is the distinction between the terms *throughput* and *turn-around time*. The former term describes the over-all machine efficiency of a system. Thus, if there were 500 orders to process per day, it might be possible to process them in 50 minutes by the sequential approach (the throughput rate is 10 orders per minute). However, the turn-around time of this same system is 50 minutes; that is, because the orders are done in a batch, no meaningful output is possible until the entire operation on all the orders is completed. There may be a requirement to be able to process selective high priority orders in one minute. It is obvious that the sequential type of system cannot accomplish this. This turn-around requirement leads into a discussion of another type of system—the direct access approach. Even though the direct access approach may have less throughput, the user may be willing to accept this if he can obtain the required turn-around time. Obviously, a third significant overriding element is the cost of the various systems methods. In practice, it is the skillful balancing of (1) throughput, (2) turn-around time, and (3) cost that is the real challenge and the most important consideration in systems design.

DIRECT ACCESS SYSTEMS

Figure 4.5 describes the same order processing job, this time uti-

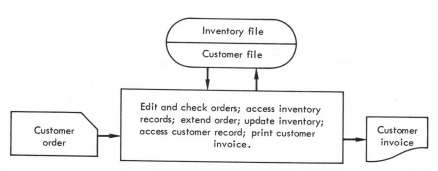

Figure 4.5 Direct access method.

lizing the direct access method. This is a great deal easier to explain, as there is but one step to the process. Orders enter the system again on punched cards but are processed one order at a time as they are received. The inventory and customer files are carried on a direct access file where they can be interrogated randomly, unlike the sequential mode where magnetic tape was passed until the proper record was found. Each item is extended and the relevant inventory record updated. The extended items are held until the complete order has been processed. The customer invoice is printed and the next order is ready to be processed.

If this method can process five orders per minute, the total time for 500 orders will be 100 minutes.

Figure 4.6 compares the relative throughput and turn-around time of the two methods. This is an oversimplified situation and emphasizes a significant contrast between throughput and turn-around time. In actual situations, the differences probably will not be as extreme. For example, it is possible that the direct access approach can have both a turn-around and throughput advantage over the sequential approach. Although the sequential approach rarely beats the direct access approach in turn-around time, it often can demonstrate an advantage even greater than the 2:1 throughput advantage it enjoys in this illustration. This is particularly so when a throughput/dollar index is used. When the throughput differential is great, the systems designer must consult with

	Throughput*	Elapsed time	Turn-around time
Sequential	10	50 min.	50 min.
Direct Access	5	100 min.	12 sec.

*Orders per minute

Figure 4.6 Sequential approach versus direct access approach.

management in order to place some type of dollar value on fast turn-around time.

The sequential versus direct access systems approach has been viewed in light of but one application—order processing. In actual practice, the information system must satisfy a host of requirements throughout a company. Turn-around time requirements of each user or function of the business must be analyzed and put into perspective.

Figure 4.7 presents a variety of user needs for information and the time frame in which the information is required. This is the type of analysis needed to determine whether the system should be sequential- or direct access-oriented. The information necessary to make this analysis emanates from the systems study described in the previous chapter.

The systems designer should bear in mind also that in many cases it need not be an either/or decision, but it may be that a combination of sequential and direct access storage is the more desirable solution. It is the composite of these needs that determines the systems design. Again, cost is a very important element. Though difficult to ascertain, an additional column—the relative dollar value and priority of meeting the turn-around requirements of each user—might well be added to the chart in Figure 4.7.

User	Information required	Type of information	Turn-around time required
Bank teller	Customer balance	Detail from customer record	Less than one minute
Insurance agent	Policyholder service	Several details from customer record	One minute to 24 hours
Salesgirl	Customer credit	Detail from customer record	Less than one minute
Credit mgr. (loan dept.)	Customer credit	Detail from customer record	One hour
Design engineer	Component to meet certain specifications	List of part numbers from result of file search	One hour
Salesman in remote office	Inventory availability	Inventory status of particular items	Less than one minute
Top management	Summary reports	Summarized data based on detail files	One week
Production manager	Component/tool availability	Inventory status of specific items	One hour
Market manager	Market potential for new product	Market analysis	One week

Figure 4.7 Information response requirements.

There are other considerations in determining whether the sequential or direct access approach is more suitable. Figure 4.8 places these in context with the first three, which have been discussed. Turn-around time is always in favor of the direct access approach whereas throughput and throughput per dollar must be qualified to mean those applications that have large enough batches so that they can be processed at one time. Another cost advantage results from the fact that the sequential job can be broken up into smaller and more digestible pieces. Because of this, it usually is possible to accomplish the job by using less computer memory. The fewer but larger and more multifunctional runs of the direct access approach also require more programming complexity and, therefore, either more programming time, more experienced programmers, or both. A check is placed in the appropriate column to show an advantage of the sequential method in this area.

Audit control is another consideration that favors the sequential approach. This can be illustrated by referring to Figures 4.4 and 4.5. Step 3 of Figure 4.4 indicates a master file as both input and output to the processing. Because of this, there is a natural audit trail of the old inventory file in case it has to be re-created. This is not true in the direct access file, where a single file is changed so that there is no record of the previous one. This may or may not be a crucial factor in particular situations; however, the sequential method offers the better facility for an audit trail.

The next factor is an important one and favors the direct access method. Even though current needs may not dictate quick response time, the nature of business operation in general appears to be headed more in that direction. The direct access approach permits flexibility to handle a future need for quick response that may be unforeseen today. Therefore, the direct access method may prove valuable insurance for the future. An expensive changeover would be required to convert the sequential system to direct access if conditions later warranted it. It can be stated most assuredly that many companies are going from sequential to direct access but the number that goes the other way is few.

	Sequential	Direct access
Turn-around time		√
Throughput	√	
Throughput/dollar	√	
Programming ease	√	
Audit control	√	
Future flexibility		√

Figure 4.8

At the outset of this discussion, an analogy was drawn between sequential and direct access methods on one hand and the job of the production foreman and production workers on the other. Although it is true that in many cases the sequential approach, like that of this production worker, is more efficient, it also is true that business more and more is operating like the production foreman. Thus, the nature of business operation is changing very rapidly and the information systems that parallel these operations must be flexible and ready to change as well. Competitive pressures are making response time a most valuable commodity of a company. The company that can fill an order on the spot, process a claim from a remote location, and expedite a particular manufacturing order at the last minute has a strong competitive edge. Therefore, although the data processing system with the high volume, batch-oriented, highly efficient operation still will play an important role, the general nature of business will dictate a greater emphasis on direct access systems.

TRENDS IN COMPUTER SYSTEMS

It is appropriate at this stage to view the trends that are taking place in computer systems. These trends may not be appropriate for Three B's' specific situation but, because they represent what companies more experienced than Three B's are thinking and moving towards, they are worth looking at. A discussion of these trends points out some important considerations that must be analyzed during the systems design phase.

Electronic data processing can be viewed as having three dimensions. Figure 4.9 indicates that these are hardware, software, and application.

The hardware consists of the physical computer devices that can be seen and touched such as a punched card reader, a central processor, or a line printer. When one thinks of a computer system, this is more often than not what comes to mind. However, this dimension more aptly should be called a subsystem because the hardware by itself does not accomplish anything for a business. The second dimension, the software side, consists of the programming languages and operating systems that enable the programming personnel to communicate with the hardware. This dimension is called software in contrast to hardware be-

Figure 4.9 Three dimensions of EDP.

cause the product is in reality a series of instructions that are fed into the computer originally from punched cards. Thus, the product is not hardware in the sense of the physical units just mentioned. However, more and more, companies have awakened to the fact that the software is equally as important (or even more important) as the hardware. The machine itself is a dormant mass unless the proper software is available to drive it.

Whereas the computer programmer looks at the computer through its software, the systems analyst, business manager, and operating personnel look at the computer through its application. An application is defined as an end product such as order processing, which produces a customer invoice or inventory control that produces a stock status report. By themselves, hardware and software are merely academic capabilities until they are applied to live applications in a live business environment. A computer's value is a measure of how well it handles premium billings for a life insurance company or prints a production schedule for a manufacturing company. The application can be considered software in its own right as it too eventually must be expressed by a series of instructions that are fed into the computer in the form of punched cards. However it is relevant to make a distinction between the two classes of software. Suffice to say that all three dimensions must be going for you—hardware, software, and application—to make the computer more than a sleeping giant. The software and applications properly blended by a skillful user begin to wake the giant.

HARDWARE TRENDS

Let us now take a look behind the trends. Figure 4.10 illustrates the changes in the hardware dimension in the ten-year period that began in 1964 (the advent of the computer industry's third generation). The figure indicates the dollar equipment cost for the typical user in 1964 contrasted to the expected cost for a user in 1974. As can be seen, the central processor, comprised of the memory and processing unit, accounted for more than half the dollar value of a typical user in 1964. Early computers were used for mathematical and scientific purposes, which necessitated a machine with large amounts of memory and extremely fast processing speeds. The most competent engineering talent was applied to the central processor and the resultant product facilitated the solving of large mathematical problems. However the cost was high, particularly in comparison to the input, output, and storage devices, which were used as ancillary equipment. The cost of the central processor has been reduced markedly with the advent of business data proces-

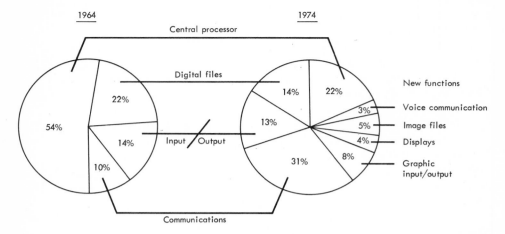

Figure 4.10 Equipment cost for a typical company.

sing, large volume production methods, and the continued reduction in the cost of its major elements. It is expected that by 1974 the central processor will account for about a fifth of the total cost.

Another element of cost expected to drop dramatically is the digital files consisting mainly of sequentially-ordered magnetic tape and random-ordered direct access files. Although the economies of scale have not operated in this area to the same extent as in the central processor area, the proportion of cost to the average user is expected to drop from 22% to 14%. Input/output devices are defined as the major batch type on-site devices, such as card readers, paper tape readers, and printers, which are hooked directly to the computer. There have been fewer breakthroughs in this area than in the others, while the volume of basic punched card input and printed output has continued to expand despite a good deal of systems work aimed at reducing it. The use of optical character reading devices has shown a steady growth and accounts for a progressively larger share of the entire input/output area (about 15% of the input/output cost or 2% of the total equipment cost by 1974).

A big growth area is in communications hardware. This represents the cost of control units, multiplexors, and terminal equipment, which is not represented by the new functions section of the chart. The new functions include remote terminal devices, most of which are in use today but were not in 1964. Voice communication covers the voice answer-back terminals beginning to pick up in recent years. Voice input is still in the experimental stages but a modest amount of this might be on the scene by 1974. The ability to digitize media that historically has been put on microfilm is another fast-growing area. The reduction in space and, more importantly, the speed of retrieval make this a natural adjunct to computerized systems. Thus, the chart shows that image files will represent 5% of the computer cost in 1974. Displays refer to the cathode ray tube method of visually projecting data at a remote site. CRT devices are in common usage today and will account for 4% of the computer dollar spent in 1974.

Graphic input/output is a rapidly growing area and is expected to reach 8% of the computer expenditure in 1974. On the input side, this category of device takes the form of a light pen or in some cases tactile impressions (the touch of a finger). An engineer can design a production part on a screen and be materially aided by the computer in so doing. On the output side, the devices are able to project graphs and charts similar, for example, to Figure 4.10 itself.

This is the projected shift in the allocation of the hardware cost dollar. Significant is the trend to communications and communication-oriented devices. However, one should not necessarily assume that the other hardware elements are becoming insignificant. The large proportion of communication cost is due in some degree to the fact that the economies of large scale production have not as yet taken place to the same extent as with central processors and storage devices. It is also true that the major cost breakthroughs have come with electronic components and not as much with mechanical components. There is a greater proportion of electronic components in central processor and storage devices than in communications equipment. Indeed, it will become apparent that direct access storage devices are essential for most communication-oriented systems.

SOFTWARE TRENDS

Figure 4.11 illustrates another important dimension of EDP—the software dimension. In 1964, the major developments were still primarily in assembly languages and compiler languages. Assembly languages allow the programmer to communicate with the computer in simple mnemonics like ADD & MOVE whereas compiler languages allow the use of structured English language statements. Thus the purpose of assemblers and compilers is to allow the machine to go about its job in binary language, the language it knows best, while the programmer can talk in English language, the language he knows best. The language software effects the translation from English to binary.

Although it is difficult to obtain accurate cost figures on software development from the computer manufacturers, the relative investments in language software are estimated at 40% and 35%, respectively, of

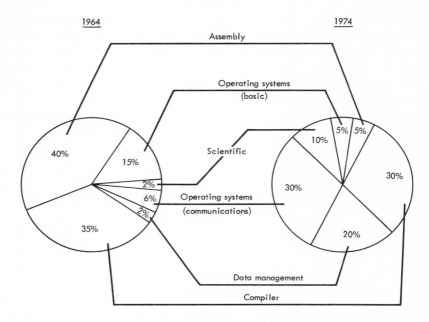

Figure 4.11 Software development costs.

the total expenditure on software in 1964. It is important to keep in mind that the major expenditures for software were from computer manufacturers at that time. A significant shift has occurred to a point where independent software houses account for a far greater percentage of software costs. These independents are doing contract software work for the manufacturers and also provide proprietary software directly to computer users.

An important event took place on June 23, 1969 when IBM announced a new pricing policy whereby certain of its software systems as well as education and systems support services would be priced separately. Although software that had already been released continues to be included in the price of the hardware, the intent is to move gradually to complete separate pricing. This "unbundled" pricing structure enables the independent software houses to compete more effectively for the user's software business. Other computer manufacturers have had mixed reactions; some stayed with the existing pricing structure whereas some have inaugurated a degree of separate pricing.

Assembly systems are expected to be a very minor part of software expenditures in 1974. They will be replaced by higher level languages. COBOL (*CO*mmon *B*usiness *O*riented *L*anguage) is being improved continuously and compilers like PL/1 (*Programming Language* One) also are becoming significant. Many computer users still will use assembly language in 1974, but for a decreasing portion of their work load. Whereas the ratio of assembly language to compiler language usage was 90% to 10%, this is expected to be reversed by 1974. This is a very significant trend. The ease of programming and of program update and change and the ability to protect one's programming investment in going to a new computer auger well for the accelerated use of compiler languages.

Another important shift is in the use of operating systems. The function of such a system can be compared to the maintenance and set-up crew for production line machinery. Their main duty is to do the routine but important housekeeping chores to ensure that the equipment is as productive as possible during the work shift. Operating systems were simple in 1964. They had only to clear memory, initialize the peripherals, handle routine error situations, load memory with the first program to be executed, and proceed to do the same with each program throughout the productive shift.

The objective is to reduce the amount of manual intervention and gain as much productivity as possible from the machine. With the advent of communications-oriented processing and the desire to continually increase productivity, operating systems have taken on a new look. They now must be able to recognize demands from a host of remote terminals, to allocate the necessary hardware resources to these demands, and to satisfy these demands while at the same time running the daily production-line jobs at the central site. This requires a rather complex monitoring and control capability—a capability that represents the major challenge of today's operating systems and the even more sophisticated ones that will be on the scene in 1974. As can be seen from Figure 4.11, the basic operating systems will fall from 15% to 5% in 1974 whereas communication-oriented operating systems will have a five-fold increase.

The growth in scientific software reflects an expanding use of computers in advanced mathematical problem-solving. In 1964, this software was the province of a relatively small number of engineers and operations research analysts using mathematical techniques to assist in engineering calculations and research projects. By 1974, techniques such as linear programming and queueing theory will be more widely used in general business operations. Scientific software that facilitates this analysis will be most significant to these companies. Scientific software, although still only 10% of the total software development cost in 1974, will show a five-fold rate of growth from 1964 to 1974.

Data management systems are a response to the user's need to store large volumes of information in a central data base in order to provide total systems capability. The total systems concept was described in the previous chapter. This information must be indexed so that relevant pieces of the information base can be obtained as a unit and in the time frame required by the business situation. This is no mean task. Figure 4.11 indicates an extraordinary growth (from 2% in 1964 to 20% in 1974) in this category of software. Data management also must tie in quite closely with the operating system, as much of the inquiry and update activity to the file takes place from remote locations over communication lines.

APPLICATION TRENDS

The third dimension of EDP, the application dimension, is illustrated in Figure 4.12. Trends in computer application indicate that general administrative applications, such as payroll accounting or customer invoicing, will decrease sharply as a percentage of computer time in this ten-year span—from about 75% to about 30% of the total. In contrast mainstream applications, such as inventory control and production

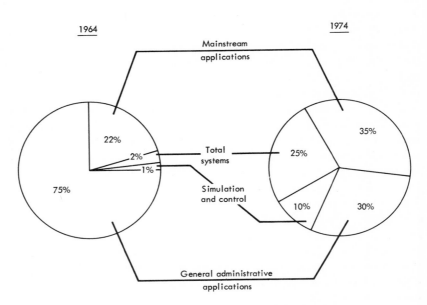

Figure 4.12 Application allocation of computer time.

scheduling for a manufacturer, will grow. The general administrative applications are directed at the clerical functions of a company and are mainly record-keeping functions. They are generally historical after-the-fact systems. In contrast, the mainstream applications are more dynamic in nature so that they may pinpoint inventory shortages before they begin to affect production or spot potential production bottlenecks before they occur.

Total systems or integrated information systems—where the administrative applications and the mainstream applications are welded together in a single unified system supported by a common data base of information—are expected to have a most rapid growth pattern. The 25% figure in 1974 does not mean that the systems making up this figure will be integrated completely but rather that they will be based on a common framework or plan employing a major degree of integration.

Simulation and control systems are a still more sophisticated category, characterized by the space and missile programs of today. A space vehicle relays information about its flight to a ground computer. Based on a flight simulation model stored in the computer, the data is analyzed immediately and signals are issued by the computer to adjust the flight of the space vehicle to hit its target. The type of modeling and simulation in which management can test policies and procedures before they happen in order to ensure the highest payoff when they happen is an example of simulation and control systems in a business environment. These applications are expected to grow to 10% of computer time by 1974. Thus, a marketing policy can be tested before the product is introduced to the market place, and a production schedule can be evaluated before it reaches the production floor.

This discussion points out some key trends and considerations that must be explored during the systems design study. Though a company must, of course, assess its own specific needs and the extent of its ability to invest in EDP, it would appear remiss for system designers not to at least review these overriding trends.

COMMUNICATIONS PROCESSING

An important systems design consideration is the degree of communications processing planned now and expected in the future. Viewed in its broadest sense, communications covers the entire area of getting information from computer memory and data storage devices to the ultimate user. In its more accepted sense, it means receiving and sending data over communication lines from remote sites to the central computer site. The broad and narrow senses of communications processing are related because direct input of data from remote sites can preclude or reduce the need for on-site input equipment. This is true also on the output side. Because of this relation, communications will be discussed here in its broader meaning.

Most companies operate over a geographical area—some have salesmen in major U.S. cities, others have sales and procurement offices throughout the country, and still others have separate manufacturing plants or warehouses located far apart. In many cases the people in these outlying offices either supply the crucial input data, receive crucial output data, or do both. Therefore, it behooves systems designers to broaden their design perspective when considering input and output devices and communications processing. The concept of turn-around time as described in the previous section must take this into account. Turn-around time must mean total turn-around time, defined as providing the final document or data in the hands of the user in the time frame he requires it. In the order processing situation, the ultimate purpose of quick order processing is to get the order to the customer when he needs it. The time requirement is not met completely by being able to process the order through the computer in 12 seconds. The order then must reach the warehouse, where physical items comprising it are picked, loaded, and shipped to the waiting customer. If the 12-second order spends two days getting to the warehouse, the system might just as well utilize the sequential approach. Suffice to say, *total* turn-around time is the crucial element and communications processing plays a key role in determining total time.

Communications processing takes many forms and shapes. The proliferation of communication equipment and devices makes this area a rather difficult one to comprehend. There are many stages, ranging from the very simple remote sales office that transmits sales orders on paper tape by means of a teletype station, to the nationwide network of hundreds of remote stations in two-way communications through visual and audio display units. It is easier to understand the different forms of communications processing by proceeding from the simple or very basic through the different levels of interactive processing to the more complex multisubscriber time sharing form. Figure 4.13 illustrates six stages of communications processing.

BATCH PROCESSING

The simplest form is basic batch processing as characterized by the sequential approach described in the previous section. All input is put

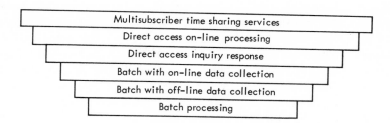

Figure 4.13

in machine readable form at the computer site. Orders may be taken by telephone but eventually they are key punched into cards before entering the computer. Likewise all output is in the form of printed copy, which is either handcarried to the ultimate users or sent by mail. Determination of input and output methods becomes a relatively simple matter of measuring the relative data recording costs (operator and supply) against volume figures and weighing the pros and cons of punched cards versus paper tape versus direct transcription to magnetic tape or disk. The output consideration is resolved by selecting the high-speed printer(s) that can handle the volume in the time frame required and meet print quality criteria. Thus, there is no mystery to batch data processing. It is the oldest form of computer use and still is the work-horse for many types of applications.

BATCH PROCESSING WITH OFF-LINE DATA COLLECTION

Moving one step up the ladder, we have batch processing with off-line data collection. Data collection involves the gathering of input data from a variety of terminal points. Examples are cash registers in a retail store, factory data collection devices, and paper tape terminals. There are on the market today cash registers that produce either a paper tape, magnetic cartridge, or punched card as a by-product of the transaction at the sales counter. This then is fed through the appropriate data transmitter at the end of the day to the computer site where it is received, usually on magnetic tape. After the reception is completed, the receiving magnetic tape is switched to the computer where the input is used for customer billing and inventory control. The major advantages of this type of operation, compared to more conventional methods, are reduced turn-around time and increased input accuracy.

Factory data collection devices represent another class of off-line equipment that is growing in use. A data collection device is a unit that can accept a prepunched card or an employee's embossed identification card and also has the facility for accepting variable information by means of a set of keys or dials. The data is then recorded on an off-line magnetic tape. After a day's operation, the tape can be switched and read by the computer to calculate the payroll and produce job and cost accounting reports. The worker records activities as they occur rather than at the end of the day, thus increasing the level of accuracy and ensuring a faster information turn-around time.

Teletype networks are used by many businesses in a variety of industries. Orders are transmitted back and forth by paper tape, insurance premiums are paid at a local office where a record of payments is transmitted over a teletype terminal to verify the payment at the home office, and a record of daily movements is transmitted by a trucking company to the home office for billing purposes. All these are examples of the wide use of off-line paper tape terminals throughout the country. The cash registers, factory data collection devices, and paper tape terminals illustrate the first step in communications processing. These devices usually cannot handle the entire input and output load but must be supplemented by conventional punched card and printing equipment at the computer site.

BATCH PROCESSING WITH ON-LINE
DATA COLLECTION

The next stage in communications processing is to switch the off-line data collection to on-line. This can be done in either a dedicated or a nondedicated mode. In the dedicated mode, a computer is dedicated full time to receiving data from remote sites. This, of course, implies a very high volume of input data to justify the expense. Another form of dedication is that in which the computer is assigned full time to data collection but only at prescribed hours throughout the day. Thus, it may be that the computer is doing nothing but collecting data during the hours of midnight to 8:00 A.M.

In the on-line mode, the data goes through the computer's memory and then on to tape or disk. Because the data does go through memory, the opportunity is there to have a program in memory that edits and checks the data for various error conditions. This is accomplished as the data enters the system so that the error can be noted immediately and sent back to the transmission point. This aids in reducing the turn-around time still further, as it may be that the erroneous data must be corrected before the processing can commence.

Figure 4.14 illustrates the off-line and on-line data collection meth-

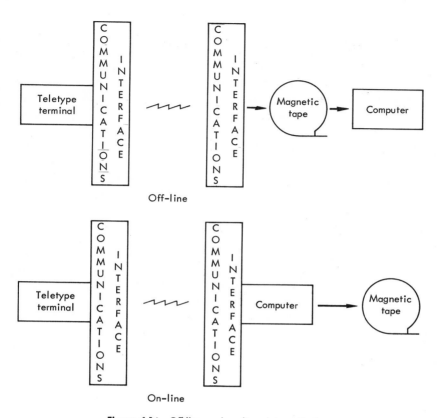

Figure 4.14 Off-line and on-line data collection.

ods. The dedicated data collection method has been described; however, the computer need not be dedicated completely to this task. The data collection function can be intermittent throughout the day and it may be desirable to transmit whenever there is data. Although slightly more complex, the computer can be programmed to run daily production programs and to be interrupted whenever there is a demand to transmit data. The production program is interrupted, control is turned over to the data collection program, the data is edited and placed on magnetic tape or disk, and control is returned to the production program. This is an example of two programs operating in the interrupt mode and will be described in a later section on multiprogramming. Both the dedicated and nondedicated forms of on-line data collection still are in the batch mode, because the data is collected and batched before final processing of it occurs.

DIRECT ACCESS INQUIRY/RESPONSE

The direct access method of data processing was described. Having data in random storage facilitates immediate access to the data and the development of a fast response system. Examples of inquiries are credit checking, order reservation, inventory status, or a customer request for information. A salesman in a remote spot wants to know if he can fill an order for a particular item. He queries the computer and in a matter of a few seconds, the computer interrogates the direct access inventory file and reports back the answer. Similarly, a person's credit can be checked from a remote spot. This type of communications processing is similar to the nondedicated on-line data collection with the exception that the response is immediate. Normally the computer is processing the daily work load, is interrupted whenever there is an inquiry, processes the inquiry, and returns to its main-line function. This type of system can include the data collection function also. The inquiries can have two levels of priority—those that must be handled now and those that can be handled later. The nonpriority items can be batched and processed later as in the methods described previously.

The direct access approach affords a programmed dialogue between the inquirer and the computer that can have significant benefits. The following interchange indicates the advantages of this approach:

Inquirer:	My customer wants a 4378A gauge.
Computer:	Please recheck the order number. I don't show such a number.
Inquirer:	My customer wants a 4387A gauge.
Computer:	Out of stock. Order can be filled in two weeks. Can I suggest a substitute?
Inquirer:	Yes.
Computer:	How about 4387B gauge? It differs only in color.
Inquirer:	Customer will accept. Please reserve.
Computer:	Order accepted.

The computer is programmed to check for the routine types of errors such as the above inversion of numbers and to suggest alternate solutions to problems such as the substitute item that is similar to the one ordered. The substitution logic must of course be preprogrammed. Programmed instruction in schools is patterned after this type of dialogue—the student answers questions and, based on the answer, the computer either moves on to the next question or looks back to display an additional series of questions emphasizing the concept the student has missed. This tutorial method of instruction is a sound approach provided (and this is a big proviso) that the instruction logic is properly programmed. This is true also in using this method in a business environment. If the programmer developing the decision logic suggests a substitute item that has completely different characteristics than the one ordered, the system soon will fall apart.

DIRECT ACCESS ON-LINE PROCESSING

This stage in communications processing may seem similar to the previous one but there is an important distinction. The previous stage involved two separate independent job streams—the inquiry programs were not linked to the production programs taking place in the background. In this mode, the inquiry program and the background jobs are interdependent and operate on common files. This stage of development is distinguished from the previous stage by its greater degree of implementation complexity. Prior to this step, an inquiry entered the system and was answered; however, it did not simultaneously trigger the processing. For example, the salesman wanted to know the inventory status of a gauge, but this did not initiate the order processing cycle for that particular customer. However, with direct access on-line processing, the order can be initiated by the remote point, the inventory record reduced by the order amount so that other systems now using the inventory file will receive the adjusted balance. Thus, the programs are interdependent. This appears a most desirable development but there are serious implementation problems that must be overcome. Because one of many remote sites can initiate action that can affect other applications, the proper interfacing and control techniques must be utilized. It is possible for a salesman to enter a large order (possibly in error) that triggers the immediate scheduling of a large production lot. Because of the high priority placed on this order, the production schedule is changed to accommodate this order. The snowballing effect of erroneously entered transactions in an interdependent on-line communications system becomes painfully evident. Suffice to say, the proper checks and balances must be established before embarking on such a systems approach.

Although the problems are difficult, this stage of communications processing represents the high point of information systems. A well-planned and -implemented direct access system embodies the flexibility and dynamic nature required by fast moving companies. It represents a paper work business system that indeed accurately reflects the physical operation of the company. Here is the way such a system works:

1. A worker reports the completion of a particular job by means of the data collection network.
2. He is told the next job (Job 43) on which to work.
3. Job 43 was substituted for the previous one (Job 86) in the work queue because the foreman inputted to the system, just a minute ago, that the machine needed to accomplish Job 86 was out of operation.
4. The system indicates a maintenance work order that is printed on the remote printer in the plant engineering department.
5. At the same time, an important customer indicates that an alternate supplier has failed to meet a delivery and he needs a particular part within a week. An inquiry from a remote site checks the availability of raw materials and tools to machine the particular part, receives an affirmative reply, and initiates the order at that point.

This interaction of subsystems is the key to a responsive and dynamic total information system. It is a goal to shoot at, but it cannot be instituted overnight. The old cliché of "Too many cooks spoil the broth" is valid here in that a system of this type involves the interaction of many people representing different functions of the business. If not properly controlled, these cooks can, indeed, have a material effect on the resultant product. The answer is that most companies that have instituted such a system have utilized a phasing approach that recognizes the normal learning curve in which the company gradually builds the technical capabilities and the working environment to implement the direct access on-line system. Many companies have used the phasing plan of proceeding up the ladder illustrated in Figure 4.13.

MULTISUBSCRIBER TIME-SHARING SERVICES

The multisubscriber time-sharing services stage is a still higher one in the evolution of communications-oriented processing systems. This type of system can be utilized within a large corporation or by smaller companies on a shared computer. This stage is somewhat similar in operation to the direct access on-line approach but is distinguished by independent users each developing their own computer programs and data files.

The multisubscribers may be a group of engineering departments, of research departments, or of market analysts. This type of approach often is used in a large, highly decentralized operation where the computer is viewed as a utility serving the needs of its users. Thus, Engineer A has a problem to resolve and feeds his input data to the computer. His individual code number and the code number of his problem call his particular program from the library, interrogate the required data files, and execute his program. At the same time, Engineer B, Market Analyst C, or Inventory Control Clerk D also call the computer to accomplish specific jobs required by their operations. The computer is oriented from both a software and hardware side to handle a multiplicity of diverse jobs.

This particular approach is very popular in large universities that have many and diversified departments, each of which can benefit from shared computer usage. The approach is consistent with maintaining the autonomy of the department while avoiding the cost of each department having its own computer. Universities have made their time-shared services available to industry in certain instances and independent time-sharing service centers have become quite prominent in the market place.

Therefore, a company has its choice of developing its own time-sharing system or utilizing outside sources for this service. Many large companies have their own communications-oriented internal system but supplement it by using outside services for special jobs that their own system is not geared to handle. In actual practice, there are various gradations and combinations of inside and outside approaches. This leads to another significant question, which must be answered by the system designer, the question of shared computer services. However, before discussing shared computer services, let us stop to analyze a systems consideration that is most important in implementing the types of communications processing systems described.

MONO VERSUS MULTIPROGRAMMING SYSTEMS

Computers originally were built to handle processing in a sequentially-oriented manner. A typical job might consist of reading data from punched cards, processing the data within the central processor, and printing the results on a high-speed printer. The program would read a card (or several cards), accomplish the necessary calculations, print the results, then go back to read the next card(s), and so on. The program would loop through the same sequence of steps until the last card had been processed.

In accomplishing this job, there is an inherent hardware imbalance. The central processor, operating at electronic speeds, can digest the data many times faster than the electromechanical punched card readers and printers that are hooked to it. The situation in a typical business application is characterized by a large amount of input and output and a very small portion of processing, considering the speed of modern day processing units. A schematic of the operation is shown in Figure 4.15.

Total time = 3 hours, 5 minutes

Figure 4.15

The use of buffered devices, whereby the card reading and printing can be overlapped, reduces greatly the over-all processing time. Several buffers or intermediate storage areas are provided to hold data for a specific transaction (one card or several cards worth of information). While the central processor is processing and printing the results of one transaction, the card buffer can be filled automatically with the data for the next transaction (the key is that there is a buffer storage area to accept it). Thus, the total run can be reduced to the time of the longest operation, in this case the printing. A saving of one hour and five minutes is effected (See Figure 4.16).

Although buffering was a big step forward, it was not enough. The central processor, the single most expensive element of the entire system, still is operating only a fraction of the time. Furthermore, the advent of communications-oriented systems added a new dimension to computer processing. Communication devices transmit and display information at an even slower rate than basic peripheral devices because they are key driven in many instances and also are electromechanical in nature. Although it is important to satisfy demands for information when they are received, it is most expensive to tie up a complete large scale computer system to do so. The computer must tend to its daily volume jobs as well as handle intermittent communication requests. The requirement to get more utility from the processing unit and the requirements of communications processing led to the development of multi-

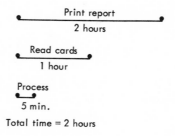

Total time = 2 hours

Figure 4.16

programming. Multiprogramming capability is the foundation of the communications-oriented operating systems referred to in Figure 4.11. Multiprogramming differs from the monoprogramming environment described in which one program is located in memory and is completed before the next one is begun.

The basic concept of multiprogramming is allocation of the hardware resources to accomplish several jobs at the same time. Figure 4.17 shows memory being partitioned into three segments. Program A is a sales forecast program that employs a good amount of mathematical processing. It utilizes a sales forecast or sales history file; calculates trends, past forecast errors, and mean absolute deviations; and builds a new forecast file. Program B is a communications program in which a number of remote sales offices can interrogate a direct access file and get the latest status on particular open orders in which the customer is interested. Program C is printing an inventory analysis report from a magnetic tape that has been produced in a previous run.

Thus we have three independent computer programs, each using its own peripherals but sharing the power of the computer's memory and processing unit. This is a most efficient and economical way to operate. It is a practical way to operate even if you do not have a communications application. This approach is called multiprogramming and it requires a sophisticated class of software called an operating system, which has been described briefly in an earlier section. The operating system allocates resources to obtain the most efficient peripheral mix and job schedule. It then facilitates and controls the simultaneous time-

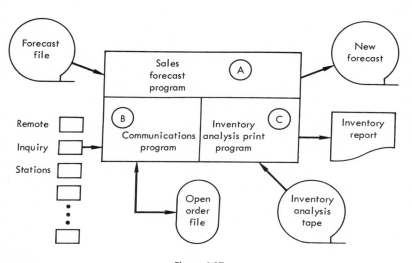

Figure 4.17

sharing of the central processor's memory and processing unit. The operating system's function is a complex one, but is a necessary prerequisite to using the multiprogramming concept. Systems designers must consider this in developing systems solutions. It also becomes obvious that an operating system is an important selection criterion in evaluating computer vendors.

With the previous discussion in mind, the focus now can be turned to shared computer services.

SHARED COMPUTER SERVICES

A company has alternatives to buying or renting its own computer. Having developed the systems requirements for the company, the systems designer must evaluate the alternatives before determining whether the company needs its own computer. Management should insist on this and should follow up to see that the proper analysis of this path is made. Often, the group making the study sees itself as running the eventual computer installation and is prone to ignore the possibilities of a shared computer service. Shared computer services make sense in many instances. Executives and EDP directors of large and small companies alike look with interest at the possibilities of contracting out large pieces and, indeed, the entire data processing job if they can be assured that it can be handled properly. Their thinking goes like this:

> We are in the business of manufacturing and marketing a product; we are not in the data processing business. We want to devote our top talent to our main line production, marketing, engineering and financial activities; we would prefer not to dilute it by taking on any more functions than we have to. Furthermore, we understand that there still exists a significant skills shortage of qualified systems and programming personnel and that the systems have become so sophisticated and complex that experienced professionals and specialists are required to design and implement them. If an outside agency can render this service or a logical piece of it, this represents an attractive and viable alternative. Another advantage is that the costs of data processing will be more apparent this way than if we did the job ourselves. We know the fee we are paying to an outside agency and we can readily measure the benefits against it. In running our own shop, these costs may tend to become buried or hidden. Therefore, we want to explore thoroughly the possibilities of shared computer service before we decide to proceed on our own.

This summation establishes the motivation to look at the variety of computer services available. If many of the large companies that have the money and the volume to justify their own installation continue to utilize outside services, certainly the smaller company should take a look. Figure 4.18 indicates the various paths open to a company contemplating initial use of EDP. The first two paths indicate the utilization of a company's own computer and the next two indicate various outside services routes. What are the pros and cons of the various choices?

UTILIZE OWN COMPUTER

The first path indicates the more conventional route of companies that enter the data processing field with a small first computer and then expand their applications and usage to the point where more power is needed. They then either add more capacity to their current system or upgrade to the next model in the computer family. This is done with varying degrees of trouble, depending on whether the original system was built open-ended and with growth in mind.

The second path offers a possibility for a company that cannot afford even a small computer. The expected usage is about half a shift, so the concept is to rent the remaining time to another small company or even to a larger company that requires additional machine time. From

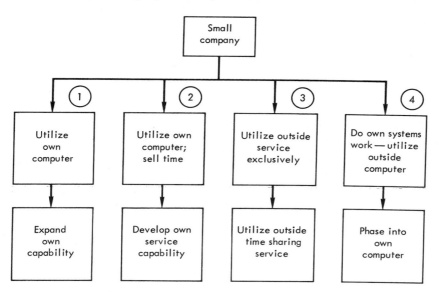

Figure 4.18

an economic viewpoint this makes a good deal of sense. Economies of scale have been mentioned whereby throughput per dollar goes up with the larger classes of equipment. Therefore, if the company can find the users, it can benefit from having the higher throughput power. The company then can expand both its own internal use of the machine and also its own service capability. In following this path, the company must realize that it is entering a new business that may be quite different from its existing one. If the company desires this type of diversification and if it understands the nature and problems of the new business, the computer service activity can be a profitable new venture. Certainly the service center business continues to be one of the fastest growing segments of the over-all EDP industry. The service activity can grow to include time sharing facilities, with the parent company one of the principal users.

The latter route should be taken only by a knowledgeable few. The service activity competes for the same personnel resources that are used to develop systems to improve internal operations. There always will be the decision of whether the most competent people should be used internally or externally. Furthermore, it usually is difficult to build both operations concurrently, particularly when you are starting both from scratch.

A solution might be to sell only computer time to potential customers, instead of a complete systems job. However, the problem will be finding and maintaining users, a problem similar to that faced by a landlord in keeping a building fully rented. Scheduling and prime time conflicts also can create serious problems. These problems will be explored more fully in the ensuing discussion of the use of outside computer services.

OUTSIDE COMPUTER SERVICES

The third and fourth paths point out two different approaches to the use of outside service facilities. Path 3 indicates a complete dependence on outside services, moving from the more conventional service center relationship (taking the data to the center to be processed) to the communications-oriented service where a remote terminal is used to communicate with the service center's computer. There are a wide variety and a wide range of communications services that can be utilized. The fourth path indicates a middle level approach whereby the company does its own systems work, including the design and programming of the applications, and uses the service center only for production running of the programs. With this in-house experience and capability, the company has an optional second step of phasing into its own computer operation when it has the volume to justify it.

The third path has the advantage of not requiring the hiring and training of a company's own internal staff. Because of the significant EDP learning curve, it is usually cheaper at the outset to utilize outside systems services. Where the break-even point comes depends on the success a company has in its personnel recruitment program. The success of following this course of action depends on the specification of the job to be done. If the job is well defined as to the input, processing, and output, and if the volume and timing considerations are spelled out, then the job can be properly evaluated and costed. The company can be reasonably assured that it gets what it pays for. Ah, but there's the rub. As evident in the previous chapter, it takes a concentrated and comprehensive systems study effort to develop the required systems specifications. A key question to be answered is whether you want to have an outside agent develop systems specifications for you. I believe firmly that the whole boat approach in which you are completely dependent on the outside service is a dangerous path to follow. It is preferable to wait until you have your own capability, at least to the point of developing your own systems specifications, before you resort to outside services.

This leads to Path 4, a combination of doing your own systems work and utilizing outside computer services for the production running. Various combinations can be utilized in this route. A company can do the complete systems job as represented by the computer acquisition cycle in Figure 1 or it can do its own systems study and leave the design and implementation phases to the service center. If the company does its own systems design, it must know the machine(s) available. This means that a competitive service center evaluation must be made prior to systems design. Another possibility is to contract the systems design effort to a firm that specializes in that activity while a second party service center runs the jobs. This two-vendor approach has many problems and is not recommended. Following Path 4 can lead to the utilization of a company's own computer system and indeed often does. This represents a desirable route, as the company has gone through the learning cycle and has made mistakes on someone else's machine—it has not been as costly as it would have been on the company's own computer. The company is now in a better position to select equipment more appropriate to its applications and can proceed with added confidence.

There is a variety of computer time sharing arrangements that can be made with a service center. These arrangements for the most part follow the same stages discussed under communications processing (see Figure 4.13). However, the degree of complexity increases dramatically at the more sophisticated levels because the users are independent of each other and efforts must be made to ensure that they remain independent while at the same time guaranteeing that they have adequate computer time when they need it. Thus, the stage of development of multisubscriber time sharing lags behind the development of time sharing services developed by a single company or by a university.

One other type of service that should be mentioned offsets to some degree the need for a company to develop its own systems specifications. So-called subscription services offer application packages geared to a specific application or specific industry. Some subscription service companies specialize in the design and implementation of packages ranging from basic payroll and accounting systems to more sophisticated application areas such as statistical forecasting or simulation. Other subscription service companies concentrate on providing packages aimed at specific industries like hospital accounting or school administration. If these packages are flexible, modular, and well designed and reflect the practical business environment, then they indeed can prove quite attractive to a company evaluating its own entrance into data processing. The rationale for subscription services from the service company's side is that it is possible to offer a lower price because of the multiuse of the packages. If the cost incentive is present, it may be feasible for a company to change its operation to adapt to the specifications of the package. However, this should be evaluated carefully. The advent of the application package and subscription service opens up another potential avenue for the new computer user.

It is desired to paint a balanced picture of the use of computer services and the avenues open to the new computer user. Up to this point, the service centers have been viewed in the ideal framework of providing what they say they provide. In actual practice, there are problems in machine scheduling, machine down-time, communications handling, input errors and the like, which are compounded by a situation where there are multiple users of a common facility. If the service facility also is responsible for altering or developing new applications, there are additional scheduling and priority problems. These are quite serious concerns and they emphasize the need to exercise sound judgment in selecting a service facility. These problems are lessened materially by utilizing your own computer. There still will be priority and scheduling problems among the using departments, but the seriousness of the problem is not as great.

The complete use or the complementary use of outside services offers certain economies and capabilities that should not be overlooked. Paths 3 and 4 are certainly viable possibilities and this source of systems and computing power should be investigated thoroughly by the systems designers.

FINAL SYSTEMS DESIGN

The job of the systems designer is to resolve and satisfy the basic systems requirements, outlined in the previous chapter, by combining state of the art technology in the most efficient and practical manner. Practical implies an awareness of the cost and the resources necessary to design and implement a system in a reasonable time frame. The designer must know his own company and the specific environment in which it operates. He must know his management, its philosophy and its outlook. The following precepts might well underlie a systems design study.

1. There is a necessary and normal learning curve in going from where you are today to where you would like to be tomorrow. It will not come about by taking one giant step.
2. The popular credit slogan of today—Pay as you go—must be accompanied by an increasingly heard business slogan—Pay *off* as you go. Management is tired of hearing how good it is going to be. It would like to see at least a small sample of tangible benefits today.
3. Be practical and avoid the go for broke philosophy. Indeed, "broke" is oftentimes what happens to the system that looks good on paper but not so good in operation. Keep the implementation considerations in mind during systems design. Creativity and sophistication are desirable, but they should be combined in a simple, usable manner. The slogan "Elegance in simplicity" might well be used as an overriding guide.

As discussed in this chapter the system must be either sequential- or direct access-oriented. It may use both sequential and direct access storage devices but the overriding orientation of each application must be determined. The degree and type of communications processing must be ascertained. It may turn out that this is a future requirement rather than a current one; however, it is important to build the flexibility into the system in order to be able to add communications processing at a later stage. For example, if direct access file storage is needed for inquiry/response purposes only and this is envisioned later, it is nevertheless necessary to build the current system around direct access so that inquiry/response can be added affectively at a later date. If only today's needs are considered and sequential storage is utilized, a major redesign job will be necessary when inquiry/response is added.

After each application is analyzed and broken down into individual computer programs or runs, the individual requirements must be summed up and viewed as a whole. Figures 4.19, 4.20, and 4.21 begin to bring the pieces back together. Figure 4.19 is a composite look at the input requirements. This obviously is not a complete list of all the input transaction types but it is sufficient to illustrate how this form can be used in systems design. Column 1 indicates the number of alphanumeric characters required to describe each input transaction. The 50 characters listed for the sales order include: (1) item number, (2) item description, (3) quantity ordered, and so on. The characters per transaction are multiplied by the number of transactions per month (in this case, the number of sales orders times the average number of line items on each order) to obtain total input characters. A future growth factor of 20% is added to arrive at the total capacity of 1,500,000 characters of input data. In a like manner, the other input transactions are accumulated to arrive at a total input load for the month. This then can form the basis for selecting the input devices required of the system. This, of course, must be evaluated in light of peak loads.

Figure 4.20 accomplishes the same type of analysis for output. The various output documents and the volumes for each are listed. For example, the company issues 5,000 customer invoices per month, each having an average of 15 lines of print. A 15% growth factor is used to arrive at the total print capacity of 86,250 lines. This is then added to the other reports to determine the over-all print requirements and the type of output device needed for the computer system.

Figure 4.21 is a compilation of the company's data base or storage requirements. It indicates that 200 characters are needed to describe each of 1,000 customers. A 30% growth factor indicates a total storage requirement of 260,000 characters. Because there is no need for direct access inquiry, the requirements are listed under sequential. A summation of these last two columns can help resolve the important issue of selecting the storage medium (speed and capacity) for the computer system.

Transaction	Characters per transaction	Number of transactions per month	Total characters	Growth factor	Capacity required
Sales order	50	25,000	1,250,000	+20%	1,500,000
Time card	60	3,000	180,000	+10%	198,000
Requisition	70	2,000	140,000	+15%	161,000
Job completion	30	22,000	660,000	+15%	699,000
Move ticket	20	30,000	600,000	+15%	690,000
Total			2,830,000		3,248,000

Figure 4.19 Input requirements.

Output document	Number of forms/mo.	Lines per form	Lines of print	Growth factor	Capacity required
Customer invoice	5,000	15	75,000	+15%	86,250
Sales analysis	50	500	25,000	+10%	27,500
Inventory status	20	1,000	20,000	+20%	24,000
Payroll register	10	1,000	10,000	+15%	11,500
Pay checks	4,000	10	40,000	+15%	46,000
Purchase orders	2,000	15	30,000	+15%	34,500
Total			200,000		229,750

Figure 4.20   Output requirements.

File	Characters per item	Number of items	Total characters	Growth factor	Capacity required	Direct access	Sequential
Customer	200	1,000	200,000	+30%	260,000		260,000
Sales history	20	1,200	24,000	+30%	27,600		27,600
Product master	250	8,000	2,000,000	+15%	2,300,000	2,300,000	
Work in process	50	2,000	100,000	+20%	120,000	120,000	
Vendor	200	200	40,000	+10%	44,000		44,000
Personnel	250	500	125,000	+20%	150,000		150,000
Total					2,901,600	2,420,000	481,600

Figure 4.21   Data base requirements.

DESIGNING THE MINIMUM EQUIPMENT CONFIGURATION

The price of an extra direct access storage module, peripheral unit, or memory module increases the total cost of a system. After the general form of the system has been determined, it should be reviewed with cost considerations in mind. The equipment should be limited to that which is necessary to accomplish the job. This procedure starts from an analysis of the largest or most complicated program of each application. The required memory capacity of a computer is a function of the complexity and size of the largest program it needs to execute. If the largest run can be simplified or broken into two runs while still meeting the systems requirements, then a saving is obtained. For example, the run analysis in Figure 4.4 indicates that run 3 is the most complex. It utilizes four magnetic tape units and involves significantly more processing than the other four runs. If this run can be simplified by breaking it into two or by utilizing one less magnetic tape unit, a saving in the over-all equipment configuration can be effected.

Points to be considered in accomplishing this are:

1. The elimination of underutilized equipment in the system by a different run breakdown or by performing minor processing operations on other available equipment.
2. The accumulation of reports, exception listings, daily registers, and the like on a magnetic tape or direct access device for later printing. This reduces the printing bottleneck and may make it possible to get by with a slower and more economical printer.
3. Determine the system configuration on the basis of the daily volume jobs. Build the system to optimally handle these key bread and butter applications. Fit in the infrequently run programs around the volume jobs and do not let them unecessarily influence the total system size.

More computer runs can reduce memory and peripheral needs but may require more time for the total job. In many cases, there is ample time even in a single shift to handle the company's application work load with the multirun approach. The price of the equipment configuration goes down, its relative utilization goes up, and over-all return on investment is improved.

SUMMARY

At this point, the first phase of the synthesis process has been completed. Refer back to Figure 1. Alternate solutions to satisfying the system specifications developed in Chapter 3 have been explored. A variety of computer solutions has been discussed, including direct access-, sequential-, and communications-oriented systems approaches. Each application area has been thoroughly dissected, broken down into computer runs, analyzed, reanalyzed, and put in context with the total system's requirements.

Finally, a composite picture of input, output, processing, and storage needs has been determined. The groundwork has been laid to evaluate computer vendors and specific computer systems to see which is most suitable to accomplish the job. Chapter 5 concludes the synthesis phase by bringing the systems design into focus with the specific hardware offerings, enabling the systems design group to determine the final computer justification and present its findings to management.

THREE B'S' APPROACH TO SYSTEMS DESIGN

Dexter Johnson's systems group has hit full stride during the systems design phase. The group considered this to be far more creative and enjoyable work than the painstaking systems study. Though Johnson thought he and his group were well qualified to develop the most efficient data processing solution to the systems problem Three B's was facing, he formed a design advisory panel made up of personnel from operating departments who had a reputation for creative and imaginative thinking. This panel met several times during the systems design to discuss various concepts. Johnson thought these sessions were most productive.

One of the concerns Johnson had was that the design they had developed was a little too imaginative for Three B's to adopt and implement in a reasonable time frame. Johnson had been guided all along by Bill Barrett's aggressive viewpoint toward data processing. He recalled Barrett's return from an executive session on computers where he had waxed eloquent about the virtues of integrated data processing concepts and on-line, real time communications-oriented systems. Johnson realized this was what Barrett wanted but he questioned whether the president knew what was needed for a company like Three B's, a babe in the computer woods, to develop a system of this magnitude. He now reflected on whether the over-all system approach was practical in light of the company's experience level.

The approach Johnson and his group utilized was a direct access-oriented system built around a more or less real time order processing and inventory control system. Salesmen would be able to ascertain inventory status and order status by placing a call to the home office. The central dispatch point would utilize a remote inquiry device to interrogate the appropriate inventory item or customer order in the open order file. Likewise, there would be dispatch points throughout the plant where foremen, inventory clerks, and production coordinators would be able to interrogate central files. Johnson knew this system approach would appeal to management. He was concerned about his ability to implement this type of system in a reasonable time frame. He realized that the more enthusiastic management was about the system, the quicker it would want results. On the other hand, he knew he had to do some selling because plant manager Harrison and several others were still skeptical about a computer system for Three B's. Johnson did not consider an outside computer sharing facility because he thought Three B's was large enough to justify its own system and he had an inherent bias against having someone else do a company's work for it. In retrospect, it may have been wise at least to explore this possibility, if only to satisfy members of management who might raise the question.

Johnson and his group spent a considerable amount of time with the computer vendors who were asking specific questions of the systems specifications. Johnson felt good when the vendors' systems personnel working on the job remarked that Three B's had one of the most com-

plete sets of specs they had ever encountered. The vendors all agreed that this should enable them to do a far better and more comprehensive system design. The EDP director knew they had taken more time than was scheduled to develop the systems specs but he knew it was better to spend the time than to shortcut this important activity. Whatever system was adopted, he knew it would have a far better chance of filling the needs of the Three B's company.

One of the three vendors indicated he needed an additional two weeks to complete his proposal. Though Johnson knew this would delay his final management presentation, he felt he needed at least three bids. Possibly, he should have asked additional vendors to bid in order to gain more leverage with those vendors who required additional time. When the proposals were in, Johnson planned to review them in light of the systems design he and his group had developed. At this point, he was beginning to feel that a less imaginative approach than the one he had developed should be the one presented to management—the strategy and psychology would be to be more conservative on what they stated could be accomplished. At least if the communications-oriented approach was mentioned, it should be indicated clearly that this was to be added as a latter phase in the implementation. He felt that the phasing plan was critical to the entire presentation and he intended to use this as a significant selection criterion in evaluation of the vendors' proposals.

Johnson now reconsidered the use of an outside consultant. His dependence on them was lessened because he had built a greater sense of confidence in his study team. However, he thought an outside agency still could be of value in evaluating the over-all degree of sophistication built into the system and the phasing plan to attain the end results— the two areas that Johnson felt were the most crucial to the entire EDP project.

SOURCE MATERIAL AND SUPPLEMENTARY READING

Ackoff, R. L. and P. Rivett, *A Manager's Guide to Operations Research.* New York: John Wiley & Sons, 1963.

"A Panel Session—On-Line Business Applications," *Conference Proceedings*, AFIPS. Vol. 34, 1969 SJCC, pp. 29–32.

"An On-Line Information System for Management," *Conference Proceedings*, AFIPS. Vol. 34, 1969 SJCC, pp. 339–351.

Data Communications in Business, Edgar C. Gentle, Jr., ed. New York: American Tel & Tel Co., 1967.

Datamation. The August 1969 issue is devoted to time sharing.

Datamation. The November 1966 and October 1969 issues are devoted to communications.

Dean, N. J., "The Computer Comes of Age," *Harvard Business Review* (January/February, 1968).

Dean, N. J. and J. W. Taylor, "Managing to Manage the Computer," *Harvard Business Review*, (September/October, 1963).

Diebold, J., "What's Ahead in Information Technology," *Harvard Business Review* (September/October, 1965). (The trends discussions in this chapter are extrapolations from material found in the above articles. The hardware trends come from the Diebold article and the application trends from the Dean, and Dean and Taylor articles. The software trends are my own projections from industry reports and my own experience.)

"Effective Program Development, The Choices," *Data Processing Digest, Inc.* (1969).

Gruenberger, F., *Critical Factors in Data Management.* Englewood Cliffs, N. J.: Prentice-Hall, Inc., 1969. 160 pp.

Parkhill, D. F., *The Challenge of the Computer Utility.* Reading, Mass.: Addison-Wesley Publishing Co., 1966.

Smith, P. T., *Computer Systems and Profits.* New York: American Management Association, 1969.

Ziegler, J. R., *Time Sharing Data Processing Systems.* Englewood Cliffs, N. J.: Prentice-Hall, Inc., 1967. 298 pp.

5

COMPUTER SYSTEM
JUSTIFICATION

Dexter Johnson now has three proposals from computer vendors who responded to his letter. As indicated, there was an extra two-week delay because one of the vendors had a scheduling problem and could not immediately assign systems personnel to complete the proposal. It became apparent as the study progressed that there were quite a few competent computer suppliers. Johnson discovered this in talking to data processing managers of other companies, whom he met at local Data Processing Managers Association sessions.

The systems group did not establish any specific selection criteria for evaluating the proposals. Because the company was evaluating computers for the first time and had no prior experience, Johnson considered the systems support and education supplied by vendors as important factors in the choice. He was more concerned about the software and applications assistance than the specific hardware features. Certainly, cost was a consideration, but it had to be strongly tempered by other elements.

As Johnson reviewed the proposals from the three manufacturers, he found himself a little concerned. All three seemed to have the necessary hardware and software, as well as the other supporting services. Johnson had a feeling that things looked better on paper than they actually were. Having had experience with a computer manufacturer, he could see the positive salesmanship and optimism interleaved throughout the proposals. The EDP director pondered over a method to test the claims made by the vendors.

He considered two possible techniques to accomplish this. One was to make his own survey of computer users to validate the claims. He knew this would consume a good amount of time and add more delay to a schedule that already had undergone substantial adjustment. The other possibility was to have the vendors' systems personnel program one of the applications for running on their machines. The application could be programmed in COBOL, a language that all vendors said was available on their systems. If the vendors were reluctant to do this, Johnson could have his own staff write the program. The key question here was whether there was enough uncertainty to warrant taking the extra time and expending the additional money to either make the survey or prepare the benchmark application.

Johnson now had a good idea of what the computer system was going to cost Three B's. The proposals were based on the system specifications that were developed during the systems study and provided a good basis for refining the cost estimates made during the feasibility study. Generally, the costs were quite a bit higher, but offsetting this was the increased potential for saving that more detailed study of Three B's' information processing system brought to light. The question of renting versus purchase came up, but Johnson did not give this much attention, as he more or less decided from the beginning that Three B's should rent its first machine.

The remaining job was to put the entire study together and make a final justification and presentation to management. As management reviewed and began to organize the massive amount of information that had been gathered, Johnson and his study group felt they had come a long way. They now felt a sense of urgency to present their findings to Mr. Barrett and the top management team. Several questions remained. These revolved around whether the vendors should be allowed to present their proposals directly to management or whether the study team should handle the entire presentation. Johnson had obtained management approval to call in an outside consultant to review the proposals. The consultant would make an independent analysis and vendor recommendation. With these considerations in mind, Johnson was sufficiently confident to request the scheduling of a two-hour meeting in two weeks to present the final computer justification to management.

INTRODUCTION

Referring once again to Figure 1, we see that the computer system selection and implementation cycle is now in the final stage of the synthesis phase. The system design phase has facilitated the development of alternate computer solutions to the systems problems and has produced the analysis needed to evaluate the alternatives and select the best one. While the company's own internal systems study group has been engaged in systems design, the systems specifications developed during the analysis phase have been submitted to competitive computer vendors. The justification subphase enables the systems group to compare its solution with those of the vendors. This provides the basis for selecting the computer system that best meets the company's needs.

The justification subphase consists of: (1) the selection of the computer vendor, and (2) the final presentation to management, which justifies the selection and states the reasons why the company should install a computer. Normally the selection process resolves the denominator or cost portions of the return on investment formula as shown in Figure 2.7 and the justification adds the numerator or benefit portion of the formula. Generally these two steps can proceed independently. This is not to say that the selection process has no influence on the benefits. Making the wrong computer selection can affect the time frame for achieving the expected benefits. For example, if the vendor cannot deliver on time, or if the availability of a particular software system is delayed, the effect on the overall computer program can be very substantial.

However, it can be stated that the major benefits of installing a computer system emanate from the individual company's ability to marry the proper systems concepts to its information processing needs. The benefits are commensurate with a company's over-all approach to data processing, the proper involvement of management, and the selection of the right people to directly control the EDP effort. The selection of the right computer hardware from the right computer vendor is certainly significant in realizing the benefits of EDP, but not as significant as the user's own role.

Various selection techniques will be discussed, ranging from the very simple to those of a more sophisticated nature. A discussion will follow of the various financial methods for acquiring computer power. General overriding selection considerations will conclude the selection section of this chapter. The justification process then will be explored, looking at various cost versus saving analyses as well as a return on investment technique. A sample management presentation will summarize an approach used by a particular study team in attempting to convince its management that a computer is a desirable investment.

THE SELECTION PROCESS

The goal of the selection process is to choose the vendor(s) that can best satisfy a company's systems requirements at the least cost. The "s" suggests that more than one vendor may be selected, each doing part of the job. This is possible and will be discussed later under the consideration of <u>multivendors</u>. It should become apparent also that selecting a computer vendor is not always a case of low bidder; indeed because of the significance of support and service, cost often is not the most significant criterion.

The EDP industry has grown and changed greatly since the beginning of the commercial computer era in 1951. U.S. Department of Commerce statistics indicate that in the decade of the 1960s, EDP has been the fastest growing industry in the country. Though most companies, if they are similar to Three B's, will be making their selection from the group of vendors who offer a general purpose, business-oriented computer, it is important to realize the scope and nature of the total EDP industry.

Figure 5.1 lists the segments of the EDP industry under the hardware, software, and application dimensions as described in the previous chapter. A fourth category, services, has been added.

In the hardware segment there are nine major manufacturers of general purpose computer systems. These nine companies (which will be listed later) provide input, output, storage, and central processors

Hardware	General purpose computers
	Special purpose computers
	Peripheral devices
	Supplies
Software	Proprietary software systems
	Software consulting
Application	Proprietary application systems
	Application consulting
	Contract programming
Services	Consulting
	Leasing companies
	Computer time sales
	Personnel recruiting

Figure 5.1

as well as communication facilities and remote terminals. In addition they offer (some manufacturers at extra cost) the software, education, and services along with the hardware. There is a much larger number of manufacturers of special purpose computers. The special purpose category includes small desk-type computers, which are used mainly for scientific purposes, as well as analog computers, which are used in production processes—for example to meter in the correct amount of ingredients to produce a specific chemical product.

Peripheral device manufacturers produce a wide variety of input, output, and storage units that may be on site with a computer system or remote to it. In this category are devices such as punched card readers, magnetic tape drives, high speed printers, factory data collection devices, cathode ray tubes, optical scanners, and the like. Initially these devices were sold to the major general purpose computer manufacturers who then would resell the devices as part of their system. However, the peripheral manufacturers have extended their marketing activities and now sell directly to the ultimate user of the system.

The supplies manufacturers produce punched cards, printing forms, magnetic tapes, and magnetic disks that are used in increasing quantities by the peripheral devices on a computer system. Although the mix of supplies usage is changing, the overall growth of the supplier market has kept pace with the growth in number of computer systems. Each of the nine general purpose computer vendors includes at least some types of supplies as part of its product line.

The software market segment has been one of the fastest growing ones. The major barrier to the continued growth of this segment is the skills shortage among systems and programming personnel. The first software houses were spawned by subcontracts from the major computer manufacturers. The manufacturer used the software houses to supplement his own in-house development of assembly, compiler, and operating systems as well as a variety of mathematical programs. The software houses now produce software for the end user. Prior to the separate pricing era, the smaller user usually relied on the computer vendor's software whereas the larger user was attracted, for example, to a scientific computer system that he felt was superior to the vendor's offering. When the full impact of separate pricing is felt, the smaller user also may be forced to shop around for his software. Some firms offer software consulting services to companies developing their own software.

The application area is one of the fastest growing market segments. With the skills shortage, firms have been organized to develop and market proprietary application systems. Proprietary implies that the system is sold to each user, who is prohibited from giving it or selling it to a third party. Application systems to do payroll, general accounting, inventory control, premium billing, and the like are available at a specified price from these companies. The offerings range from special programs that automatically generate flow charts to programs that purport to analyze the breeding habits of chickens.

Consulting services as well as contract programming assistance are available for the design and development of a company's own computerized applications. A word of caution is in order in the use of application packages either from a third party or from the computer vendor. Although it is true that the application needs of companies are similar in many respects, there are significant differences as well. Therefore, either the company using the package must adopt certain practices in order to utilize it or the package must be flexible enough to allow some hand-tailoring by the user.

The services industry segment includes consulting on many levels, ranging from advising a company on the role of the EDP function in its organization to evaluating and selecting competitive vendors to specific advice on a subroutine that is part of an application program. Leasing companies offer an additional financial method of acquiring a computer, which will be discussed in a later section. Computer time sales range from the simple service center facility to an elaborate on-line, real time subscription arrangement. The former involves only the contracting of computer time while the user does his own systems and programming work. The latter combines the use of the proprietary application package with the sharing of a computer. Thus the user can obtain a specific service like credit checking or a complete business accounting system. There are many additional services that fall between these two. Finally, another part of the services industry is represented by newly formed companies that help in the search for competent systems and programming talent. This function is performed for all the industry segments listed in Figure 5.1 as well as for end users.

This then is a brief description of the segments of the EDP industry. Companies may not fall neatly into one of the categories listed, as many are engaged in a combination of two or more activities. Also, some companies are developing unique approaches by combining these services in different ways. For example, several companies have been successful offering a complete computer package to a prospective user. Such a company will undertake the entire computer system selection and implementation cycle, even running the computer at the user's site when the job is completed. The user states that he wants a system to accomplish order processing, inventory control, and production control —the subcontractor takes it from there. The service these companies offer is called facilities management.

COMPETITIVE EVALUATION

The selection process outlined will be confined to the evaluation of a general purpose computer vendor. Although the selection methods to be reviewed can be applied to the evaluation of the other services described previously, the main concern for companies like Three B's is the computer vendor. As has been stated, there are nine major manufacturers of general purpose computing equipment. One consulting firm produced the dart board shown in Figure 5.2.

It lists the nine major computer vendors, and although it was produced with tongue in cheek, it bears a message. The message is that many companies still do not use competitive evaluation to select a computer vendor. It further states that for those that do, the selection process follows a rather subjective hit or miss pattern. One would assume that a decision as significant as the selection of a computer would involve a competitive evaluation. However this is not always the case. Surveys on the subject indicate that 20% of the computer decisions are made without a competitive evaluation. The figure approaches 40% for the smaller and less sophisticated companies. These figures are in-

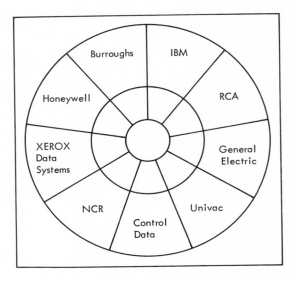

Figure 5.2

fluenced by the fact that one very large and very strong company, IBM, controls about 70% of the computer market. Because of this, the attitude of many is: "They must be doing something right, so why bother looking around." The following is a sample of comments that were made by respondents of a survey on evaluation and selection of computer systems. It may serve to add some practical insight into the selection process.

Since computer rental must be justified to management, cost is the principal factor. The next most important point . . . is ease of conversion from the present configuration. . . .

Organizations and personnel inexperienced in computers must not be allowed a strong voice in the selection of equipment for their use. If your company is supported by government contract, maintain complete documentation to support possible audits.

Although the previously listed selection factors are investigated and taken under consideration, I do not feel that our decisions are based upon completely unbiased objectivity. I feel that this situation is a universal problem among a high percentage of computer users. It is common to get the facts and then ignore or discount them. Loyalty to a company or salesmen based upon past experience of our organization or an individual seems to reign high. After eight and a half years in the business I have seen little progress in objectivity.

Selection has been: any computer as long as it is manufactured by IBM. Policy may be shifting in the near future.

We think it costs less to stay with one manufacturer.

It's a tricky business at best. Advances in hardware and software are so rapid these days that by the time you install the selection, it is almost out of date. In general, a quick selection with a good manufacturer will keep you abreast of the game. I don't think you can get ahead.

All too often, computers are selected on the basis of which salesman does the best snow job or, more simply, sticking to the manufacturer of the current equipment. We do write specifications and go out for bids, but this is, in reality, window-dressing. Probably this is true in most government-controlled situations. Almost any major manufacturer's equipment can be made to do almost any job. All it takes is money. The manufacturers seldom tell the unvarnished truth about capabilities and availability. Logical computer selection seems almost impossible.

Like most organizations, we tend to favor IBM very strongly in our EDP equipment selection. While we look to other systems, by and large this is done more as an exercise than an analytical appraisal. I believe we should be more objective than we are, but I stand almost alone in this attitude. The personnel directly involved in EDP functions are united in their IBM orientation and bias. While I disagree with this, in general I am frank to admit there is a certain built-in security in staying with them. I also find the performance of their representatives is generally superior to the competition. I don't believe this is true of the products.

Extremely complicated.

As the EDP industry continues to mature, it is safe to say that more and more companies, small and large, will be utilizing competitive computer selection. However, the next question that must be raised is what type of selection process do they use. Is it the dart board approach, or is there a logical objective evaluation procedure? The answer is: "Both."

OBJECTIVE SELECTION TECHNIQUES

We must conclude that the 20% of surveyed EDP users who indicated they made no competitive evaluation do not have an objective selection technique. This is not to say that they do not have an objective computer justification technique, because they may indeed go through a sophisticated return on investment analysis in deciding whether to install a computer system in the first place. It is to say that, for one reason or another, these companies felt a competitive computer evaluation was unnecessary or at least not important enough to warrant the time and effort involved.

The majority of companies do use some objective method, although some methods may be considered more objective than others. The surveys agree that the larger users generally use the more sophisticated objective methods, while among the large users, the government uses the most sophisticated methods. Because the government selection methods are in public view, it is logical to expect that the last statement would be true.

A very significant question suggested by this discussion is whether there is a correlation of EDP success and the use of objective methods. This is a question that probably cannot be answered by a survey. Objective methods are not all inherently sound. They still require management judgment in placing weight on certain factors and in evaluating areas like quantity and quality of support, which are difficult to quantify. However, consensus on an empirical basis indicates that objective methods increase the probabilities of making the right decision. Those who are still cynical may concede that an objective method at least allows a review to see why the wrong decision was made.

It now is time to define what is meant by an objective method. Generally, such a method has three stages:

1. Determining decision criteria
2. Establishing relative importance of these criteria
3. Rating each vendor on how well he fulfills these criteria.

DETERMINING DECISION CRITERIA

The decision criteria emanate from the basic systems specifications. It is somewhat similar to selecting an individual for a particular job opening. The first step is to have a thorough understanding of the job. As in filling the job opening, the selection criteria usually can be separated into two categories: (1) the necessary criteria or qualifications that must be met before further consideration is given and (2) the desirable criteria, or those factors that, although not deemed essential, are considered extremely important in the evaluation. It is most important to select carefully the necessary criteria because a hasty selection may arbitrarily eliminate a vendor at this stage. Examples of necessary criteria are illustrated in Figure 5.3.

In this instance vendors A and D would be further evaluated whereas B and C fail to meet the necessary criteria for further consideration. It is possible to reconsider the criteria if the majority of vendors were eliminated at this stage. However, with the breadth of product offerings of the nine major vendors, it is likely that most will meet all but the most restrictive necessary criteria.

Next we turn to the desirable criteria. Figure 5.4 lists a sample set of criteria, which are grouped under the previously discussed dimensions of hardware, software, and application. Support has been added as an important fourth element. Although this is not an all-inclusive list, it includes some of the key criteria that are considered in computer selection.

Necessary criterion	Vendor A	Vendor B	Vendor C	Vendor D
Rental cost less than $5,000 per month	X		X	X
Offer family line of computers	X	X		X
Higher level language capability	X	X	X	X
Communications facilities	X	X	X	X

Figure 5.3

ESTABLISHING RELATIVE IMPORTANCE OF DECISION CRITERIA

Figure 5.5 puts the established decision criteria into a format to facilitate the development of values for each of the general categories and for each of the criteria within the general categories. For example, the form shows that more weight has been given to application and support than to the categories of hardware and software. Although this may be true in the judgment of Three B's' systems study group, it may not be true for other companies. A larger company with prior experience in computers and with substantial in-house system expertise might place a 70% value on hardware and software.

Once the general category values have been established, the point value can be allocated among the various criteria. The sum of the individual criteria within a general category must, of course, equal the value of the general category. As can be seen, throughput/dollar is the most significant hardware consideration. In the software area, availability, ease of use, and a data management system are important criteria. The availability, ease of use, and available documentation are the key decision criteria in the important application category. In the support category, the most significant decision criteria are the education, routine consulting, and responsiveness on the part of the computer vendor. Each of these three elements receives a value of 10 and together will constitute almost one third of the weight for the selection of a computer vendor.

Hardware	Reliability Availability Throughput/dollar Communication-orientation Compatibility Ease of upgrade Modularity	Application	Availability Scope Users' library Modularity Language used Ease of modification Documentation Sophistication
Software	Reliability Availability Multiprogramming Data management Overhead requirements Compile time Execute time Meets industry standards Documentation Ease of use	Support	Education Routine consulting High level consulting Responsiveness Proximity Sales relationship

Figure 5.4

Utilizing this method forces one to focus on some very important issues, for example: "Are education, consulting, and vendor responsiveness more significant than throughput/dollar?" It should be borne in mind that these particular values are used merely for illustrative pur-

General category	Desirable criteria	Value	Vendor A Score Wt.		Vendor B Score Wt.		Vendor C Score Wt.	
15 Hardware	Reliability	2						
	Availability	2						
	Throughput/dollar	6						
	Communications-orientation	2						
	Compatibility	1						
	Ease of upgrade	1						
	Modularity	1						
		15						
20 Software	Reliability	2						
	Availability	6						
	Multiprogramming	—						
	Data management	4						
	Overhead requirements	—						
	Compile time	—						
	Execute time	—						
	Meets industry standards	—						
	Documentation	2						
	Modularity	2						
	Ease of Use	4						
		20						
30 Application	Availability	6						
	Scope	4						
	Users' library	2						
	Modularity	4						
	Language used	—						
	Ease of modification	7						
	Documentation	7						
	Sophistication	—						
		30						
35 Support	Education	10						
	Routine	—						
	Consulting	10						
	High level cons.	1						
	Responsiveness	10						
	Proximity	1						
	Sales/relation	3						
Subtotal		35						
Grand Total		100						

Figure 5.5

poses. The decision criteria, values, and scoring of the vendors, which will be discussed next, are a basic outgrowth of each company's particular situation, stage of development, aspirations, and ability and desire to invest in EDP.

The evaluation is complicated by the separate pricing issue. Some of the software, applications, and support services are extra cost items from certain manufacturers. Either these costs or the costs of acquiring these products from a second vendor should be considered in the evaluation procedure.

RATING THE VENDORS

Figure 5.6 adds the rating score given to each vendor on each of the decision criteria. In this example, a rating scale of 10 is used so that a vendor scoring the highest in each of the categories would receive a weight of 1,000. As one goes through an evaluation of this type, it becomes obvious that a good number of value judgments must be made. This is certainly true and it is apparent that an evaluation tool like this one is only as good as these judgmental factors. This is the situation with any objective method. However, the method provides a consistent framework for evaluating those elements for which there are objective methods and for pointing out those areas where more subjective evaluation is required. This so-called divide and conquer principle allows the decision maker to subdivide the problem into individual elements, thereby conquering those that can be resolved by objective means and separating out those that require more subjective methods. Several approaches that can materially aid the scoring of each vendor will be discussed in a later section.

The ratings show that vendor B looks to be the superior vendor. Although vendor A is superior in the hardware area and scores well in the application area, he falls down in the heavily weighted software and support areas. Vendor C is a smaller computer manufacturer who scores fairly well in hardware, software, and application, but very poorly in the support area. Vendor C might well be considered by a company that has its own systems expertise and is not forced to rely heavily on the vendor's support organization. Note that vendor C offers the highest throughput/dollar.

RELATIVE RISK IN SELECTION

The selection process can be looked at from a different viewpoint. The decision criteria can be stated so that a risk index can be developed.

General category		Desirable criteria	Value	Vendor A		Vendor B		Vendor C	
				Score	Wt.	Score	Wt.	Score	Wt.
15	Hardware	Reliability	2	10	20	8	16	6	12
		Availability	2	10	20	8	16	6	12
		Throughput/dollar	6	8	48	6	36	10	60
		Communications-orientation	2	8	16	2	4	6	12
		Compatibility	1	10	10	6	6	4	4
		Ease of upgrade	1	10	10	6	6	6	6
		Modularity	1	10	10	6	6	8	8
			15		134		90		114
20	Software	Reliability	2	6	12	8	16	6	12
		Availability	6	6	36	8	48	6	36
		Multiprogramming	—	—	—	—	—	—	—
		Data management	4	6	24	8	32	6	24
		Overhead requirements	—	—	—	—	—	—	—
		Compile time	—	—	—	—	—	—	—
		Execute time	—	—	—	—	—	—	—
		Meets industry standards	—	—	—	—	—	—	—
		Documentation	2	4	8	8	16	8	16
		Modularity	2	6	12	8	16	6	12
		Ease of use	4	4	16	8	32	6	24
			20		108		160		124
30	Application	Availability	6	8	48	10	60	8	48
		Scope	4	10	40	8	32	8	32
		Users' library	2	8	16	8	16	2	4
		Modularity	4	8	32	6	24	8	32
		Language used	—	—	—	—	—	—	—
		Ease of modification	7	7	49	8	56	8	56
		Documentation	7	7	49	8	56	8	56
		Sophistication	—	—	—	—	—	—	—
			30		234		244		228
35	Support	Education Routine	10	6	60	10	100	3	30
		Consulting	10	6	60	10	100	3	30
		High level cons.	1	4	4	6	6	2	4
		Responsiveness	10	6	60	8	80	3	30
		Proximity	1	6	6	10	10	6	6
		Sales/relation	3	6	18	10	30	8	24
	Subtotal		35		208		326		124
	Grand Total		100		684		820		590

Figure 5.6

For example, one of the listed decision criteria is availability. The importance of this as a decision criteria was established and a vendor rating on the availability of the system proposed was determined. Now let us look at it from the viewpoint of the consequences of not having the equipment available at the expected time and rate the possibilities of this event occurring. Figure 5.7 presents such an analysis.

In this analysis, five major risk factors have been identified and the relative negative consequences of each to the company have been indicated. Each vendor has been rated on the probability of the event occurring. Vendors A and B already have available hardware and software, so there is no risk associated with these areas. Vendor C has not yet delivered the hardware, so there is a 20% risk of this occurring. It is only 20% because there is a four-month time interval between vendor C's scheduled hardware availability date and the date on which the company requires delivery. There is only a 10% chance that vendor C will not deliver the promised support because he is willing to sign a statement describing his specific support commitment. Vendors A and B are unwilling to do this.

Using this approach, vendor A looks best, followed by vendors B and C. This type of analysis is really the corollary of the previous one and adds another important dimension to the rating process. It has the advantage of focusing a company's attention on the negative side of things—on the consequences of events not occurring as scheduled or promised. Unfortunately this often represents the real world of business. This type of approach can be viewed as a kind of security index.

METHODS FOR DETERMINING VENDOR RATING

The need to rate the various vendors on the basis of their ability to satisfy various decision criteria has been emphasized. This section will

Factor	Value	Vendor A		Vendor B		Vendor C	
		Score	Wt.	Score	Wt.	Score	Wt.
Late delivery	20	0	0	0	0	2	40
Excessive downtime	10	2	20	2	20	4	40
Promised support does not materialize	25	2	50	4	100	1	25
Software does not work	20	0	0	0	0	2	40
Cannot use application packages	25	2	50	4	100	4	100
Total	100		−120		−220		−245

Figure 5.7

discuss various methods that can be used to assist in this process. To begin with, this may be the logical time to consider an outside consultant. It is no doubt true that if the company's own internal staff is unable to structure a problem, then it probably is unable to properly comprehend and utilize whatever decision is reached by the consultant. However, if the company has a solid awareness of the job to be done by the computer and has established its own decision criteria using the described decision framework, a consultant now may be very useful. A consultant may possess the necessary knowledge and contacts with companies using competitive systems so that he can present a reasonable and fairly accurate competitive appraisal. At the same time, the company's internal staff may want to proceed with its own independent evaluation.

There are four basic techniques for deriving the data necessary to objectively rate the vendors on the various decision criteria:

1. Literature search
2. Vendor bid to system specifications
3. Application benchmark
4. Simulation.

The degree of objectivity of these techniques corresponds in reverse to the order in which they are listed. The literature search is the least objective whereas simulation is the most objective technique. Generally speaking, the smaller companies tend to use the less objective techniques. Simulation is used only by the larger companies. A company does not necessarily restrict itself to the use of a single method but may use several in its evaluation procedure. It is not uncommon for a large government installation to utilize all four techniques in evaluating competitive bids for a large computer contract. The discussion now will focus on the four methods, analyzing the strengths and weaknesses of each approach.

LITERATURE SEARCH

The most basic way of gaining information about a vendor's product is to obtain, read, and analyze thoroughly the available literature. This can be a challenging and difficult job, as each of the nine major vendors has literally hundreds of hardware, software, and application products, each product in turn having many options and features. The individual making the literature search must know what he is looking for and must be able to focus quickly on the pertinent literature. Another problem is that although this method is the most basic, it takes a knowledgeable and capable systems analyst to comprehend the literature and to cull out the salient facts and features. It is easy to overlook an element or to derive the wrong meaning from a manual or systems brochure. For example, an operating system is a complex piece of software with subtle capabilities and features. The evaluation of competitive operating systems based on reading the specifications can prove a difficult task.

The individual conducting the literature search should also bear in mind that the EDP industry is still a futures business although it is becoming less so with age. Futures means that the documentation and specifications concerning a product still lead the availability of that product by varying time intervals. Because of this, the availability, reliability, and performance of the product must be determined independently of the published documentation. Performance specifications still are difficult to determine before the product has been field-tested thoroughly. For this reason it is wise to evaluate the stated performance specs in a live working environment if possible. The degree of credibility to be given to specifications depends on the complexity and the uniqueness of the particular product. A company must decide on how conservative or progressive it wants to be in this respect. Business is built on calculated risks and the selection of a computer system is no exception. Too stringent a requirement may rule out a vendor who has announced a real innovative approach but does not yet have demonstrable hardware.

 It is possible to qualify the statements made by vendors in their literature by conducting a survey of companies using the vendor's product. This, of course, brings up the question of time and the problems of developing a realistic customer sample. One way to do this is to ask each vendor to name five customers of his who are about your size, in your industry, and use the class of equipment in which you are interested. There may be a problem in finding users that fall into these categories, particularly if they must be in the same geographical area. In addition you can be assured that the accounts selected will be ones experiencing success with the vendor's product. Despite this, the survey can be helpful in further qualifying key considerations.

An alternate or complementary approach is to utilize the product analyses that are compiled by independent consulting groups. There are services available that maintain the pertinent literature on each manufacturer along with an analysis of the specifications of major products. This approach can be quite helpful, but it must be remembered that EDP products still are proliferating at a rapid rate and it is possible that a service of the type mentioned may not have the most current information.

Rather than conduct its own literature search, a company may ask the vendors to respond to a series of questions directed at their products. The vendor can answer the questions directly and/or append the literature that is pertinent to the issue. The government utilizes this technique very effectively, sometimes as a screening process to reduce the number of vendors prior to a final in-depth evaluation. The following is an example of a set of questions distributed to various vendors by the National Library of Medicine:

Firms having capabilities to furnish the required services are invited to submit the following information:

1. qualification and interest of firm;
2. experience in similar projects;
3. names and qualifications of professional staff who would be assigned to the project;
4. facilities and equipment available for the project.

The criteria outlined below will be used in evaluating a firm's capabilities:

1. equipment production and experience,
   A. third generation computer hardware and concepts,
   B. time-sharing capabilities and procedures,
   C. inquiry and response capabilities (CRT data collection, etc.) and hardware,
   D. communication equipment (long line) hardware or interfacing;
2. software production and experience
   A. vendor supplied software,
   B. applications software by area and degree of definition (see No. 5 below),
   C. data base conversion and management,
   D. hardware-oriented computer program conversion,
   E. documentation;
3. training
   A. courses and materials (types),
   B. facilities and location,
   C. instructors available (experience level);
4. maintenance and technical assistance,
   A. maintenance of vendor-supplied software,
   B. maintenance of vendor-supplied equipment,
   C. maintenance of vendor-supplied applications software by area (see No. 5 below),
   D. technical assistance in computer program conversion,
   E. general and technical manuals and publications,
   F. user groups (size meetings, etc.);

5. experience in information storage and retrieval projects,
   A. studies: systems analysis, systems design and simulation;
      1. library,
      2. biomedical,
      3. bibliographical,
      4. communications networks,
      5. graphic image,
      6. others;
   B. systems implementation: systems analysis, systems design and models;
      1. library,
      2. biomedical,
      3. bibliographical,
      4. communications networks,
      5. graphic image,
      6. others;
6. corporate capabilities in subject specialties, number, and experience;
   1. library science,
   2. information handling,
   3. linguistics,
   4. statistics,
   5. forms design;
7. research and technology programs,
   1. man-machine interaction studies,
   2. education and training devices,
   3. natural language programming and data manipulation studies,
   4. other pertinent programs.

Respondents will not be notified of the results of the evaluation by the National Library of Medicine on the qualification data submitted, but sources deemed qualified will be considered when proposals are solicited.

VENDOR BID TO SYSTEMS SPECIFICATIONS

The vendor bid to systems specifications is the technique being employed by the Three B's Company. An obvious prerequisite is the availability of a system specification to give each vendor. If a comprehensive specification has been developed, the bid to systems specifications can prove to be a most desirable selection technique. It places a heavy burden on the vendor, but it does help qualify the degree of interest the computer manufacturer has in obtaining your business. It also helps to assess the responsiveness and systems talent of the vendor, qualities that may be high in your selection criteria. The use of this procedure usually will necessitate a good deal of interaction between the company's system staff and the vendor's systems representatives. No matter how clear and concise the systems specifications are, there always are areas that have to be clarified or areas where more data is required. Because the proposal may suggest a systems design that is superior to any the internal staff can develop, it usually is desirable to cooperate with the vendor's requests for more information.

If the necessary system specification has been prepared, it will pay a company to spend the time and effort to work with vendors on the development of proposals. The bid to system specification approach is a superior and far more objective method of evaluating competitive systems than the literature search and can be used to more accurately weigh the selection criteria discussed previously.

APPLICATION BENCHMARK

The application benchmark evaluation technique involves the development of an application (be it order processing or an inventory update) that is indicative of the total computer work load. The specifications for the particular application then are given to each computer manufacturer who expresses the desire to bid on the job. The manufacturer's systems and programming staff go to work on the job in order to meet the demonstration deadline established by the company. The company's evaluation team records the computer operation time of the application and uses the comparative times and resultant costs as the prime determinants in selecting a vendor. The major concerns of this type of evaluation are whether the benchmark job selected is indeed representative of the total job and whether the evaluation is weighted too heavily by the systems and programming skills of the manufacturer's people who were assigned the benchmark rather than the overall hardware/software/systems merits of the vendor.

There are different gradations to this approach. The selection of the benchmark need not be a complete application. One computer run of the application or possibly only a test problem can be selected. The test problem might be a series of complex mathematical equations to test the internal processing power of the central processor or it could be a tape or disk sort to test the speeds of these storage devices and the software systems the vendor has designed for them.

It usually is not desirable to base the entire evaluation on the benchmark. However, it can be a most valuable supplementary method. The benchmark can help validate the claims made in a vendor's literature or proposal and can prove the availability of specific products and services that are particularly significant in the evaluation. If the vendors are reluctant to expend the systems and programming effort for the benchmark (and even if they are not) it may be desirable for a company to program its own benchmark using COBOL. This will give the company's own programming staff some valuable experience and will enable the staff to get a closer look at each vendor's machine.

SIMULATION

The simulation technique is the newest, most sophisticated, and, probably for these reasons, the least used. However, as the various simulation approaches become better defined and more flexible in operation, their use will grow, particularly with larger companies. Simulation as used in computer evaluation is defined as testing the cost/performance of a company's information processing requirements on a variety of computer systems. Normally the simulation takes place on a computer. As with the bid to systems specifications techniques, the systems requirements must be thoroughly analyzed and determined before simulation can be used.

There are two types of simulation. The first type of simulation is the most sophisticated and is still in its early developmental stages. Figure 5.8 illustrates how such a system works. The basic input to the simulation are the basic systems specifications pertaining to the input, output storage, and processing of each application. In addition the mode of operation (direct access or sequential, which reflects the response time required) is indicated. The computerized simulation program then processes this data against the various available hardware devices and their costs, comparing the times of all the resultant computer runs, and arrives

		INPUT			OUTPUT			STORAGE		PROCESSING	
MODE	APPL'N	VOLUME	PEAK	CONTENT	VOLUME	PEAK	CONTENT	ITEMS	CONT	TYPE	CONT.
S	ACCT'G.										
D	ORDER PROCES'G.										
D	INV'TRY										

A system costing $4952 per month will do the job in 152 hours/month

Figure 5.8

at the optimum configuration. (In this case, $4,952 per month.) It is apparent that the simulation process must be capable of performing a good deal of systems design work in order to arrive at the optimum solution. Such a simulator must also have access to the prices, capacities, and capabilities of a wide spectrum of competitive hardware devices. Although simulation has not as yet developed to its fullest potential, this basic example should illustrate the significance that simulation can have on the computer selection process.

The second type of simulation is a simpler version of that shown in Figure 5.8, is available, and is used more frequently. Here the user defines his application and does the systems design work himself; that is, he predetermines the number of computer runs and a range of hardware configurations needed to do his job. The input to the simulator (see Figure 5.9) is a run by run breakdown of each application, defining the input and output of each run as indicated in the first nine columns of the form. Another input is the speed, capacity, and capability of each device of each computer system whose performance one wishes to simulate. The simulator then computes the input/output time, the run set-up time, and the available central processor time of the selected system configurations.

Figure 5.9 shows four runs from the payroll application. The total run time of the first run listed is 36.15 minutes. This particular run is input/output bound as it requires only 3.68 minutes of processing time. This leaves 32.47 minutes of available central processor time, which might lead one to look at the possibilities of multiprogramming. The set-up time of two minutes covers the time to mount the tape drive and prepare the card reader for operation.

Figures 5.10 and 5.11 are two examples of possible hardware configurations for accomplishing a particular work load. Configuration A, costing $4,540 per month, is a sequentially-oriented tape system with total monthly run time of 178.4 hours. Configuration B is a direct access-oriented disk system renting for $5,240 with a monthly run time of 142.9 hours. This is extremely relevant information in deciding which system to select. The beauty of simulation is that timing and cost summaries can be developed quickly for a number of different configurations and conditions. For example, a company may want to see the effect of higher speed tapes and disks on the resultant cost and time figures, or it may want to reduce the cost of the system to rock bottom while going to second shift operations.

Four techniques to assist the vendor evaluation process have been presented. They range from the very basic literature search to sophisticated simulation approaches. The decision to install a computer is an important one to a company and the requirement to install the right one

Timings Reference Equipment Configuration A
General Manufacturing Corporation
Payroll Application

RUN GMC-1 WEEKLY. READ CARDS 202. WRITE TAPE 203.

OPERATION	FILE	NAME	ITEMS	CHAR/ITEM	ITEMS/RECORD	CHAR/KEY	NO. KEYS	MEDIA	I/O TIME	CP TIME	SET UP
READ	202	TIME CARDS	28921	18	10	8	2	C	36.15	2.92	1
WRITE	203	TC-1 TAPE	28921					T	1.03	.76	1

TOTAL RUN TIME: 36.15 MINUTES   AVAILABLE CP TIME: 32.47 MINUTES

RUN GMC-2 WEEKLY. SORT TAPE 203.

OPERATION	FILE	NAME	ITEMS	CHAR/ITEM	ITEMS/RECORD	CHAR/KEY	NO. KEYS	MEDIA	I/O TIME	CP TIME	SET UP
SORT	203	TC-1 TAPE	28921	18	10	8	2	T	5.80		1

TOTAL RUN TIME: 5.80 MINUTES

RUN GMC-3 WEEKLY. READ 201, 203. PRINT 104

OPERATION	FILE	NAME	ITEMS	CHAR/ITEM	ITEMS/RECORD	CHAR/KEY	NO. KEYS	MEDIA	I/O TIME	CP TIME	SET UP
READ	201	PAYROLL MASTER	25000	73	2	8	2	T	4.11	1.44	1
READ	203	TC-1 TAPE	28921	18	10			T	1.03	1.61	2
WRITE	205	CHECK TAPE	25000	73	10			T	2.04	.98	-
PRINT	104	TRANSACTION REG.	5000					D	12.77	1.20	-

TOTAL RUN TIME: 12.77 MINUTES   AVAILABLE CP TIME: 7.54 MINUTES

RUN GMC-4 WEEKLY. PRINT 206. READ 205. WRITE 208.

OPERATION	FILE	NAME	ITEMS	CHAR/ITEM	ITEMS/RECORD	CHAR/KEY	NO. KEYS	MEDIA	I/O TIME	CP TIME	SET UP
READ	205	CHECK TAPE	25000	73	10	10	3	T	2.04	1.44	1
WRITE	208	WEEKLY SUMMARY	800	37	5			T	.06	.03	-
PRINT	206	CHECKS	25000					D	42.74	5.46	1

TOTAL RUN TIME: 42.74 MINUTES   AVAILABLE CP TIME: 35.81 MINUTES

Figure 5.9

Timing Summary

CONFIGURATION A: TAPE SYSTEM
PRICE   : $4540 PER MONTH

APPLICATION	DAILY		WEEKLY		MONTHLY	
	Run Time	Set Up	Run Time	Set Up	Run Time	Set Up
PAYROLL	.5	.1	2.2	.3	4.0	.5
ACCOUNTING	.9	.2	.8	.1	6.3	.7
INVENTORY	.4	.1	1.0	.2	5.8	1.0
ORDER PROCESSING	2.2	.3	.5	.1	1.1	.3
SALES ANALYSIS	.7	.2	.5	.1	8.6	2.0
OTHER	.5	.1	1.2	.2	10.9	3.0
TOTAL	5.2	1.0	6.2	1.0	36.7	7.5
MONTHLY TOTAL	114.4	22.0	27.3	4.4	178.4	33.9

Figure 5.10

Timing Summary

CONFIGURATION B: DISK SYSTEM
PRICE   : $5240 PER MONTH

APPLICATION	DAILY		WEEKLY		MONTHLY	
	Run Time	Set Up	Run Time	Set Up	Run Time	Set Up
PAYROLL						
ACCOUNTING						
INVENTORY						
ORDER PROCESSING						
SALES ANALYSIS						
OTHER						
TOTAL	4.2	.8	7.8	.9	42.7	6.0
MONTHLY TOTAL	92.4	17.6	7.8	4.0	142.9	27.6

Figure 5.11

is equally important. The company should consider this when choosing a selection method. It is true that the more advanced techniques are more time consuming and expensive (if a company is selecting its first computer, obviously it is going to have to use an outside service or a service center computer if it utilizes the simulation method). However, with the stakes as high as they are, additional concern and attention to the selection process may be well worth the effort. Several firms offer computer simulation services to assist a company in evaluating and selecting a computer vendor.

FINANCIAL ALTERNATIVES IN ACQUIRING COMPUTING POWER

Several events in the history of EDP are responsible for the advent and growth of purchase as a financial alternative in acquiring computer power. Prior to 1956, IBM, the major computing company, only leased equipment to its customers. However, in 1956, IBM agreed to a consent decree that satisfied the Justice Department. The decree made it mandatory for IBM to offer its computers for sale as well as for rent. In addition, the Justice Department directed that the sales price have a commercially reasonable relationship to the rental price. The latter was necessary lest IBM establish purchase prices that in effect would act only to encourage people to continue to rent.

Up to this time, rental had become the traditional method of acquiring computing power and continued to be so even after the consent decree of 1956. The EDP manager found the rental approach psychologically easier to sell to his management when compared to justifying a large one-time capital expenditure. Likewise, it was easier to justify an incremental increase in rental to enlarge his system. When coupled with the high obsolescence rate of early computers and the uncertainty on the part of the buying public, the rental acquisition method continued to dominate.

However, with the advent of the second generation of computer equipment in 1959 and the third generation in 1964, it soon become apparent that computer technology was not changing as rapidly and dramatically. The generations were lasting longer while the differences between the third and second generation were less apparent than the differences between the second and the first. Knowledge of the fourth generation at this stage indicates that the same will be true of this generation. Along with the stabilization of the industry came the continued maturing of the using public. Computer users who have gone through two or three generations of computer usage feel a growing confidence in their ability to evaluate and select the equipment that is appropriate for their needs. Thus the sense of security and protection associated with the renting of computers is not as important as it used to be. The ratio of rental to purchase has gone from 80/20 just a few years ago to a current ratio of 70/30. Barring any material changes in the pricing policies of computer manufacturers, the trend appears likely to continue in the direction of a still higher purchase to rental ratio.

The rental versus purchase question is becoming more a strict financial decision than it has been in the past. The basic financial facts are these. The purchase price to monthly rental ratio averages about 47 to 1.

One might conclude that he could benefit financially if he keeps the machine at least four years. However, there are other factors to consider. The purchaser must pay maintenance charges that are included in the rental price. He must pay taxes and insurance on the equipment. The purchaser also must realize that he will have interest-producing money tied up in the computer investment and will be able to effect less tax credit because rental costs usually are greater than the combination of maintenance, tax, insurance, and depreciation cost. Adding these factors to the financial picture creates a break-even point of close to six years. This assumes no resale, trade-in, or salvage value of the purchased system. Assuming that there is some residual value will add a favorable factor to the purchase acquisition route. However, after six years it is felt this value will be slight. Thus this analysis would say that if you can reasonably expect to utilize the equipment for six years, you should consider purchasing it.

Another possibility is to purchase those pieces of equipment that appear to have the longest life and to rent the remainder. This has led many companies to purchase their central processors while continuing to rent their peripheral devices and auxiliary storage devices like magnetic tape units and disk units. An analysis and decision based on these considerations can present an attractive middle route.

A third financial avenue for acquiring computing power is an offshoot of the renting route. The user can rent a computer, but he does so through a third party leasing company. The rates can be 10% to 15% less than the manufacturer's rental price, depending on whether the lease is short- or long-term. Obviously the leasing company must charge more for the short-term lease as it must find a second or third lessee for the returned equipment if a short-term lease is not renewed. The leasing company makes its money by betting that the life of the computer is longer than that reflected in the manufacturer's ratio of purchase price to monthly rental (after the leasing company includes the other cost factors of purchase as described.).

The computer user can decide to purchase some of his equipment from the manufacturer and lease other equipment from the leasing company. The 10 to 15% savings must be weighed against the full system support and consultation from the computer manufacturer. Although the manufacturer still offers certain standard services to the leasee of a leasing company, he does not offer the specialized support services that might be quite significant to a company. Likewise the third party leasee loses any leverage he might have in dealing with the manufacturer. Some companies that find the need, for either back-up reasons or other, to have two identical computers believe that they may have the best of both worlds by renting one from the manufacturer and one from the leasing company. Thus they get the one at a lower rental price and still maintain the specialized support from the manufacturer on the other, which, because the machines are the same, means support for both.

Other financial alternatives to acquire computer power such as service centers and time-sharing services have been described in the previous chapter. More and more users are finding that a combination of their own facilities augmented by outside services is the most satisfactory approach. As the EDP industry matures, the trend is definitely towards the combination of several types of financial approaches to acquiring the necessary facilities whether this be a combination of purchase and rental, a combination of purchase and third party leasing, or a combination of a company's own facilities and a service center.

SINGLE VERSUS MULTIVENDOR

A consideration that often arises during the selection process, particularly in the case of the larger company, is whether to rely on a single vendor to provide the entire system or to utilize multivendors. When the EDP industry was in its infancy—before the proliferation of hardware, software, applications, and support services, and before separate pricing—this was not a concern. The potential computer user decided on a single vendor and that was that. However, there are a number of different choices open to him today, and it may be sound economically to explore the possibilities of buying a computer system from more than a single vendor.

For the most part, the nine major computer manufacturers can provide a complete system to a potential user, and a complete system is what the user really is looking for. Therefore, one school of thought states that it is far easier to deal with a single supplier and not to buy, for example, a central processor from one vendor and communications equipment from another.

Because these two devices must interface and a software system must talk to both of them, the maintenance situation becomes a sensitive area. If something goes wrong, the source of the problem may not be readily obvious. The user may find the communications equipment vendor and central processor vendor accusing each other while his system is unproductive. Therefore, the user prefers a single vendor who is responsible for the entire system. Another reason for the user favoring a single vendor concept is the sheer complexity of the decision making process. If there are nine computer manufacturers, nine peripheral device manufacturers, nine communications equipment manufacturers, and so on, the job of competitive evaluation and selection becomes a monumental one. The user sees a need to bound his selection process or he may find himself spending an inordinate amount of time on this part of the job.

Looking at the single/multivendor question from the viewpoint of other schools of thought, there are significant reasons to consider multivendors. Although it has been difficult for new companies in the EDP industry to compete with the major manufacturers across the entire spectrum of their product line, they have been able to selectively enter a segment of the market and apply a great deal of ingenuity and creativity to a particular device. Thus there is a wide array of products, particularly in the peripheral and communications areas, that have a great deal of appeal not only from the capability side but also from the cost side. Another factor that has aided the multivendor concept has been the development of the standard interface. As with any new industry, the standardization process in the EDP industry has been slow. One strong element of standardization has been the Bell Telephone Company. Because all computers have to utilize the common carriers to speak to one another, they must meet certain standards. An input device made by vendor A is designed to send data over a telephone line. A central processor manufactured by vendor B is designed to accept data from its own input device over a telephone line. Because the interface is the telephone line, the computer is able to speak to either its own device or any other device that is capable of sending data over the line.

In addition to the common interface imposed by the Bell System, most of the major computer manufacturers have developed connecting interfaces that enable a user to connect to their computer devices that do not go across communication lines. With the proliferation of specialized peripheral devices like graphic terminals and audio systems, it becomes difficult for the manufacturer to stay competitive in every area. Therefore, in some cases he chooses not to try, but rather to provide interface devices that allow the hook-up of foreign peripherals.

The multivendor concept is not limited to the hardware area but is evident also in the software and support areas. The previously mentioned separate pricing announcement by IBM has accelerated the growth of these services.

At any rate, this states the issue and the arguments of those in the single vendor school versus those in the multivendor school. In the long run, the significant point to remember is that a computer is only one part of the ultimate system. The user must put together the right blend of hardware, software, and application in order to benefit his business operation. The elements must work together; the applications utilizing the software, which in turn utilize the various elements of hardware. The user must be thoroughly convinced that the pieces of his system that he buys from separate vendors will blend together to serve his purpose, otherwise it might be more prudent for him to stick with a single supplier.

JUSTIFICATION

Preliminary computer cost figures were estimated during the feasibility study. Whatever the selection technique used, a company should be able to pinpoint these costs with far higher accuracy after it has completed its vendor evaluation. The remaining job is to review the benefits or savings and compare these with the costs in arriving at a final justification.

The concept of life cycle costing is being used increasingly as a justification technique by government as well as commercial evaluators in comparing contractor proposals. The major concept of life cycle costing is that it may be desirable to pay more initially for a product that can be shown to be cheaper over the life of the product. This method imposes the need to make a longer-range projection and justification of a product rather than to just look at the situation over a period of a year or two. A typical example of this method can be seen in the automobile industry or in any industry in which the original manufacturer has a maintenance responsibility for his product. It is generally agreed that improved quality control methods have had a great deal to do with the five-year warranties that are common in the automotive industry. Thus, the car manufacturer puts more money into the cost of manufacturing the product because he calculates that it more than offsets the added maintenance costs. It makes sense to spend a little more to ensure the quality of a transmission because of the high labor cost in reconditioning one. The life cycle costing concept in this case necessitated a five-year cost projection in order to determine the true effect of the five-year warranty.

The life cycle costing concept is equally appropriate in evaluating a computer installation. A one- or two-year projection does not tell the entire story. This is particularly true with a system that is directed at improving business operations rather than a system directed at reducing costs. The latter shows a higher short-term return whereas the former may not be significant until the later years of the project. Therefore, it is wise to look at computer justification over at least a five-year cycle.

Figure 5.12 presents a five-year cost summary in a hypothetical situation. The first column (labeled zero) is the year prior to the computer installation and the other columns refer to the first four years of operation. The chart separates the one-time costs from the recurring costs. It assumes that the EDP costs will continue to rise along with the normal expansion of business and with the introduction of computer processing into more facets of the company's operations. One might assume that EDP costs should be reduced with time, but this has not been the case historically. Although the productivity of the EDP function continues to improve, the saturation level for computerized information processing is still below 50% for most companies in most industries. Assuming that there continues to be benefit in computerizing information systems, EDP costs will not drop until the saturation level begins to be approached.

Figure 5.13 presents a savings summary for the five-year period, broken down into tangible and intangible categories. There obviously are no savings prior to the computer installation and less than some would imagine in the first year of operation. The first year is a transition year when the new system phases out the old, usually with some overlap and duplication. Note, however, the rapid buildup of savings in the second and subsequent years. In this particular instance, the current data processing costs are $130,000. It can be seen that the major portion of these costs are not eliminated until the second year of operation. It is obvious that the company is spending a good deal more on data processing with the computer system. The key to the justification of these costs rests with the savings in clerical costs outside of EDP, inventory reductions, overtime reductions, and the like.

Figure 5.14 illustrates graphically the cost versus savings situation (only the tangible savings are included). It indicates that savings do not exceed added costs until the second year of operation or three years after the computer program has been initiated. Figure 5.15 is a cumula-

	0	1	2	3	4
Initial systems & programming	60,000	20,000			
Site preparation	6,000				
File conversion	3,000	3,000			
Parallel operation		4,000			
Other	1,000	1,000			
Total One-time Costs	70,000	28,000			
Hardware rental		62,000	80,000	90,000	100,000
Systems & programming		60,000	70,000	60,000	60,000
Operations	10,000	50,000	50,000	60,000	65,000
Outside services	2,000	2,000			
Other	1,000	1,000			
Total Recurring Costs	13,000	175,000	200,000	210,000	225,000
Total	83,000	203,000	200,000	210,000	225,000

Figure 5.12   Cost summary.

	0	1	2	3	4
Reduction in Current Data Processing Costs		50,000	110,000	115,000	125,000
Clerical Costs Outside Data Processing		10,000	20,000	30,000	50,000
Inventory Reduction (15% Carrying Cost)		40,000	125,000	150,000	160,000
Overtime Reduction		5,000	20,000	22,000	32,000
Production Variances			5,000	40,000	50,000
Other		1,000	1,000	1,000	1,000
Total Tangible Savings		106,000	281,000	358,000	418,000
Profit on Sales (Increased Customer Service)		5,000	50,000	100,000	100,000
Improved Sales Analysis			100,000	100,000	100,000
Increased Management Control					
More Meaningful Data					
Other					
Total Intangible Savings		5,000	150,000	200,000	200,000
Total Savings		111,000	431,000	558,000	618,000

Figure 5.13   Savings summary.

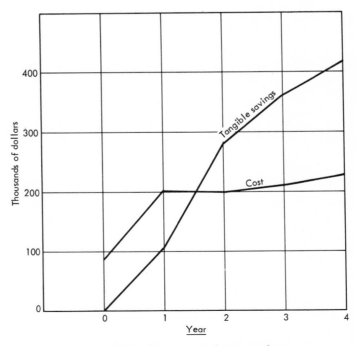

Figure 5.14   Costs versus savings comparison.

tive summary of costs and tangible savings and shows that the break-even point does not occur until the third year of operation or the fourth year from initiation of the computer program. However, the savings curve is continuing to rise while the cost curve is beginnng to level off. The short-term picture may not seem too impressive, but the long-term picture is extremely attractive. The particular illustration used may be more long-term oriented than is true in practice, but it serves to illustrate the need for life cycle costing in considering computer justification. Embarking on a computer program must be viewed as a long-term project with little opportunity (or reason) to return to the old system once the new program is underway. The justification process should be keyed to this long-term framework.

RETURN ON INVESTMENT ANALYSIS

Another way to view computer justification is to measure its over-all impact on the profitability of the company. The thinking is that if a

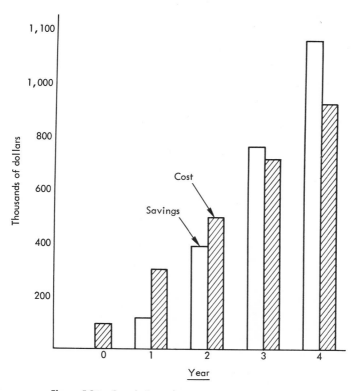

Figure 5.15 Cumulative costs versus savings comparison.

computer is a beneficial tool, it will increase the profits of a company and/or reduce investment and thereby have an effect on improving return on investment. Profitability and return on investment are the two key yardsticks of measuring business performance. Figure 5.16 illustrates a simplified schematic of a return on investment analysis. The top portion is a profit and loss statement for the company, starting with sales on the first line, subtracting cost of sales to arrive at net earnings before taxes, and then subtracting taxes (a 48% rate is assumed) to arrive at net earnings after taxes. Cost of sales is comprised of fixed costs (depreciation, rent, equipment cost, and the like), variable costs (labor,

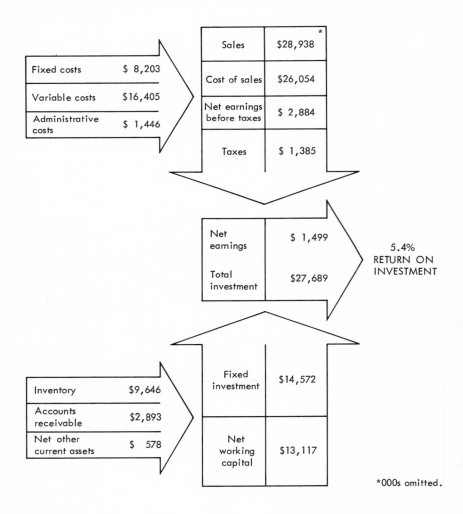

*000s omitted.

material, and so on), and administrative costs (legal, personnel, accounting, for example). Thus, the $1,499,000, is the company profit for the year and forms the numerator of the return on investment equation.

The investment or denominator of the equation is comprised of fixed investment (money tied up in machinery and buildings), and net working capital, made up of current inventory, accounts receivable, and other current assets. The ratio of net earnings to total investment is equal to the company's rate of *Return On Investment* (ROI). ROI is really what a company is trying to improve, as it is the true measure of how well it is using the stockholders' money. If a computer can have an appreciable effect on improving this rate of return, then it is most certainly a desirable investment. For illustrative purposes, assume that Figure 5.16 represents the company's ROI at the point in time it is evaluating the possibility of a computer. The figures exclude the last three zeros so that the company in question is netting approximately $1.5 million on $29 million sales and has an ROI of 5.4%.

The supposition is made that a computer system that will add $100,000 to current data processing costs can reduce inventory an average of one third. The company recognizes that it has a much lower inventory turn than other companies in its industry and is convinced that an advanced statistically-oriented computerized inventory system can materially improve the situation. Whether the expected reduction is 33%, 40%, 10%, or 5%, this technique can be utilized to show the effect on ROI. It begins to place the computer in the direct context of ongoing business operations. Figure 5.17 shows the effect of this action on the company's ROI. Administrative costs have been increased by $100,000 (added cost of the computer and the staff to operate it) and inventory has been decreased by a third. In addition, because the reduction in inventory reduces the inventory carrying costs (storage, movement, taxes and insurance, and so on), 10% of the $3,215 (inventory reduction) or $321 has been subtracted from variable costs. The net effect of putting the computer to work on inventory control is to increase net profit, reduce investment, and increase ROI from 5.4% to 6.6%.

Figure 5.18 represents a situation where the computer program is directed at increasing the productivity of plant operations. Variable costs represent the biggest cost element and there would be real leverage on profitability by improvements in this area. If a computer program is focused on an improved production scheduling and control system built around a standard cost system to reduce production variances, and a scheduling system to reduce overtime, idle time, and the like, it may be possible to effect a 5% improvement in variable costs. The improved use of facilities increases productive capacity. It is further assumed that

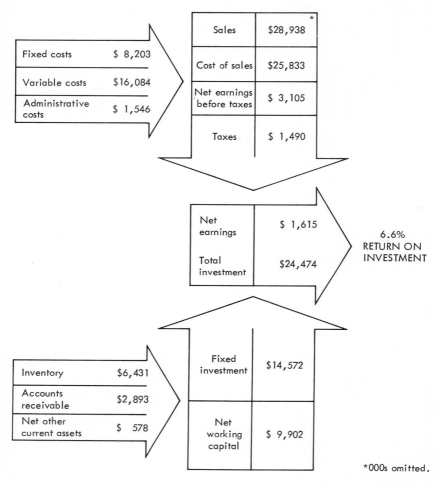

Figure 5.17

the introduction of computerized sales forecasting techniques and advanced market analysis enables the company to increase sales by 5%. This changes the return on investment analysis in Figure 5.18 as follows:

1. Sales up 5% over sales listed in Figure 5.17.
2. Variable expense in Figure 5.17 is 55.6% of sales. A 5% reduction results in 50.6% of sales or $15,374.
3. Increase of 5% ($1,447) in sales will cause an increase of $321 in inventory and a 5% increase in accounts receivable ($145).

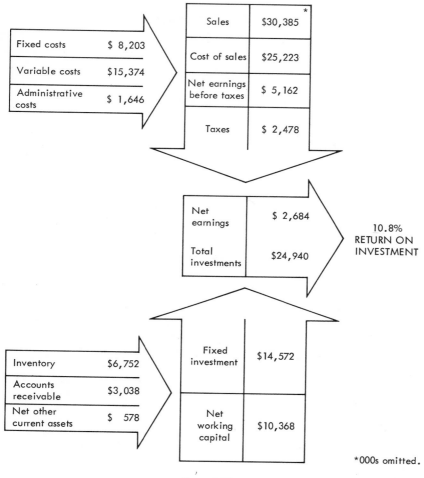

Figure 5.18

4. Administrative costs increased $100,000 to handle expanded computer applications.

The effect of this is to increase the ROI from 6.6% to 10.8%. The changes illustrated here may seem dramatic, yet they show the potential the computer can have on the basic operating and financial ratios of a company. The study team that is preparing the computer justification should, of course, apply figures that are pertinent to the particular system under study. The point being stressed here is the desirability of looking at the computer as an integral part of the business operation. This puts the justification in concrete business terms that can have a very favorable impact on management.

THE MANAGEMENT PRESENTATION

The normal considerations in making a management presentation must be considered in presenting the final computer justification. The presentation must be geared to the audience, with major emphasis on assuring that the tone is not too technical in nature. It must highlight the key considerations, reach definite conclusions, cover and counter the major management concerns, state the financial considerations, and offer a plan for moving from where the company is today to where it wants to be in the future. The approach should not be to either oversell or undersell, but to present the facts as they are in a realistic framework and with good perspective of the actual working environment in which the company operates. The level and quality of visual aids and presentation materials must fit into this over-all framework.

The Addendum at the end of the chapter is an example of a computer justification presentation. This particular presentation was given to the management of the food processing division of a large grocery chain that also has its own retail division. It recommends a central computer to handle the data processing workload for the food processing division and the retail division as well as the home office operation. The presentation culminated some nine months of systems feasibility, systems study, and systems design. The reader may judge for himself the organization, content, and effectiveness of the approach used.

SUMMARY

The synthesis process now is completed. The previous chapter covered the design of a system to best satisfy the established system specifications. This chapter explored various approaches to selecting a computer vendor. The approaches centered on: (1) determining decision criteria, (2) establishing relative importance of these criteria, and (3) rating each vendor on how well he fulfills these criteria. The following methods of vendor rating were discussed: (1) literature search, (2) vendor bid to system specifications, (3) application benchmark, and (4) simulation. Other issues explored were the alternate ways of acquiring computer power and the consideration of a single or multivendor relationship.

Finally, the justification process was reviewed, illustrating the cost versus benefit analysis and also the return on investment approach. The justification presentation was discussed and a sample company presentation included as an addendum to the chapter. The remaining consideration of the synthesis process is a go/no go decision on the part of management. A go decision will be the signal to proceed to the next chapter and a discussion of the implementation phase of the computer system selection cycle.

THREE B'S' APPROACH TO COMPUTER JUSTIFICATION

As Dexter Johnson planned for the presentation to management, several things went through his mind. First he was glad he had decided to have his group program the benchmark problem in COBOL. He was able to run the program, after some modification, on each of the three vendors' machines. This gave him a better basis on which to make a competitive decision and also gave his own staff a good deal of added confidence. Secondly, he thought it a good move to bring in a consultant to make an independent evaluation of the three vendors. Johnson was reassured when the consultant ranked the vendors in the same order as he had, although he did not know what he would have done had the consultant made a selection different than his.

Looking toward the presentation, the head of Three B's' systems group felt confident that management would agree to his recommendation. Johnson had done his homework and knew how the key executives felt about installing a computer. Sales vice president Paul Peters had been convinced the most easily because he was disillusioned with the length of the order processing cycle. Peters knew something was needed or Three B's would begin to lose customers who could get better service elsewhere. Johnson's boss, Harry Hanson, was reluctantly willing to go along because he knew he would have little to do with the program—in fact, Hanson was considering early retirement to permit his successor to be involved with the data processing program from the outset. The key antagonist was Warren Coolidge, vice president of production, who was being influenced greatly by Burt Harrison, the plant manager. The plant manager still opposed the computer program although he recognized the serious production problems facing Three B's. Harrison felt the combination of better manual systems and utilization of a service center would solve their problems. Johnson felt he had accomplished something in interesting Harrison enough in computers to attend a three-day management course. He felt he could win over the plant manager, but unfortunately there was not enough time between the current date and the date of the presentation.

The date of the presentation arrived. The approach and tone were direct and forceful. Johnson used figures to show how more than 90% of companies of Three B's' size already had computer systems. He stated that he could not see how Three B's could remain competitive and resolve the information and control problems facing it without the use of a computer. The computer would be the catalyst in the much needed business system reorientation. An integrated system framework would be established that would lead to the use of advanced statistical decision-making techniques and communications-oriented approaches. The computer would tackle the key money areas of the operation. It would cost money, more than the company currently was spending on data processing, but the long-range results would justify the added costs.

The tone was aggressive and hard-hitting. True, Coolidge brought up some roadblocks, but it was obvious from the start that Bill Barrett was pleased and excited by the presentation. He asked Coolidge if he were prepared to go along with the recommendations. Coolidge slowly assented. Barrett commended Johnson and his team for their effort and told them they had the company green light. The president indicated that Johnson should notify the winning vendor and do whatever was required to get the implementation effort under a full head of steam as soon as possible.

ADDENDUM: OUTLINE OF COMPUTER JUSTIFICATION
PRESENTATION TO FOOD PROCESSING DIVISION MANAGEMENT

I. Background of the Study
II. Benefits of a Computer Center to the Food Processing Division
    A. The Money Making Jobs
    B. The Cost Cutting Jobs
III. Justification for the Central Computer Concept
IV. Significant Considerations
V. Plan of Action
VI. Summary

    I. *Background of the Study*
       A. The objective of the study effort initiated nine months ago was to explore the feasibility of combining the following three data processing operations into one computer center.

          a. Small scale computer at retail division
          b. Punched card installation at food processing division
          c. Bookkeeping operation at home office

  B. A three-man study team was formed. After an initial period of education and orientation, the team split up with each member concentrating on the systems requirements of one of the installations listed.

  C. The study team met regularly to review and correlate the data each member was gathering. The study focused on: (a) existing applications and their cutover to the new system, and (b) new applications. The major emphasis was on accomplishing the current work load with some improvements, but at less cost than each division was currently spending for its data processing.

  D. A separate presentation will be given to the retail division and to home office. The aim here is to present the results of our study to answer the basic question of the feasibility of a computer center to handle the work of the food processing division.

II. *Benefits of a Computer Center to the Food Processing Division*

  A. *The Money Making Jobs.* I would like to present reasons why I think the Food Processing Division needs a computer by using two relevant examples of how a computer can help make money-making decisions.

   1. I discovered that a major responsibility of a production coordinator is to schedule production for the coming quarter. The situation is one of balancing the cost of carrying inventory with the cost of production set-up and at the same time keeping in mind the other factors that affect scheduling, such as cost of stock out and cost of overtime. Illustration 1 lists some of the key elements

Scheduling Factors

Item	Plan A	Plan B	Optimum
Cost to Carry Inventory			
Cost of Changeover			
Cost of Stock Out			
Cost of Hiring & Laying Off			
Cost of Overtime			

Sales Forecast

Item	Month 1	2	3	Total
A	100	90	110	300
B	80	85	60	225
C	40	35	45	120

Illustration 1 Production scheduling.

needed to make a decision of this type, including a sales forecast for the quarter. The current method of accomplishing this is by a trial and error method of trying different schedules, looking at the pros and cons of each, and then picking the one that seems best. In the busy schedule of a production coordinator, it may be possible to try two or maybe three different alternatives, but the coordinator never knows how close he is to any type of optimum situation. The computer offers us a way to materially improve our production scheduling activity. It can materially improve the accuracy of forecasts and develop a production plan based on the forecast, taking into account the listed cost factors.

2. Illustration 2 describes another tool we have been seeking for a long time—flexible budgets. It indicates that static budget we currently utilize where we establish a figure, $8,000, based on a set level of operation. In reality, we all realize that the budget is not static but is flexible, depending upon the number of shifts that actually occurred during the budget period. This is a highly simplified instance of a 30-shift actual operation where the static budget shows the department was under its budget, whereas the flexible budget would tell the truer tale. There is a great deal of calculation that goes into first determining the flexible budgets and then reporting and measuring the actual results against budget. The computer offers us a way to develop and implement a flexible budget system.

B. *The Cost Cutting Jobs.* We took a look at the data processing job that currently accounts for 60% of our data processing time—sales order processing. We used this as a benchmark, developed the systems design, programmed part of it for the computer, and actually ran it under test conditions. Illustration 3 gives a general

Indirect Labor Expense

A. STATIC BUDGET $8,000
(Based on a 40-shift operation)
B. FLEXIBLE BUDGET $ 750 + $200/Shift

Actual Results
30-Shift Operation

		Budget	*Actual*	*Variance*
A.	Static Budget	$8,000	$7,500	$ 500
B.	Flexible Budget	$6,750	$7,500	$(750)

Illustration 2   Flexible budgets.

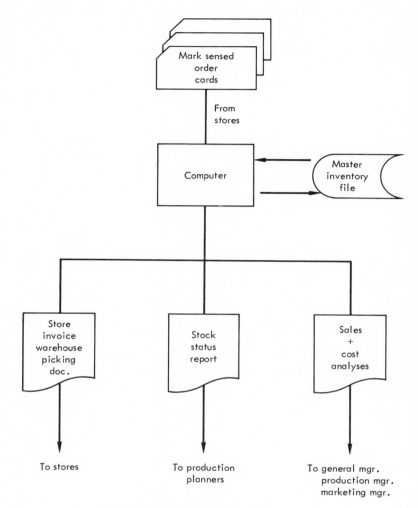

Illustration 3   Order processing.

schematic of the job. This convinced us that we can do
the basic bread and butter jobs and, as you will see, can
do them more cheaply than we currently are doing
them.

III. *Justification for the Central Computer Concept*

It should be stated here that we have decided on an American
Computing Corporation 250 system. There is a separate evaluation report explaining our rationale for this choice. Suffice
to state, we feel ACC offers the best combination of hardware, software, application, and support for our needs. There

was one vendor who offered a better price, but he was ruled out because his offerings fell short in the application and support areas.

The rationale behind the idea of a computer center is very simply explained in the following three statements:

A. *We can do the job better.* Not only can the central computer do our current jobs, it can do the job better. We are confident that the order cycle time can be reduced by 24 hours as a result of computer processing. Currently an order requires two days to be processed because of lack of computing and printing power and the one-shift operational policy followed by the Food Processing Division. The central computer will have the printing speed and processing capacity to complete the job within a one-shift operation and can utilize the evening shift if necessary. Thus, orders coming into the center by 8 A.M. will be processed and returned to the Food Processing Warehouse by 8 A.M. the following day. This means that goods will be on trucks a day earlier than previously. In addition, more meaningful inventory reports and sales analysis reports can be produced as a by-product of computer processing. Furthermore, the production scheduling and flexible budget approaches are but two examples of what a computer system can accomplish in the more advanced areas of application.

B. *We can put on new jobs faster.* The establishment of a computer center will enable us to utilize systems analysts and programmers of a much higher caliber than the individual divisions could afford. Also, our study has brought out the interdivision similarity in many systems areas. For example, the payroll and accounting systems appear "naturals" to be handled by a common set of programs. This will allow our staff to become more productive and thus be able to computerize more expeditiously your current backlog of jobs. We think we can get these jobs on the air a lot sooner than you could with your current staff and budget.

C. *We can do it more cheaply.* Illustration 4 .tells the cost story. It shows that a computer center can save you $1,400 per month. You can see our estimated budget of $15,000 per month, and the allocation of hours to each of the using divisions. The estimate of 54 hours is a conservative one— frankly, we think we can handle your current work load in less than 40 hours. It is significant that the hours you will be charged do not increase in proportion to the increase in your volume. Because we will be using second

Cost Proposal

Projected Computer Center Costs/Month

1.	Equipment	$ 7,000
2.	Systems/Programming Personnel	5,500
3.	Operations	2,500
		$15,000

Projected Hourly Charges

		Hours	Charge
1.	Food Processing Division	54	$ 5,400
2.	Retail Division	78	7,800
3.	Home Office	18	1,800
		150	$15,000

What Will the Food Processing Division Save?

1.	Personnel (five people)	$ 3,500
2.	Equipment Rental	$ 3,300
		$ 6,800
	Computer Center Charge	5,400
	Savings	$ 1,400

Illustration 4

shift operation, and second shift rental is greatly reduced over first shift, your hourly equipment rate will drop materially as our volume increases.

IV. *Significant Considerations*

From our informal discussions with you, we think the following represent the key considerations (potential problem areas) concerning the center.

A. *Centralized Control.* The computing center will be operated as a service function. You will define what you want to be done, what your system objectives are, and what you need for output to help you run your business. Our job will be to design the system so as to take maximum advantage of the existing hardware and to minimize the cost of doing the job. We will review with you the costs and implementation schedule for each application that you want to consider.

B. *Competition for Computer Time.* You may feel that another division's job will get priority over yours. There is, of course, limited time on the computer, but we feel this is a job of proper scheduling on our part. You will note the projected work load is only 150 hours per month. We still have unused capacity on a single shift, and we can always go to second and third shifts. Also, bear in mind that with the economies of operating a center, we can always add capacity and power if the work load demands it.

C. *Risk of Machine Breakdown.* We feel that this has been materially overemphasized. The computer we are suggesting utilizes advanced and exceedingly reliable solid state circuitry. Although we have all our eggs in one basket, so to speak, we think the basket is a strong one. Certainly we currently experience and will continue to experience machine downtime. However, we think it will be less than the composite of the small computer and punched card installations utilized by the Food Processing Division and the Retail Division. Also, we have the option of using a similar computer in this area as a back-up in case it is necessary.

D. *Communications.* Because we are within ten miles of the administrative headquarters and 15 miles of the warehouse, we plan initially to rely on carrier service to communicate input and output back and forth. However, we have underway a study looking into the feasibility of communications equipment to tie the facilities together. We think this may become necessary within two years when we computerize those applications requiring immediate data turn-around.

V. *Plan of Action.* Illustration 5 presents the plan of action. After gaining approval from the Food Processing Division, the Retail Division and Home Office, we must begin to organize the Computer Center department. This will involve some transfers of people. An education effort then will commence to train the personnel who will be added to our current staff. We would then proceed to convert the order processing application and when this is under control, divert manpower to convert the other applications. We would expect to complete these by the

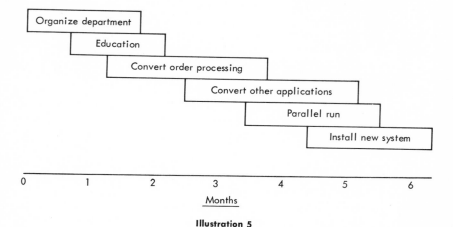

Months

Illustration 5

end of the fourth month, run the new systems one month in parallel with the old, and then install the new system. We would shoot to replace your equipment and reassign your data processing people by the end of the sixth month. This is an ambitious schedule, but with the proper cooperation, we think we can make it.

VI. *Summary*

We have attempted to explain just why we feel that a centralized computer center will have outstanding benefits for the Food Processing Division and have tried to get across and extend to you a bit of the enthusiasm that we feel for this project. We are excited about the Center, for we can look ahead and see sizable financial savings and major operational control advantages for our company. The Food Processing Division has always been a forward-looking division, and I know that management has always demanded the best. We feel that a computer will give management the best and will move you closer to the important goals that we have discussed at this meeting. When you are driving down the road it is much more rewarding to look through your front window than through your rear vision mirror. Paperwork systems up to now have concentrated on the rear vision mirror approach; they tell us how we did. Today's business situation makes it essential to look ahead. With the capabilities of today's electronic computers, operating managers have the tools to look ahead. We want to know how we did, but more important, we want to know how we are going to do. We firmly believe that the computer is a prime tool to accomplish this.

SOURCE MATERIAL AND SUPPLEMENTARY READING

Datamation. The August 1968 issue is devoted to the subject of computer leasing.

Datamation. The February 1967 issue is devoted to the subject of computer selection.

Harvard Business Review, "Special Reprint Series on Computer Management," (16 articles).

"Life Cycle Costing for ADP Equipment," *ADP Newsletter* (November 18, 1968). Published by the Diebold Group, Inc., New York, N. Y.

Miccio, Dr. J. V., "Electronic Data Processing: Its Controls and Economics," *Data Management* (June, 1967).

Production. "Panel Discussion—The Mighty Control System Has Everyday Problems," section entitled *On Justification*: J. J. Murphy, July, 1968.

(The section on return on investment analysis in this chapter is based on this article.)

Raiffa, H., *Decision Analysis*. Reading, Mass.: Addison-Wesley, 1968. (This book provides further detail on the decision-making matrix approach described in this chapter under the heading Objective Selection Techniques.)

Sharpe, W. F., *The Economics of Computers*. New York: Columbia University Press, 1969. 571 pp.

Study of the Acquisition of Peripheral Equipment for use with Automatic Data Processing Systems, report to Congress by the Comptroller General of the U. S., June, 1969.

Wall Street Journal Study, Management and the Computer. Dow Jones & Co. Inc., 1969.

6

THE IMPLEMENTATION PHASE

Dexter Johnson now has the official approval of management to make plans for the computer installation. As he looks back at the work that has been accomplished, he feels a sense of satisfaction in the fact that he has followed a realistic, practical approach. He has not promised management immediate results. Rather, he has stressed the importance of management's continued involvement in the implementation effort. With management endorsement, Johnson knows that it is up to him to accomplish the job. The burden rests squarely upon his ability and that of his team to turn the systems specifications into operational computer programs.

Johnson reflects on an interesting point. Although it has never been stated officially, it appears to him that the president has tacitly assumed that Johnson has been his EDP director all along. Nonetheless, the president has never asked Johnson whether he is willing to take charge of the installation effort. The acting EDP director felt at the outset of the study that this might be a temporary assignment, as his real interest

was to move up the ranks in the controller's department and try for
Harry Hanson's job when Hanson retired. However, as the study
evolved, Johnson's interest in the EDP operation grew—he could see
more clearly the potential of EDP for Three B's. At first, Johnson considered EDP merely an adjunct to the punched card installation and
still a part of the controller's responsibility. However, as the systems
study expanded to include the entire business information system of
Three B's, and as the detailed work focused on the sales and inventory
systems as contrasted to the basic accounting functions, Johnson realized the real significance of his role. He has reached the conclusion that
he wants to stay with the activity and head the department. Another
interesting situation was that Johnson was taking directions more from
Barrett than from his boss, Harry Hanson. Although it was not definitely
stated, Johnson felt the new EDP organization would report directly to
the president when the computer system was installed.

With the implementation job facing him, Johnson reviews the resources he has to accomplish the task. He believes that Osbourne and
Farnum have progressed very well and should prove a strong nucleus of
the programming team. However, the first program either had written
was their portion of the COBOL benchmark. Both would need additional training in programming the new computer. In addition, the EDP
director would have to hire at least two additional programmers. With
the scarcity of systems and programming talent, Johnson knew he would
need more depth in case there were turnover during the implementation
cycle. Even if Johnson found the experienced personnel he was looking
for, they too would have to be trained, at least to a certain degree. Thus,
training would be an important factor.

The scope of the job at hand, the need for a detailed plan of action,
and a schedule with measurable milestones along the way were the
crucial issues facing the acting EDP director. Barrett had indicated he
would like to review the over-all schedule as soon as Johnson was able
to draw one up. Johnson decided to spend the next week reviewing and
analyzing various project control techniques to determine which approach was best suited to their particular situation. He would discuss
this with the computer vendor as well, because he knew this step was
necessary before they could establish a computer delivery date that made
sense. He realized that the practice of many companies was to schedule
the delivery of the computer to coincide with the earliest possible time
the manufacturer could promise it. The schedule was then established
in a backwards fashion from this predetermined delivery date. Johnson
did not consider this a desirable way to operate, for although equipment availability was a consideration, it was not the prime one. The
major consideration was a determination of a realistic schedule that
reflected the goals, objectives, and resources of the Three B's company.

INTRODUCTION

Figure 1 indicates that the implementation phase consists of three sub-phases—programming, operation, and maintenance/modification. The programming subphase begins with the development of a comprehensive plan for the entire implementation effort. It includes the selection and training of the systems analysts and programmers and the actual detailed design and programming of the selected computer applications. The operations subphase includes the testing of the written programs (usually called debugging) and the initiation of productive operations once the programs have been fully tested. The operations phase ends with a review of the resulting programs, measuring the savings or benefits obtained against those that were projected during the justification process. This is a continuing activity, as the savings and benefits usually are stretched out over several years. The maintenance/modification subphase will be explored in the subsequent chapter.

Like any other machine, the computer does not prove itself until it is in productive operation. The paper profits may look impressive but they must be proven in practice. This is the function of the implementation phase.

During implementation, the systems specifications must be distilled into the binary language of the machine. The broad systems goals and objectives must be translated into step by step procedures, which in turn are translated into individual computer instructions. The over-all job is broken down into progressively smaller and smaller pieces until it can be run on the computer. Figure 6.1 indicates the basic objective of the implementation phase as translating a broad statement of an application objective (as illustrated by the inventory control application) into the binary language of the computer (as illustrated by the string of zeros and ones). The illustration is not meant to imply that the programmer

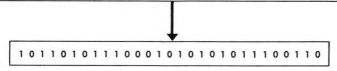

Inventory Control Application

Edit all inventory transaction such as receipts and issues. Update the inventory master file with these transactions and print out an inventory status report indicating the ending balance of each item while highlighting those items that fall below a previously determined reorder point.

1 0 1 1 0 1 0 1 1 1 0 0 0 1 0 1 0 1 0 1 0 1 1 1 1 0 0 1 1 0

Figure 6.1

himself must record the lengthy series of binary computer instructions. As has been seen, there are software language systems available that enable the programmer to describe the application in terms closer to the English language statements used in the illustration. The language system itself handles the translation into binary. There is a host of software aids, application aids, and general systems techniques to assist in the accomplishment of this task. The job of implementation is to take advantage of these aids and techniques in order to accomplish the implementation job in the shortest possible time.

The job of the EDP director changes substantially during the implementation phase. Whereas the technical content of the job is of primary importance during the system study and systems design efforts, now the managerial content becomes the pertinent element. The EDP director, much like the production line foreman, must see that the job is done, is done properly, and is done on time. To do so, he must concern himself with the functions of scheduling and controlling the activity.

A definite plan and schedule must be established. The objectives must be determined with measurable final results and measurable milestones. The director must monitor and control this schedule to ensure that it is being adhered to. Finally, the director must take the proper action to get back on schedule if it becomes apparent that his group is falling behind. This is not to say that the EDP director does not have to be technically competent. Certainly he must know the nature of the work his programmers are performing and be able to review and assist them in this work. However, unless the director is also a good manager in the sense of getting a job done, the computer implementation phase is apt to stretch out far beyond what is reasonable for the job.

THE IMPLEMENTATION SCOPE

The first requisite of establishing a schedule is to have an understanding of the over-all scope of the job at hand. Figure 6.2 breaks down the implementation job into four major paths. The first path is involved with preimplementation considerations, such as establishing the schedule and assembling the resources necessary to accomplish the schedule. The second path is the most time consuming and most important part of the implementation cycle. It is here where each program within each application is analyzed in depth, programmed, tested, and productively run on the computer.

The conversion path is concerned with the phasing out of the old system as the new system is installed. The operations path is directed at the administrative functions of acquiring supplies and preparing for the

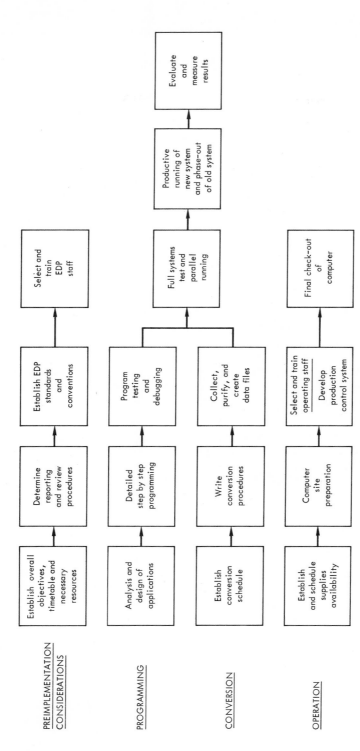

Figure 6.2 The implementation phase.

187

physical installation of the computer. Each of these four paths will be discussed in turn.

PREIMPLEMENTATION CONSIDERATIONS

It is surprising that there still are EDP shops that do not utilize any formal method of establishing an implementation schedule. This is true despite the fact that many companies and many EDP directors have passed through three generations of computer hardware. The following recorded dialogue may serve to set the stage for a discussion of preimplementation considerations.

Interviewer: You've been head of the data processing department for three years now. You were in charge of the feasibility study, recommended your existing computer, and managed the entire program since installation a little over a year ago. As you look back, what do you think your major problems have been?

EDP Director: My major problem has been the lack of communications with management. Somehow, despite everything, they don't seem to understand how to make the most effective use of EDP. We should have meetings where the basic problems are recognized, explored, and resolved, but for some reason we don't. I have a difficult time selling them my program.

Interviewer: What would you say are your secondary problems?

EDP Director: Next in importance is the problem of hiring and keeping good systems and programming people. Somewhat related is the problem of getting applications on the computer in a reasonable time frame. I have an existing application backlog that is about 20% of my current work load.

Interviewer: Do you use any type of project control techniques to schedule the implementation of applications?

EDP Director: We don't have a formal method. I can pretty well estimate how long it's going to take from previous experience. I can tell you at any one time how far along each application is and the estimated operational date. However, because business keeps changing and the information system changes along with it, the completion date is always highly problematical.

Interviewer: Do you have historic records of the time and cost of computerizing the applications that are currently operational?

EDP Director: No, but I can tell you within reasonable limits what each application cost us.

Interviewer: Do you supply management with any progress report or have meetings to discuss the status of your department?

EDP Director: We don't have regularly scheduled sessions. When we first began to prepare for the computer, we had scheduled meetings with my boss (the controller) and several of the key operating managers. However, I don't think that management could understand what was going on and they didn't seem very motivated to find out. We met for a couple of months but gradually the operating managers dropped out until it was just my boss and me. Since the two of us discuss problems on a day to day basis when any crisis arises, there didn't seem to be any need for a formal status review, so we dropped the regularly scheduled sessions.

Interviewer: Do you think it is possible to utilize a project control method to plan and control a project like a computer installation?

EDP Director: To a certain extent, yes; but you must remember this type of operation is not like a production line process. We are dealing with skilled personnel who are in great demand and who can leave you tomorrow for a better job if they react unfavorably to too rigid a control system. Also keep in mind that systems and programming work is still an art and not a science—as such, it is very difficult to establish a schedule in which one has a great degree of confidence.

This brief interview describes the basic problems facing the management of the EDP function, and it is felt that these problems are fairly typical. Although the problems in applying scheduling and control techniques can be understood, they can hardly justify not having a schedule. The first thing that must be done in the preimplementation phase is to develop an over-all plan and schedule based on the scope of the job as outlined in Figure 6.2. The major portion of the job is the programming phase. A definite system for controlling this portion will be described later in the chapter.

It is important to establish necessary communications with management early in the game. Develop a schedule that management understands, agrees to, and can monitor with the EDP director. It is important both to the EDP director and management that a vehicle be established that can be used to discuss problems as they arise. The EDP director should not look at the lack of a formal plan and scheduled review sessions as a vote of confidence in his own ability to get the job done. Rather, he should actively solicit and support a management review panel. Missed implementation milestones often can be traced to management inaction. An active, responsive management review panel can help to resolve problems and break road jams to keep the project on schedule.

It is also important to develop the necessary standards and conventions before embarking on the implementation phase. This facilitates a common understanding of the work of the programming group and a more ready interchange of ideas and concepts among the individuals. It is not recommended that an inordinate amount of time be spent on this activity. There are examples of good programming standards throughout the industry and an EDP staff should be able to adopt a suitable set. It is far easier to slightly modify an existing set than to start from scratch on your own. The staff should concentrate its ingenuity and efforts in the systems and programming areas. Standards and conventions should be established quickly and adhered to. It is immaterial

whether a decision box looks like   or like

A   B

What is important is that an EDP procedures manual be maintained so that each new member of the EDP staff can quickly review and follow the established standards.

As has been stated, the problem of selecting and training systems and programming personnel is accentuated by the severe skills shortage that exists in the industry. Many a tardy installation schedule can be traced directly to this situation. It is important that the EDP director not get so deeply involved with the technical content of his job that he neglects the important people function. He should bear in mind always that his staff represents his most valuable asset—an asset that is hard to replace. It is important to remember that continuity of effort represents an important element in progress. The people resource is obviously a vital factor in establishing the initial schedule. The schedule should be predicated on the number of systems and programming personnel budgeted for the function and on the time needed to staff and properly train new programmers and systems analysts. A training program should be established but it should have sufficient flexibility to allow tailoring to the particular background and level of the individual. The EDP director must realistically weigh the time, cost, and effort required to hire experienced personnel with that of hiring inexperienced people and training them on company time.

PROGRAMMING

This path covers the main line design, programming, and testing of each application to be run on the computer. Because this activity usually involves about 80% of the implementation effort, attention will be focused on a specific scheduling technique to assist the planning effort in this area.

The first requirement of a scheduling technique is to divide the total job into identifiable and measurable subjobs that can be assigned to individual programmers or programming teams. A logical breakdown is by application and program, the definitions of which are as follows.

> *Application*—An application represents a major business information system or problem to which a computer is applied; for example, payroll or inventory control.
>
> *Program*—A computer program is a set of instructions that will direct the computer to do a specific task.

An application is accomplished by writing a series of computer programs. An application such as payroll may be comprised of the following individual programs, which are related and linked but can be assigned and completed separately:

1. Time card editing and validating
2. Gross earnings calculation
3. Net earnings calculation
4. Print pay checks
5. Print deduction register
6. Print payroll register.

The next requirement of a scheduling technique is to determine the events or tasks necessary to complete a particular program or application. By showing the events required to complete the job and the sequence in which they occur, the schedule of the total job can be determined. The following list describes 20 events that must be completed before a computer application can be considered productive. Obviously there are shortcuts and ways around certain events but for the most part, each event is a requirement for efficient operation. Some of the events may have already been completed as part of the systems study or systems design phases. However, it is appropriate to include them here because the programming of the job normally requires a degree of detail that goes beyond the earlier requirements.

1. *Program narrative*—This is a succinct English language description of the purpose and objective of the particular program. The major forms of input, the basic computer transformations made to the input, and the resulting output are described. The narrative is so written that a person unfamiliar with the particular application can understand it. In addition to the narrative for each program within an application, the

over-all application is described and a general flow chart of the entire application is developed.

2. *General flow chart*—This is a broad general-type flow chart that uses problem-oriented language rather than machine-oriented language. The flow chart is developed so that it can be followed by a systems man not intimately acquainted with the computer being used or with its language. It is in suitable detail to show all operations but not in great enough detail to use for programming.

3. *Input/output formats*—All input and output documents, including punched cards, punched paper tape or optical font formats, and printed or visual display reports, are laid out in detail on the appropriate standardized forms.

4. *File design*—The basic information and master files must be determined and formatted for either direct access or sequential storage media.

5. *Control techniques*—An often overlooked aspect of installation planning is a technique for establishing the necessary audit trails, cross-footing, batch balancing, sample checks, and whatever else is required to ensure the reliability of data within the system. Control techniques should not be left for insertion at the last minute. This will result in expensive backtracking.

6. *Volume and timing estimates*—At this stage a fairly precise estimate of volumes and the resultant computer running time should be made. For example, it is important to see the effect that multiprogramming and simultaneous input/output processing will have on over-all operational time.

7. *Detailed flow chart*—This is a flow chart based on the general flow chart (2) and uses standardized flow chart symbols. It is written in a style that is closer to machine language than to systems language. Every step and path or branch of the program should be charted with the necessary connectors and switches. This flow chart is the basis for writing computer instructions.

8. *Allocation of computer memory and storage units*—An accurate allocation of computer memory should be made to determine whether the particular program is consistent with anticipated memory capacity. Necessary tables, buffers, constant areas, total areas, and the like must be accounted for. Likewise the data files must be analyzed to determine if there is ample storage capacity.

9. *Write computer instructions*—This is the step-by-step recording of computer statements on standard instruction sheets using the prescribed conventions. This activity is often called coding and should be highly disciplined, with corrections being made in a consistent manner. The instructions will follow the detailed flow chart on a step-by-step

basis, with any changes in the coding immediately noted in the flow chart and vice versa.

10. *Key punching*—This involves the punching of the coding or instructions into 80 column punched cards or directly onto magnetic media.

11. *Compilation*—This is the process that translates the computer instructions into the binary language of the machine. The translation or compilation process takes place in the computer utilizing a vendor's software system.

12. *List and describe subroutines, programming aids, and special features*—It is good practice to list and describe all aids of this nature that are being used in conjunction with a particular program. The manner in which these routines will be used, the necessary linkages or calling sequences should be fully described. All special features of the program should be listed to facilitate testing, rewriting and eventual operation. Any deviation from standard practices should be cleared with EDP management and if approved should be well documented.

13. *Preparation of sample test data*—Every effort should be made to make initial test data as straightforward and clear as possible. In the early testing stages, it is difficult enough to debug a program without having test data errors as well. Create test data that is simple yet comprehensive and well thought out to ensure that all paths of the program are given a thorough evaluation. Testing is a major part of the total job. Insufficient test data will cause more serious problems as programs approach final operation. The general rule holds that the earlier the error is found, the easier it is to correct. Although later testing with volume test data will be a necessity, many effects of volume data can be simulated with well-worked out sample data.

14. *Desk checkout*—Desk checkout is important because it can be performed if the machine is not available and can greatly expedite eventual machine checkout. There are two types of desk checkout: the first for logic and the over-all use of the programming language, the second for detailed clerical exactness (proper instruction codes, use of symbols, sequencing, and so on). Mistakes of the latter type can be detected during compilation. Desk checkout can simplify and reduce the amount of machine testing necessary. Desk checkout will include the use of sample test data and the carrying of it on a step-by-step basis through the program, noting the results at various stages. This, too, can be very effective in simplifying and speeding up the later task of machine checkout.

15. *Machine testing*—This is a vital part of any implementation plan and historically has been understated when schedules are prepared. Programmers must be trained thoroughly in the full use of software testing systems. Proper utilization of these concepts can materially re-

duce testing time, whether the testing takes place at the company's own facility or at a remote facility.

16. *Operating instructions*—Presumably the programmer will not be the operator when the program is in production running. Therefore, the programmer must create detailed operating instructions so that an operator not intimately familiar with the program can run it. Things such as forms used, preparation of input data, storage media used, and any manual switch settings should be clearly defined. In addition, the operator should know when a program is successfully completed, the different error conditions, what reruns are necessary, and so on. The instructions should be clear and complete to enable the operator to meet any problems that may occur in the operation of the program. In addition, plans for operation of the entire computer section should be formulated so that the ground rules for running the completed productive system are fully understood.

17. *Procedures write-up*—If a program or an application were started and finished within the computer room, there would be little need for a write-up telling people what to do. But in most cases, the input is produced by other departments. This necessitates the writing of comprehensive procedures explaining just what is involved in the new system and what it means to each individual who has something to do with the system, whether it be in originating input or in using the output.

18. *Preparation of volume test data*—After the sample test data has been completely checked out, the program should be tested against volume test data. This volume test will simulate closely the actual operating conditions and it can test parts of the program that are only reached by running through a large volume of data. It may be that this volume data will be actual data that is being run in parallel through the existing system and modified to serve as input into the new system as well.

19. *Volume checkout*—For the most part, this will follow the same principles laid out in machine testing (15) but it will normally be testing final results rather than intermediate results. This stage is called full systems test because an entire application consisting of many programs is tested as an entity.

20. *Establish maintenance procedures*—After a program is tested completely it is inevitable that further changes will be instituted; in some cases major ones. A plan should be formulated to establish a procedure for incorporating these changes into the system. Careful documentation and planning are required because a seemingly harmless modification can cause serious unforeseen difficulties in other parts of the program.

These then are the 20 project events that each program of each application must go through to be considered operational. The events can be divided into smaller subevents or they can be combined into fewer events. The breakdown described here represents a middle level of detail. A broader approach is to combine the 20 events into three event levels: (1) design, (2) programming, and (3) testing, as indicated next. This can prove a more meaningful categorization for reporting the status of the project to higher management.

Project Events	*Event Levels*
1. Program narrative	
2. General flow chart	
3. Input/output formats	Design
4. File design	
5. Control techniques	
6. Volume and timing estimates	
7. Detailed flow chart	
8. Tentative allocation of memory and tape units	
9. Coding	
10. Key punching	Programming
11. Compilation	
12. List and describe subroutines, programming aids, and special features	
13. Preparation of sample test data	
14. Desk checkout	
15. Machine testing	
16. Operating instructions	Testing
17. Procedures write-up	
18. Preparation of volume test data	
19. Volume checkout	
20. Establish maintenance procedures	

Figure 6.3 illustrates a simple reporting structure, listing the applications and programs down the left hand side of the form with the 20 events listed across the top. By reviewing the check marks in the various blocks, the particular status of a program can be ascertained; for example Program 1 has proceeded through 14 events whereas Program 3 has progressed through only three events. However, there is a missing dimension —the time dimension. There has to be a technique for projecting how long it should take to complete the 20 events for each program.

One such technique involves the projection of a schedule by estimating

Event Number

Application/program	1	2	3	4	5	6	7	8	9	10	11	12	13	14	15	16	17	18	19	20
Inventory Control	X	X	X																	
1. Edit & transcribe input	X	X	X	X	X	X	X	X	X	X	X	X	X	X						
2. Update inventory file	X	X	X	X	X	X	X	X	X	X										
3. Produce status report	X	X	X																	
4. Extend costs	X	X	X	X	X	X														
5. Produce evaluation report	X	X	X	X	X	X	X	X	X	X	X	X								

Figure 6.3

196

the number of instructions comprising each program and the number of instructions per day that a programmer can write. Thus, if a program is estimated to have 1,000 instructions and a programmer can write 20 instructions per day, then it will take 50 man days $\left(\frac{1,000}{20}\right)$ to accomplish the job. The critical factors in such an approach are the determination of the numerator, (programming steps) and the denominator (number of instructions per day or programming factor). Let us take a look at how these key factors can be developed.

DETERMINING NUMBER OF PROGRAMMING STEPS

Every computer program has in common the fact that it is comprised of programming statements or instructions. This then becomes a common yardstick for estimating programming workload. There are several inherent problems in estimating the number of instructions of a program that is not yet written. First, it is true that each program is different from all others in some aspects. Second, systems modifications may result in changing the number of instructions, and third, the degree of existing system documentation and definition (the starting point) will differ among companies and among applications. Yet, despite these considerations, it is possible to estimate the number of programming steps. The important thing is to have a starting point upon which to base the plan. The starting point need not be an exact figure but can be an estimate. The accuracy of the estimates will improve as more experience is gained and estimates are measured against actual results. The degree of difficulty in making estimates will also lessen with experience.

After an application has been divided into programs, the objectives of each program can be stated. Next, the input and output and the transformations that convert the input to output should be examined. From prior knowledge of already programmed runs, a good estimate of the number of instructions then can be made. Another aid in estimation is to find a previously coded program of a similar nature and to compare the complexity of the program with the run being estimated, using the former as a benchmark.

DETERMINING THE PROGRAMMING FACTOR

The programming factor is the number of completely checked out and documented programming steps that can be produced in a normal working day. There is a variety of ways to arrive at such a figure and it obviously is going to depend on a number of elements that are unique to the particular program and the particular programmer. However, the key consideration again is to have a starting point. Experience will improve the accuracy of the programming factor. A factor that is used in the software industry is 12. This means that a program will require one man-day for each 12 program statements.

At first glance, this figure may seem highly conservative. One can observe a programmer writing as many as a hundred program statements a day. But it must be kept in mind that the programming factor covers all the related activities incident to the actual writing of programming instructions, the 20 events previously listed. The programming factor is directly influenced by the complexity of the program being written and the skill of the programmer.

MODIFYING THE PROGRAMMING FACTOR

1. *Program complexity index*—It is readily apparent that programs differ in degree of difficulty. This is why allowance should be made to modify the programming factor according to a *Program Complexity Index* (PCI). The PCI recognizes three gradations in program complexity.

Gradation	Program Complexity	# of Statements Added	Resulting Programming Factor
1	Simple	+2	14
2	Average	0	12
3	Complex	−2	10

Gradation 1 indicates an extremely simple run consisting, for example, of a very basic card to tape conversion where efficiency of object code is not a major criterion. Gradation 2 indicates an average program, for example, a simple file update or a fairly straightforward report run. Gradation 3 indicates that the program is very complex, typical of a major file update where object code efficiency is very important. A simple program (PCI of 1) adds 2 to make the basic programming factor 14. A medium complexity program (PCI of 2) maintains the programming factor of 12, and a complex program (PCI of 3) subtracts 2 to make the basic programming factor 10.

2. *Programming efficiency index*—Another factor that may modify the basic programming factor is the *Programming Efficiency Index*

(PEI). This factor reflects the basic level of experience of a company's programming staff. The PEI also recognizes three gradations.

Gradation	Programmer Efficiency	# of Statements Added	Resulting Programming Factor
1	Inexperienced	−2	10
2	Average	0	12
3	Experienced	+2	14

Gradation 1 indicates an inexperienced programmer fresh from programming school who has written only one or two programs. Gradation 2 indicates an average programmer who has written several programs before. Gradation 3 indicates an experienced programmer who has written many programs and has a high level of skill. Gradation 1 subtracts 2, gradation 2 maintains the programming factor of 12, and gradation 3 adds 2 to the basic programming factor. A company may want to insert its own programming efficiency index based on its own learning curve. For example, a company may find that a programmer can write a program 50% faster after he has written several programs. Therefore the various gradations between one, two, and three may differ from the −2, 0 and +2 that are used here.

   3. *Percentage allocation of events*—Along with the number of computer instructions and the programming factor, another key determinant of the schedule is the particular percentage allocation of each of the major event levels. Experience shows that the general breakdown normally is in the following range:

Design	45%
Programming	35%
Testing	20%
	100%

However, a company should utilize percentages that better suit its own situation. For example, if a system is being converted on an as is basis, most of the design phase no doubt is already completed. However, caution should be exercised because it is very rare when a system is not changed during a conversion and therefore a design element introduced. Also bear in mind that a considerable portion of the design phase must be completed by the time a schedule of this type can be produced.

This would have to be in order to break down applications into programs and to be able to estimate the number of instructions.

A typical example will show how the various programming factors are combined to produce a schedule. Assume a programming job is estimated at 500 instructions. Further assume that it is a highly complex program (programming complexity index of 3) and is assigned to a programmer with an average efficiency level (programming efficiency index of 2). A look at the following table indicates a resultant programming factor of 10.

		Programming	*Efficiency*	*Index*
		1	2	3
Programming	1	12	14	16
Complexity	2	10	12	14
Index	3	8	10	12

The number of instructions (500) divided by 10 equals 50 man days. A 45%, 35%, 20% breakdown will produce the following schedule.

$$
\begin{array}{rrcl}
\text{Design} & 45\% \times 50 & = & 22.5 \text{ man days} \\
\text{Programming} & 35\% \times 50 & = & 17.5 \text{ man days} \\
\text{Testing} & 20\% \times 50 & = & 10.0 \text{ man days} \\
\hline
\text{Total} & & & 50.0 \text{ man days}
\end{array}
$$

The design phase should be completed 22.5 calendar working days from the starting date, the programming phase 17.5 calendar working days after the end of the design phase, and the test phase 10 calendar working days after the end of the programming phase. The calculations should allow for regular scheduled holidays as well as vacations.

It is appropriate to look now at how this technique can be utilized to facilitate the reporting of actual time expended on the various computer events, the analysis of the reported time versus the projected schedule time, and the action taken as a result of the analysis.

Figure 6.4 is a report using the principles listed to schedule a specific job. The title of the report is Application Status Report (1). The name of the company using the report is Three B's, Inc., (2). The reporting date is July 15, 1969 (3). The name of the application is Inventory Control (4). The application is divided into two programs entitled Conversion and Update (5), and Application Status (6). The programmer's name (or senior programmer if there is more than one) is Black

Application Status Report (1)

July 15, 1969 (3)

Three B's Inc. (2)

Inventory control (4)

	A Sched. Start Date	B Sched. Finish Date	C Total Man Days	D Elapsed Man Days	E Computed % Complete	F Reported Man Days	G Reported % Complete	H Status +/− Days
Conversion & update (5) # of instructions 360 BLACK (7) PEI 2 PCI 2	(11)							
Design 45%	6/8/69	6/25/69	13.5	13.5	100%	10	100%	0
Prog. 35%	6/26/69	7/10/69	10.5	10.5	100%	8	80%	−2
Test. 20%	7/11/69	7/21/69	6.0	3.0	50%	0	0%	−3
Summary	6/8/69	7/21/69	30.0	27.0	90%	18	73%	−5
Application status (6) # of instructions 720 THYS (8) PEI 2 PCI 2	(12)							
Design 45%	6/8/69	7/15/69	27	27	100%	15	80%	−5
Prog. 35%	7/16/69	8/13/69	21	0	0	0	0	0
Test. 20%	8/14/69	8/31/69	12	0	0	0	0	0
Summary	6/8/69	8/31/69	60	27	45%	15	36%	−5
Application summary	6/8/69	8/31/69	90	54	60%	33	48%	−10

Total # programs 2 (9)
Total # orders 1080 (10)

Figure 6.4 Application status report.

(7) for Program 1, and Thys (8) for Program 2. The various programming factors described in earlier sections then are listed. The number of instructions for Program 1 is 360 and both the PEI and PCI are 2. There is a summary line for each program. In addition, there is an application summary line listing the total number of programs, which is 2 (9), and total number of instructions for the two programs, which is 1080 (10). The percentage breakdown of the events is 45%, 35%, 20%, (11). The start date of each program is 6/8/69 (12). Based on the calculations explained before, columns A and B and C are computed and summarized by application.

REPORTING

The reporting period is determined by the particular needs of the company. The recommended reporting interval is monthly or biweekly but it can be more frequent or less frequent as the situation demands. It generally is felt that a weekly interval is not time enough to distinguish any significant changes.

Each programmer keeps an informal record of his time, accounting for eight hours of each day. He must record the program on which he is working, the hours he has worked on it, and whether the time is spent on design, programming, or testing of the program. Column F reflects the reported man days; in the case of the Conversion and Update Program, 10 man days have been reported for design and eight man days for programming as of the report date of July 15, 1969. Column G, reported % complete, is a very significant statistic and must be determined by the particular programmer and reviewed carefully by his supervisor. Often, programmers tend to be optimistic and to underestimate the complexity of the remaining part of their work. Every effort, therefore, should be made by the reviewing party to make certain that these figures represent realistic measurements. This will become easier with increasing experience.

ANALYSIS

The remaining columns of the application status report will be explained now. These are the columns that produce the analysis of actual status against the projected schedule. Columns A, B, C, F, and G have been described already. Column D indicates the elapsed days between the scheduled start date of each event group and the report date. All figures from Column C across are in man days. Column E, computed % complete, is derived by dividing Column D by Column C. Column H shows the status of the programming effort. It compares Column G with Column E and translates the difference into man days. The formula is (Col. G — Col. E) times Col. C.

A look at the report as a whole now brings to light exactly what is indicated. The report date is July 15, which is very close to the scheduled completion date (July 21) for the conversion and update program. The schedule shows that the design and programming phases should have been completed and the test phase should be 50% complete. The reported % complete shows that the design phase is completed, the programming phase is 80% completed, and no work has been initiated yet on the test phase. Column H indicates the program is five days behind schedule. One of the reasons for being behind schedule is the comparison of Column D and Column F. This shows that the programmer assigned to the job has not been able to devote the scheduled time to it (after 27 elapsed days, only 18 days have been expended). The program summary line indicates a reported completion percentage of 73% against a scheduled 90%. The second program also is behind schedule. The five man days behind schedule probably is caused by the fact that the programmer has been able to spend only 15 days out of a scheduled 27. The summary for the application shows a reported 48% complete against a scheduled 60% or 10 man days behind schedule. The summary figures are calculated by weighting each program by the proportion of number of orders it is to the total number of orders in the applications. Thus Program 1 is $\frac{360}{1,080}$ of the job and Program 2 is $\frac{720}{1,080}$ the job.

ACTION

Action is no doubt the most important part of any system. If no action is taken as a result of reviewing the application status report, then the system serves only as a speedometer. What is needed is an accelerator to depress in order to pick up speed and arrive at the destination on time. For remedial action to be possible, the plan must have flexibility built into it—flexibility to schedule overtime or weekend work, assign more people to the task, or simplify the design of the job. In the particular situation described here, it may be that the programmers have been out of work because of illness or have had other assignments that interfered with their programming efforts. It appears obvious that if this continues, the schedule will not be met. However, the programmers apparently have been able to make good progress when they have been working.

The action here may be to institute a plan whereby the programmers cannot be called on for other work until these two programs are completed. If this cannot be arranged, it may be necessary to assign additional help to the programs. However, this may not be feasible if it takes time to familiarize the new programmers with the particular programs. It may be better to accept the delay. At any rate, the report pinpoints the problems and allows the manager to decide upon the most practical alternative to solve the problem and maintain the schedule.

This describes how a project control approach can assist EDP management during the implementation phase. The following is a summary of the benefits of such an approach.

1. *Forces systematic thinking*—A computer is a systematic and logical entity. Sometimes the planning effort that goes into installing a computer is not a very systematic and logical effort. Project control institutes the use of efficient planning habits and a continuing awareness of the elements that go into a computer installation. It makes one ask the question: "What must I do to complete the job?" It assures that various factors are not deferred or completely ignored in the lengthy time period that precedes the installation of a computer. Too often a supervisor or manager will commence work on a particular project without ever sitting down and looking at the over-all job to be accomplished. In an attempt to move ahead quickly, the initial planning considerations often are overlooked. This almost always results in needless retracking and duplication of effort at latter stages of the schedule.

2. *Establishes more realistic schedule*—A schedule always should be based on the work to be done and the manpower available to complete the work. A contrived schedule based only on the earliest possible delivery date has been a major cause of installation disappointment. A schedule should be built forward and not backward. Project control enables a company to develop a realistic schedule based on the resources available to it—or it can indicate what additional resources are necessary to meet a required date. Establishing a degree of realism and developing the schedule are essential to the successful completion of that schedule. The effectiveness of a working force in accomplishing an over-all job can be reduced materially if the target dates established have no relation to reality. In very short order all semblance of a schedule and any type of organization are lost.

3. *Provides base for estimating manpower needs*—Project control allows a company to measure adequately its manpower needs; for example, the schedule may indicate that an important deadline would be missed if the current staff of programmers is not augmented by new hiring. Project control allows the company to see immediately that either more programmers are needed or that the projected target date will have to be extended. It establishes the important but often overlooked relationship between personnel resources and time in completing a job.

4. *Measures programmer productivity*—The question of measuring programmer productivity is a frequently avoided subject. Computer programming is a relatively new field, and work measurement for programmers always has seemed a very nebulous subject. However, if utilized properly, project control can serve to evaluate programming productivity and can point out ways to increase productivity by comparing performance and passing on useful procedures and techniques of the different programming groups. By requiring programmers to account for their time, project control instills a discipline and an awareness on the part of programmers of how effectively their time is utilized. It lends a sense of urgency in making progress on a particular application. Caution must be exercised by the manager who reviews the application status report— caution to make certain he realizes that the quality of a program is a criterion as well as is the time to write it. Although the effectiveness of a particular program is never determined fully until it is completely checked out and timed, an experienced manager should be able to ascertain the quality of the work. Project control is not intended to place a straitjacket on a programming force. Its primary aim is not to force the following of a rigid reporting and evaluating procedure. Rather, it is designed to give some indication of the amount of effort it takes to accomplish a job and, in a broad sense, to be able to measure one job against the other.

5. *Provides historical record*—There is a continuing need in the computer field to develop statistical or historical data that can be used to refine future schedules and plans. The advancements in cost accounting systems have not been utilized fully in the expensive and time-consuming task of implementing a computer system. It is surprising that many companies do not know how long a particular job took or the actual man hours expended on the job. This is particularly important when the computer is operated as a service center charging time to the particular departments using the facilities. Programming for a computer is not a one-time operation; there always are new applications that are programmed and converted to the computer. Therefore, the development of historical information is extremely important in order to continually refine the time and cost estimates of getting these new applications on the air.

6. *Indicates schedule progress*—One of the more important benefits derived from project control is the production of a schedule and the measurement of progress against that schedule at periodic intervals. Project control affords the means to develop the schedule, record actual time against the schedule, analyze the phases that are behind or ahead of schedule, and point out the action necessary to get back on schedule. The action taken as a result of the analysis is an important part of the over-all technique. A good schedule not only establishes projected target

dates but also has built-in flexibility or the means to get back on schedule in the event that a target date is missed. Project control enables the company to know when such action is necessary in order to meet the target date.

7. *Anticipates problems*—Project control can make a valuable contribution to a company by helping it anticipate problems before they actually occur. This is normally called the big picture look—that is, continuing to look at the over-all schedule to foresee the next stage and prepare for it in advance. Without a definite schedule, a manager is unaware of what actually is around the corner or what he should prepare for in order to meet the schedule. For example, if he looks ahead and sees that testing on volume test data will begin at a certain date, he knows that he must make preparations to produce the volume test data prior to that date.

8. *Provides documentation and uniformity*—Inherent in project control is the type of systematic thinking that provides documentation and uniformity. Both are extremely important. The results of a computer installation normally are commensurate with the methods used to obtain them. Shoddy work habits produce shoddy results and cause a great deal of rework and wasted effort; documentation must be thorough and precise and no back-of-envelope type of techniques can be tolerated. It is normal in the EDP area for companies to have some programmer turnover during the installation effort. Where the documentation is poor, it is not uncommon for the new programmer to be forced to restart from the beginning. There can be no continuity of effort without effectively documenting the work being done.

Project control also aids in developing a degree of uniformity among various programmers or programming teams. It ensures that every programmer is working under the same ground rules. This facilitates movements between teams and communications within the computer group. The contribution of project control in the area of uniformity and documentation is extremely significant.

CONVERSION

A most important part of the implementation job is the transition from the old system to the new one. This is referred to as the conversion task and includes the activities listed in Figure 6.2. The conversion area is an often overlooked one, but it is vital to the success of the computer installation. A company converting to a computer system has information systems currently being performed by manual methods, bookkeeping machines, or punched card equipment. Unless the new system is a carbon copy of the old one, there will be new procedures for preparing the input for the system as well as interpreting the output. Even if the new system is identical to the old (and this is highly unlikely), the new system undoubtedly will utilize different file storage media. The manual or punched card master files must be converted to magnetic tape or some form of direct access storage. The conversion tasks must be carefully sequenced with the programming effort described in the previous section to ensure a smooth implementation.

There are two major concerns to the conversion task; the first associated with those activities within the EDP province and the second associated with those activities outside of EDP. Conversion schedules and procedures must be determined for each.

The inside EDP concerns are directly related to the change in input, output, and file storage elements. As the basic source documents are determined, a procedure must be written that describes the step by step action necessary to transcribe the source data into electronic media. Likewise, the procedures for dispersing the output must be developed. The most significant concern within the EDP area is the conversion of existing files to the new media or the initial development of files themselves if they do not already exist. This can be a very costly and time-consuming activity and can be made even more costly by not establishing the proper schedule and procedures. A master customer file or master inventory file is comprised of a large number of alphanumeric characters. Consider an inventory file of 10,000 items, each item having 200 characters of descriptive information. This represents 2,000,000 characters that somehow must be converted to magnetic storage. Once the data is suitable for key punching, it will take a keypunch operator working at an average rate of 8,000 key strokes an hour 14 weeks to punch and verify the information onto punched cards. Then the information on the punched cards is transferred onto magnetic storage.

The 14 weeks total assumes that the information on each item is available. The time can be extended materially if, for example, vendor lead time must be determined for each inventory item. This involves a letter or a phone call to each vendor if the information is not already available. Thus one can see that file conversion is no small task. Normally file conversion is a phased plan whereby data that is fixed and rarely changed is converted first and the more volatile data is converted later in the process. The data that changes on a daily basis often must be converted the day before or the night before the new system goes into productive operation. This is a tricky business and calls for careful attention to the formulation and execution of a conversion schedule.

The outside EDP conversion considerations involve those departments and people who are affected by the new system. These may in-

OPEN LETTER TO STORE MANAGER

We are introducing a system of Direct Store
Ordering for all Divisions. This is a
system whereby orders bypass the Division.
We, of course, cannot at this time see
all possible problems. We are attempting to
enumerate some of the changes that will
affect your department. These are as
follows:

1. You will receive a new shipping form
   to check in orders. This will have
   line number and quantity on it as well
   as total pieces. This form will have
   no description or item retail. You
   will use your order catalogue for
   the piece and description if
   necessary. However, every case has
   the line number clearly printed on it.
   The shipping form will indicate
   items that have been scratched.

Figure 6.5

clude, for example, the purchasing department who receive automatic
purchase requisitions from the computer for those items that fall below
a certain minimum point, or the sales department who must indicate
the individual salesman, his territory, and his region on each order received. Thus the purchasing department is receiving a new form of output and the sales department must provide additional input data. These
changes to the procedures of department personnel outside the EDP
area must be anticipated and a plan developed to train and indoctrinate
the people involved in the new procedure. A good starting point is to
write a letter to each affected party explaining how the new system is
going to affect his operation. Figures 6.5 and 6.6 are examples of such

2. You will have a new ordering catalogue
   and system of ordering. This is a
   mark sense method, which is described
   fully in another write up.

3. You will receive a store bill the day
   after your shipment arrives (in some
   instances, on the same day) which
   will have the item number, extended
   weight, extended retail and quantity
   as well as the total weight, retail,
   and pieces. This billing will give
   you immediate credit for items
   scratched. That is if the shipping
   form showed a case of Item 4000
   scratched, you will get credit for
   this on the bill you receive. It
   should be very easy to tie in what
   you receive with what you are billed.

4. We should be able to reduce the time
   lag between your order placement and
   the delivery of your merchandise.

Figure 6.5   (cont.)

letters, written for the store manager in one instance and the transportation manager in the other. The letter is merely a starting point in the program to indoctrinate personnel in the operation of the new system. Detailed procedures manuals and in-depth training sessions are necessary to ensure a smooth changeover.

Figure 6.2 indicates that the conversion activity must dovetail with the programming effort at the time of full systems test and parallel running. Parallel running involves the simultaneous operation of the old and new system using actual live data. The results of the new are compared to the old to determine if the full system operates as a consistent entity. If the new system differs radically from the old, it may not be

OPEN LETTER TO TRANSPORTATION MANAGER

We are introducing a system of Direct Store
Ordering for all Divisions. This is a system
whereby orders bypass the Division. We, of
course, cannot at this time see all
possible problems. We are attempting to
enumerate some of the changes that will
affect your department. These are as
follows:

1. You will have loading information
   (weight, pieces, cube) faster. This
   should enable you to schedule your
   loads better and also get this
   information to the food processing
   division to assist them in loading.

2. The computing center will teletype
   you the weight, pieces, and cube for
   every store. You will use this data to
   load and route trucks and teletype
   the truck loads back to the center.

3. You will now receive in addition to
   weight and pieces, the cubic volume
   of each store order. This should
   enable you to do a better loading job.

4. The weight and piece totals you
   receive will be more accurate than
   you are now receiving because the
   figures will be net of deletions and
   substitutions of items.

Figure 6.6

possible to effect parallel operations. The old file must be completely converted and the data collected, edited, validated, and purified just prior to the full systems test. The next step is the productive running of the new system and the phaseout of the old. After a period of time, the results of the new system should be evaluated against the results projected during the justification process. This is the final step of the implementation phase.

It is here that management can determine if computer performance has lived up to its expectations and if the projected implementation costs were stated realistically. If management is satisfied with the results, the stage is set for the refinement of existing applications and the implementation of new ones. The proof of the pudding is not in the tasting; it is in the second helping.

OPERATION

The operations path covers the planning and implementation of the physical operating environment in which the computer performs. The physical operation of a computer can be viewed as analogous to a production work center. In the case of the computer, the basic product is paper, usually in the form of printed business reports. Like the production center, the computer center transforms raw material (punched cards and punched paper tape) into finished product. There are various work-in-process stages, such as when the data from cards is transcribed onto magnetic storage media for later processing.

The first step in the operations area is to establish and schedule the availability of the necessary raw, in-process, and finished materials for the computer center. The need for punched cards, magnetic tapes, removable storage disks, and output paper forms must be projected and orders placed so that delivery coincides with the programming and conversion requirements described earlier.

Despite claims to the contrary by some data processing people, the use of punched cards, magnetic storage media, and printed forms continues to expand at a rapid pace. The data processing people claim that the use of systems techniques like management by exception, whereby the computer prints only those results that exceed a predetermined norm or standard, reduces the need for paper. However, the principle has not caught on as universally as some think. In reality, it has been the proliferation of additional applications and the added volumes that have caused the growth in the computer supplies industry.

The plan and schedule for preparing the computer site must be considered in light of the desired computer layout and existing facilities. Modern computers have greatly reduced space, airconditioning, and special flooring requirements. Unless unusual conditions exist or the particular user desires a special custom-tailored installation, site preparation is not a complex planning job. If the equipment is ordered to replace existing gear, a phaseout plan must be established, because it is rare when the new system arrives concurrently with the departure of the old equipment. Temporary facilities may have to be provided. The cost of site preparation can run from $2,000 to $20,000 and up, depending on user requirements. Simple raceways can be used to cover cabling or the computer can be placed on an elaborate raised floor that covers the cables and gives the computer room a more professional look. If the computer room is going to be used as a showplace and shown to clients and customers, then it may be well worth the added cost to dress up the site.

Consideration must be given to storage space for supplies and storage media as well as to the input preparation area. It may be advisable to locate the data preparation activity adjacent or at least in an area that is convenient to the computer room. The computer manufacturer usually can provide a company with alternate floor plans and assist in site preparation. The placement of equipment should take into account human factors to increase worker efficiency and provide a pleasant working environment. Figure 6.7 presents a basic planning checklist and site preparation schedule.

A hiring and training program must be established prior to the computer installation. If the company plans to utilize internal personnel, then the hiring process can be eliminated; however, a training program still is required. The computer manufacturer offers operator training courses to teach new operators how to run the equipment. Normally this is not a difficult job and personnel with some logic ability and machine aptitude can learn to operate the equipment in short order.

It is important to develop a good set of operating procedures. As in the analogy of the computer center to the production center, this set is akin to a production control system. The computer represents an expensive asset and should be operating at maximum efficiency. A daily job schedule should be established and measured against actual results. This is particularly important if the computer is being operated as a service center with each department being charged for its usage of computer time. Figure 6.8 shows a weekly job summary report indicating the total productive and nonproductive time for each application run during the week. It indicates a productivity rate of 88.1%, which is not very good. Of the 4.6 hours of nonproductive time, the majority is a result of input errors and machine downtime. This suggests areas where corrective action is required.

Other types of reports emanating from a production control system are equipment utilization summaries indicating the productivity of each

Planning Checklist

Make layout drawings of the proposed site, showing the placement of system components.

Insure that proposed floor loading agrees with your building specifications and with applicable city ordinances.

Ascertain the location and type of the primary power source (e.g., in-plant diesel generator, public utility) and the length of power runs.

Determine need, if any, for additional electrical power and arrange for its installation at the site.

Make drawings of wiring now installed and to be added.

Make a drawing of air ducts now installed and to be added.

Determine need for additional air conditioning and arrange for its installation.

Verify site dimensions and building access dimensions.

Order power receptacles and, if required, raised flooring.

Establish a plan to vacate the selected area prior to site preparation.

Arrange for insurance coverage if required.

Installation Schedule

Three Months Before Delivery

At least three months before delivery of equipment, all details concerning the layout of the site should have been approved.

Two Months Before Delivery

Definitive system layout drawings and specifications should have been made and approved.

One Month Before Delivery

Primary-power equipment should be on order. Associated equipment including primary-power receptacles should arrive concurrently.

Two Weeks Before Delivery

All electrical and structural elements of the installation should have been installed, including raised flooring and air conditioning.

System Checkout Schedule

After the site has been prepared and the system installed, two days will suffice to prepare the systems for regular operation.

Figure 6.7

Job Summary
Week Ending—August 29, 1969

Application	Total	Pro-ductive	Nonpro-ductive	% Prod.	Nonproductive Due To:			
					Input Error	Oper. Error	Mach. Down.	Other
Payroll	4.1	3.8	.3	92.7%		.3		
Order processing	14.3	13.5	.8	94.4	.2	.2	.4	
Accounting	12.4	11.0	1.4	88.7	.4	.2	.6	.2
Inventory control	6.1	4.0	2.1	65.5	1.2		.9	
Total	36.9	32.3	4.6	88.1%	1.8	.7	1.9	.2

Figure 6.8

piece of equipment and actual run time compared to scheduled run time. This points out the efficacy of computer time scheduling. Techniques of this type are the basis of sound operating practices. They are similar to cost accounting procedures applied to production operations.

The final checkout of the computer once it has been delivered is the final implementation step in the operation area. Figure 6.2 shows how this step precedes the full systems test and parallel running. The necessary supplies will have been ordered and received to permit full system test. After the new system is tested fully and the old system is phased out, the old equipment can be removed and the computer moved into its permanent location if it has been occupying a temporary one pending release of the old gear.

THE PLACE OF EDP IN THE COMPANY ORGANIZATION

The responsibility for the EDP function traditionally has fallen to the controller or the chief financial officer of the company. This was a natural development because the earlier computers were utilized primarily in the accounting and administrative areas. However, the mix of computer usage has been changing with the introduction of the computer in areas such as inventory control, production scheduling, forecasting, and investment analysis. In many companies, the computer is devoted more to operational problems than to administrative ones. Therefore, top management has taken another look at the place of EDP in the organizational structure in light of the broadening scope of computer application. In more and more cases, the EDP function is being removed from the financial arm of the company and is being placed on the same status with the other major departments. The EDP department still must serve the financial or controller's department; however, it must serve the other departments as well. As previous discussion has pointed out, the real profit making computer applications are outside the accounting and administrative area. Placing the EDP function outside the realm of any single operating department would emphasize the concept of the computer as an information utility serving the needs of all operating groups. It also would serve to give EDP the status it needs to effectively implement information systems that affect operating management.

Figure 6.9 is based on an industry survey and illustrates the reporting structure of the EDP function. As can be seen, the EDP department reports to the controller in 39% of the companies surveyed. The EDP function reports to a vice president in 49% of the cases; 19% of the time to the vice president of finance, and 30% of the time to another senior vice president, oftentimes an executive or administrative vice president. In 12% of the cases, the EDP department reports directly to the president. The trend in reporting structure definitely is going away from the controller and towards the senior vice president or the president. Five years ago, more than 60% of the EDP departments reported to the controller and less than 2% to the president.

The emergence of the TCE or *T*op *C*omputer *E*xecutive, particularly in the case of the larger companies, is becoming a dominant development. The TCE is called the director of information services, director of computer systems, or vice president of business information systems. The TCE reports directly to either the president or a high officer of the company, as shown, and is a member of the top management executive committee. In other words, he is a top officer and decision maker within the company. As the other department heads control important company assets, so the TCE controls an asset that is becoming an increasingly important resource in business operation—the information resource.

The growing importance of the TCE and the computer function makes it mandatory to select the right man for the TCE job. First of all he must be a top manager and have a comprehensive understanding of the company's business operations. As has been stated, technical skills are of vital importance because the operation of an EDP department still is a complex and difficult task; however, it is important to realize that technical skills are not enough. It would appear that the TCE should be a manager and executive first and a technical computer man second. With this in mind, some companies are moving selected members of operating management into EDP operations as a staging point for possible promotion to the position of TCE.

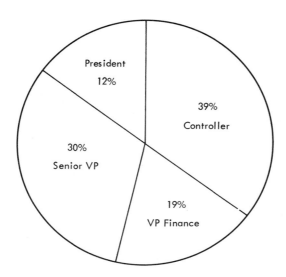

Figure 6.9   EDP Reporting Structure.

Within the EDP organization itself the evolution is toward more specialization of effort. This is particularly true in the larger companies. The EDP field still is not a well-defined profession and the definition and categorization of jobs continue to be in the evolutionary stage. There is a proliferation of job titles and job terminology that makes the subject of EDP organization a confusing one. Figure 6.10 illustrates a newspaper advertisement that appeared in September, 1969. It indicates quite well the increase in specialization of job function. The salaries are as they appeared in the advertisement and serve to give the reader an idea of the general salary structure of various jobs that exist in the industry. The TCE in this case is called the director of MIS (*M*anagement *In*formation *S*ystems). He has a manager of OR (*O*perations *R*esearch) who is responsible for the systems work in preparing mathematical and scientific applications for computer processing.

The manager of systems, on the other hand, handles the systems work for the regular business applications. The major application areas, marketing, finance, and manufacturing, are subdivided and each is headed by a systems project leader. The TCE also has a programming manager reporting to him. Thus, there is a dichotomy between systems and programming. The systems people develop the detailed systems specifications and systems design of the application and then turn it over to the programming group, which converts the specs into computer code. The programmers in turn rely on the operators working for the operation manager to physically run and test the resultant computer code. As can be seen, the systems people usually are higher paid than the programmers, who in turn are higher paid than the operators.

This set-up is typical of the growing specialization of the EDP function that is taking place within the larger companies. In the smaller companies, the job title of systems/programmer is used to indicate that the same individual has the responsibility for both the systems and programming work and probably the operations role as well, at least during the testing and checkout phase. There are pros and cons to greater specialization. Specialization implies more rigid standards and conventions and places greater demand on effective communication between the parties responsible for the different elements within the same application. Also, too great a degree of specialization may make it more difficult to communicate with operating departments within the company. Communication barriers have a tendency to grow in proportion to the number of layers in an organizational hierarchy. However, when the installation is large enough to afford it, the specialization method of work organization appears to be the more efficient. In addition, it provides an added avenue of advancement for EDP personnel, which is particularly important in an industry in such short supply of personnel. The

MANUFACTURING COMPANY
STAFFING NEW LARGE-SCALE COMPUTER CENTER

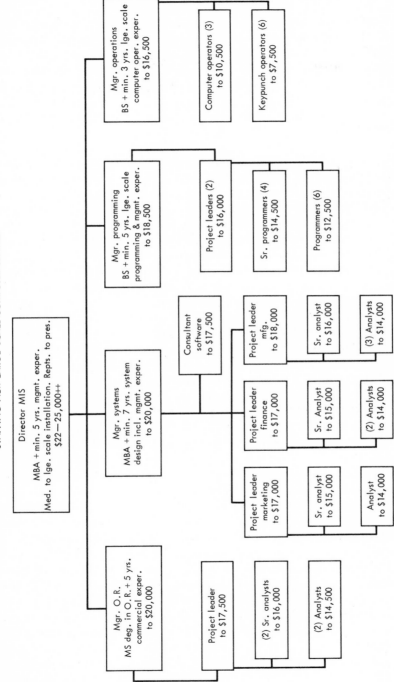

Figure 6.10

system and programming analysts must be kept challenged and motivated because opportunity knocks (as evidenced by the ad) next door. It has been estimated that there is a shortage of 100,000 systems analysts and programmers in the EDP industry. This fact obviously must be a guiding ground rule in organizing an EDP operation.

SUMMARY

This chapter has described the tasks that are pertinent to the implementation phase. Four major activity paths have been discussed as follows:

1. *Preimplementation considerations*—directed at the activities that must be initiated prior to commencing work: establishing an overall implementation schedule and developing the required communication channels, for example.
2. *Programming*—directed at the major activity path concerned with establishing the plan to design, program, and fully test the applications that are to be computerized.
3. *Conversion*—directed at a plan for the systematic phaseout of the old system and the phasein of the new.
4. *Operations*—directed at ensuring that the proper physical operating environment, including supplies and site preparation, is available when the computer arrives.

Then the subject of EDP and its place in the company organization is explored, presenting the trends of the TCE and specialization of activity within the EDP operation. It is apparent that the implementation job involves the management of a technical area of activity. The key words in the previous sentence are management and technical and both are paramount in successfully implementing a computer program. As technical as the job is, it is important to remember that a successful computer operation must become part of the company's business environment. It is not a separate and unique entity that exists outside the mainstream of business activity. The EDP function can be viewed as such but then the probabilities are that it will not perform to its full potential. Surveys of computer users clearly conclude that communication and motivation are as significant as the technical content of the EDP operation. Communications involve establishing the proper rapport between the EDP department and all levels of operating management as well as with the workers within the operating departments.

Motivation refers to both internal motivation of the personnel within the EDP department and the motivation of people outside the department who use computer results. Operating department personnel should be motivated to cooperate, participate, and better utilize the computer facility. A common attitude, but one to be avoided, is a passive waiting (even hoping) by operating department personnel for the computer to make an error. Fearing encroachment of the computer in their sphere of operations, they feel that a machine goof will affirm once again the superiority of the human being. The computer is another business tool, albeit a most significant one, that needs strong human thinking, care, and cooperation to operate effectively. The computer is an extension of the businessman's ability to plan and control his environment. The EDP staff should bear this in mind and not foster an attitude that anthropomorphizes the role of the computer.

THREE B'S' APPROACH TO THE IMPLEMENTATION PHASE

The computer has been installed at Three B's for two months now. Dexter Johnson is preparing to present a status report to the president, Bill Barrett. It is pertinent to note that three months prior to the computer delivery, Barrett announced that the EDP function headed by Dexter Johnson would report directly to him.

Two weeks ago, a third of the punched card equipment was removed. This was less than the estimated two thirds, but Johnson could see the removal of another third in another month. The accounting applications as well as the entire order processing application were in successful operation on the computer. The accounting applications converted fairly easily but there had been some trouble with order processing. Although the EDP staff had written explicit instructions to the warehouse personnel describing the procedures to be used in picking orders, there was considerable confusion for several weeks. Several orders were delayed and others had to be returned because the wrong items were shipped. The sales vice president, Paul Peters, was disturbed over the matter, but a concentrated two-day training session for warehouse personnel and a few discussions with the salesmen succeeded in resolving the crisis.

The inventory control application still was not completed. Johnson estimated it would take another three to four months to complete the job. The major delay occurred in gathering the necessary data to build the inventory file. Johnson also knew that the development of a procedure for updating the file once it was built was equally important, but it had not been accomplished as yet. Reorder points and reorder quantities are a function of elements such as forecasts of item movement, vendor lead times, and cost to write a purchase order. Gathering this data proved difficult and time-consuming. Burt Harrison, the plant manager, was upset that his inventory control clerks and purchasing agents were devoting a good deal of their time to gathering the necessary data. Nonetheless, Johnson felt that Harrison could see the potential value of the inventory control system to his operation and would continue to cooperate, though still voicing some opposition to the amount of effort involved.

In reviewing the modified PERT schedule that was used to control the project, Johnson realized that he had missed the projected target dates by three months. However, the recording of actual progress against the schedule had enabled him to pinpoint the major reasons. The schedule was predicated on hiring two systems/programmers in addition to Farnum and Osbourne. Johnson was able to hire only one of the two. Johnson did not devote the necessary time to the recruitment task until Osbourne resigned three months prior to scheduled delivery. Faced with a serious schedule slippage, Johnson was able to hire two experienced programmers a month after Osbourne left.

The upshot was a lengthy session with the computer vendor and a decision to delay computer delivery three months. Although the entire three-month delay could not be blamed on the personnel situation, it proved to be the principal element. Johnson appreciated the cooperation on the part of the vendor in agreeing to reschedule the system. The hardware was delivered according to the new schedule and was turned over to Three B's in good working order two days after it arrived on the scene. The vendor also met all requirements on promised software. Johnson felt relieved about this because he realized that any other problems would have compounded the ones they already had. He credited the on-schedule delivery to the comprehensive evaluation and selection process that Three B's conducted.

Despite the schedule delays and the fact that all applications originally planned to be in productive operation on the computer at this time were not yet running, Johnson felt satisfied about the installation. He was confident that he could present a favorable status report to Barrett and the executive committee. First, Three B's had passed the major hurdle in its computerization program. It had a computer that was operational in some key application areas. The program had not yet hit pay dirt, but he was certain that further experience with the sales order processing application would result in a material improvement in the order cycle time. Furthermore the basic inventory records had been converted to magnetic media and it was just a matter of time until the additional data was captured and the inventory control application would be in full operation. He was certain that the inventory ap-

plication would be a real profit maker for Three B's. Johnson knew it was a good decision to take the time to properly spec and design an integrated system approach that facilitated future expansion and growth. The same basic data base could be used to schedule production and institute a standard cost system. Johnson also could envision the day when salesmen would place orders and obtain confirmation directly from the central computer and when factory foremen would analyze production variances by means of a visual display device enabling them to make production line adjustments before the particular production run was completed. The groundwork had been established; there was virtually no limit to how far they could go.

SOURCE MATERIAL AND SUPPLEMENTARY READING

Awad, E. M. and Data Processing Management Association, *Automatic Data Processing. Principles and Procedures.* Englewood Cliffs, N. J.: Prentice-Hall, Inc., 1966.

Brandon, R. H., *Management Standards for Data Processing.* Princeton, N. J.: D. Van Nostrand Company, Inc., 1963.

Broucek, G. R., "An Automated System for Internal Audit and Control," *Management Services* (May/June 1967).

Charles, P. L., *The Management of Computer Programming Projects.* New York: American Management Association, 1967.

Computer Planning & Control. Babson Park, Massachusetts: Computer Institute for Management, 1968. (I was responsible for the development of the COMPACT system described in Chapter 7 of this publication. The programming section in this chapter is based on this system.)

Datamation. The October 1968 issue is devoted to software packages.

Davis, G. B., *Auditing & EDP.* New York: American Institute of Public Accountants, Inc., 1968.

Farina, M., *Cobol Simplified.* Englewood Cliffs, N. J.: Prentice-Hall, Inc., 1968. 458 pp.

"Managing the Programming Effort," *EDP Analyzer* (June, 1968).

"Over-all Guidance of Data Processing," *EDP Analyzer* (August, 1968).

Reichenbach, R. R. and C. A. Tasso, *Organizing for Data Processing.* New York: American Management Association. Research Study 92.

Sherman, P. M., *Techniques in Computer Programming.* Englewood Cliffs, N. J.: Prentice-Hall, Inc., 1969. 352 pp.

Withington, F. G., "Evolving Place of EDP in the Organization," *Datamation* (June, 1969).

7

MAINTENANCE AND
MODIFICATION

It has been four months since the computer has been installed and Dexter Johnson believes the operation has suffered a setback. The status review did not go well. The operating managers, in Johnson's view, nit-picked the entire operation to pieces. Each operating manager brought to the meeting a list of errors and discrepancies that were evident in his area of operation (obviously prepared by administrative people in the respective departments). In addition, each had a list of suggested additions and modifications for incorporation into the various applications. Although Johnson acknowledged that some of the complaints were significant, he was discouraged because he thought the magnitude painted a distorted picture for Three B's' president, W. W. Barrett.

Only two months ago Johnson was satisfied with the progress that had been made, but now he pondered what had gone wrong in the subsequent two-month period. Errors were being revealed now that the system was in volume operation and undergoing the test of daily productive use. Managers had discarded their old reports and files and were relying completely on the computer. Johnson also realized that department personnel were seeing monthly and periodic reports for the first time. He knew a complete business cycle would be required to eliminate all the bugs in the system. The EDP director discovered the existence of undetected errors in the old system, now being brought to light by the computer. As a result of the increased audit functions built into the new program, certain sales and inventory transactions were being rejected by the new system and returned to the originator for correction. The errors were not detected in the old system until far later in the cycle, if at all. The originators, unaccustomed to the volume of transactions needing correction, were slow in making them and, as a result, final inventory and sales reports were late. Although this additional accuracy would prove a later benefit, at this point in time it had a negative influence on management.

Johnson had dedicated himself completely to the computer in the past 18-month effort. He calculated that he averaged 60 hours per week in the office and countless additional hours at home poring over late evening computer printouts. The EDP group had been short-handed after Osbourne's departure and Johnson did a good deal of the programming for the inventory application. Added to his other responsibilities, this placed a considerable load on him. Although he had participated in the installation of several computers during his tenure with a computer manufacturer and had developed specific computer applications as a systems specialist, this was the first time he was personally responsible for an installation. It made quite a difference. Johnson felt discouraged as he reviewed the long lists of modifications and maintenance requests that were turned in by the operating departments.

Johnson considered his next steps. He knew he wanted to avoid getting into the same position he was in when Osbourne left, so he directed his first thoughts at his staff. He wondered whether it was adequate and whether he had the necessary backup in case of further attrition. He was concerned also with the level of documentation and quality of the programs, because so many bugs were being uncovered. An important decision facing him at this point was whether the computer installation should undergo a thorough audit and evaluation to assess the situation in order to gain a full appreciation of the scope of the problem. If necessary, a major effort would be instituted to clean up existing applications before moving on. Johnson reflected on whether an outside consulting firm (possibly the same firm used for the company's computer vendor evaluation) should be called in for this purpose or whether Three B's could conduct the review internally, possibly with a combined group representing the EDP department and the operating departments.

A well-conducted and thorough audit would form the basis of directing Three B's future data processing efforts. A two- to three-year long-range plan was needed.

INTRODUCTION

Refer again to Figure 1. The computer installation cycle now enters its final subphase. However, this cycle is in reality a never-ending one as old applications will be modified and corrected, new applications will be designed and programmed, and additional equipment will be required and justified. The final subphase covers the maintenance and modification function. It might be assumed that a book on computer system selection and use would end at the computer's installation. Not so! With the pressure of getting the computer installed and in operation, it is inevitable that short-cuts are utilized, temporary patches in programs are made, and a variety of expedients are employed.

During the implementation phase, the programmers will have accumulated a list of changes they know should be instituted. These have been deferred because they do not affect the day to day running of the application and can be added at a later date. An example of these changes is checking features that increase the accuracy of the input and output but do not necessarily prevent the job from running to completion. In addition to the internal list of changes and modifications, there are external lists. The users of the system will point out what they think are errors and inconsistencies in the computer reports they receive. Though some of the errors may be resolved by additional discussion and clarification, some no doubt will have to be incorporated into the system.

Furthermore, it is inevitable that undetected errors will appear later as volume running produces unique combinations of transactions and conditions that were not foreseen and therefore not tested.

A prudent course of action is to undergo a period of introspective evaluation before moving on to other applications. This will ensure that there is a solid foundation on which to base further additions and extensions. Thus the first activity of the maintenance and modification subphase is evaluation. The evaluation sets the stage for the second activity, called fine tuning, when the problems uncovered in the evaluation are analyzed and resolved.

After the necessary modifications have been made, the focus shifts to the determination of short- and long-term plans. Planning is a continuing process and should be viewed as an extension of the plan developed during the feasibility phase. With the computer installation accomplished, the original plan can be reevaluated from the vantage point of experience. It is rare when this vantage point does not produce major changes in the next planning cycle. Although systematic planning would seem obvious to a discipline that itself requires systematic and logical planning, it is not as commonplace as one might imagine. Indeed, the shoemaker's children often go barefoot.

EVALUATION

Rather than let errors and discrepancies become evident one at a time, it makes sense to conduct a formal evaluation of the entire operation. The EDP director should welcome the chance to have his operation critically appraised, particularly if, like Three B's' Dexter Johnson, he has been under constant pressure and harassment from operating management. Management also should encourage an evaluation of the progress made as an indication of what future data processing assistance can be anticipated. An evaluation will point out areas in which additional management involvement can be employed to materially improve the situation.

Several recent EDP surveys have come to similar conclusions regarding the degree to which companies utilize outside and inside groups to evaluate computer operations. Less than 20% of companies with installed small and medium scale computers conduct outside evaluations of their computer operation. In companies with large computers, one of three conducts outside evaluations. It can be seen that outside evaluation is not the rule even with companies that are expending upward of $2- to $3 million per year on data processing.

On the other hand, more companies employ periodic inside evaluations of computer operations. Two out of five small and medium companies and three out of five large companies conduct internal evaluations. The surveys indicate that outside evaluations normally are conducted by consultants or auditing firms and inside evaluations are conducted by personnel outside the EDP department, usually representatives of the operating departments or internal company auditors.

INSIDE VERSUS OUTSIDE EVALUATION

Pros and cons exist concerning the use of outside evaluation services for the purpose of assessing the efficacy of computer operations. A company must determine if it has the necessary resources and capabilities to carry out its own evaluation. It must consider the time and cost of an outside review. Also, it is important to determine whether the internal evaluation will have the impact of an independent analysis of operations.

A prime consideration is cost. A special audit team formed by the

Boeing Company to audit its computer operation included an experienced EDP manager, two people who were experienced in systems/programming work, an internal auditor, and a person with considerable accounting experience. After an analysis of the job to be done, the five-man group estimated it would take 33 man-years for a complete review and evaluation of all computer systems. This evaluation was predicated on a thorough and detailed analysis of programs, an effort that can be justified when one considers that the possible reduction in running time of just a small percent can mean the saving of thousands of dollars for a company like Boeing. Although Boeing is one of the largest users of EDP in the country, this estimate provides an idea of the upward boundary of an evaluation effort. It is obvious that the small computer user is not going to conduct such an analysis. In Boeing's case, the company decided to select an application area as a test case before making a final decision to undertake the complete study.

A Booz, Allen & Hamilton study of 108 leading manufacturers using computers points out that 62% of those firms employing regular audits confine them to the critical computer operations. The study also indicates the significant degree to which operating managers are involved in the audits. The operating managers usually serve as members of the committee that reviews and analyzes the results of the audit. It is obvious that the involvement of operating management or of people with no direct EDP experience depends on the objectives and level of the evaluation being conducted. The performance areas that are most studied will be reviewed later. The scope and selection of these areas can help determine who should conduct the evaluation and whether it can best be accomplished by inside or outside sources.

Unless the problems seem particularly severe and it is anticipated that major directional and organizational changes are required, the evaluation normally can be effectively handled by an inside group. The desirability of having a department evaluate its own performance is open to question. It has the advantage of providing the proper psychological climate for eventual resolution of the problem areas uncovered, but on the other hand it may not result in the most objective kind of appraisal. A compromise solution is to have a person in the EDP department assist with the evaluation, since someone with EDP experience is required at the detail level. However, the person selected should not have been directly involved in the application under scrutiny. It is wise to include one or more members of the department that is a major user of the system under study. That person need not be the manager or a supervisor of the department, but can be an assistant or administrative aide who reports to the manager. The head of the evaluation team should be a manager of an operating department. He probably will not be a full time member of the team but will direct the activity, maintain the perspective of the study, and see that the objectives of the study are carried out.

An evaluation team consisting of combined EDP and operating personnel should be able to point out weaknesses in the system and recommend action to improve the situation.

PERFORMANCE AREAS

It is important to have a clear idea of the objectives of the evaluation before it starts. As an example, the audit team of the Boeing Company had the following general objectives:

1. Assure that computer systems fulfill their stated objectives.
2. Assure that computer systems meet requirements in a cost effective manner.
3. Analyze all systems costs to see where costs can be reduced and capability extended.

Experience shows that when evaluations are made, companies cover the following performance areas.

1. New application and equipment planning
2. Project schedule punctuality
3. Standards and documentation
4. Systems errors and discrepancies
5. Report deadlines promptness
6. Computer report usability
7. Over-all use to management
8. Operating budget adherence
9. Computer department practices and procedures
10. Audit and systems controls within applications
11. Machine room efficiency
12. Programming efficiency

The list is by frequency of evaluation coverage. The rankings differ somewhat among small and large computer users. The first four areas are universal in their significance. Items 5, 6, and 7 are not as important to the larger companies, indicating those companies have overcome these discrepancies. However, items 8 and 11 receive higher priority from the larger users. This is not surprising, considering the dollar expenditures of the larger user on EDP.

PROBLEM AREAS

In addition to considering the performance areas most often evaluated by computer users, it is significant to view the major problems uncovered by these evaluations. The following list indicates the results of an extensive survey directed to this question. The problems are listed in the order of their frequency of response.

1. Internal communications between EDP and management
2. Skilled personnel—shortage and turnover
3. Complex and time-consuming implementation of applications
4. Scheduling and priorities
5. Short- and long-range planning
6. Software performance
7. Training
8. Equipment performance
9. Equipment downtime

This list is fairly consistent for small and large users alike. It is significant that software and hardware performance as well as machine downtime are low on the list. Although these were more serious problems in the earlier days of the third generation, they apparently have been resolved. Larger users tend to rank training higher in the problem list. It appears that with the hardware and software working, the burden is now on the user to recruit, select, and train the proper staff; improve his techniques for scheduling and establishing priorities; cut into his application backlog; and, most important, improve communications between the EDP department and operating management.

MANAGEMENT'S VIEWPOINT ON THE COMPUTER

Although the various internal and external evaluations of a computer operation are significant in improving computer usage, a key factor is management's viewpoint on computer performance. Management represents the group that, in the last analysis, benefits from computerized information services and also represents the group that pays the EDP bills. In an incentive salary plan, its remuneration may well be based on how well the computer gathers and analyzes information to aid management decision making. There have been some rather severe appraisals of computer performance. McKinsey & Company conducted an in-depth analysis of the EDP results of prominent large computer users in 1963, and compared it to a study made in 1968 of 36 major American and European companies representing 13 industries. The following paragraph summarizes the findings of the later report. The implications are quite clear.

> In terms of technical achievement, the computer revolution in U.S. business is outrunning expectations. In terms of economic payoff on new applications, it is rapidly losing momentum. Such is the evidence of a new study of computer systems management in 36 major companies.
>
> From a profit standpoint, our findings indicate computer efforts in all but a few exceptional companies are in real, if often unacknowledged, trouble. Faster, costlier, more sophisticated hardware; larger and increasingly costly computer staffs; increasingly complex and ingenious applications: these are evidenced everywhere. Less and less in evidence, as these new applications proliferate, are profitable results. This is the familiar phenomenon of diminishing returns. But there is one crucial difference: As yet, the real profit potential of the computer has barely begun to be tapped.

A correlation of computer user surveys indicates, somewhat surprisingly, that the management of smaller companies thinks the computer is doing a better job than does the management of larger companies. This difference might be a reflection that the management of larger companies is closer to computer operation, realizes its significance, and is more critical when the operation does not live up to expectations.

The composite picture given by the available data is that computers in reality have not fulfilled the prophecy that was talked about ten years ago; on the other hand, hardly anyone interviewed indicated that his company plans to return its computer and either revert to manual methods or semiautomatic data processing methods or turn to outside services.

A further query was posed to the management of companies using computers. In addition to being asked whether the computer was doing a good job, they were asked if the computer was paying off in dollars and cents. Less than half gave an unqualified yes. Most of those who did not give an unqualified yes were uncertain because of the inadequacy of criteria for measurement.

Earlier chapters have pointed out that it often is difficult to pinpoint actual dollar and cents savings that can be attributed to the computer. This is particularly true if the focus is on those applications that aid the decision making process rather than on those that serve to reduce clerical and administrative costs. Furthermore, an effective accounting system is required to keep track of data processing costs as well as the incremental costs of introducing the computer. It has been my experience that few companies maintain records that adequately reflect either the true costs of data processing or the benefits and savings produced by the system. There is a natural bias built into any questionnaire and a wish fulfillment syndrome on the part of the manager being interviewed in a survey. He may answer yes to the question of whether the computer is paying for itself, but often it is only a subjective answer and he may have second thoughts upon reflection. The problem in conducting surveys is that the interviewer does not follow up the question of payoff by asking for the records that support the answer. Considering this bias, I feel most assuredly that better yardsticks will show that companies, as yet, have not tapped the real potential of data processing.

An open letter from the director of marketing to the manager of data processing concludes the discussion of management's viewpoint on the computer. The memo reflects the opinion of a prominent member of top management as he reviews three generations of computer hardware at the Brown Company. The reader will see similarities between the problems described at the Brown Company and those of Three B's, though the Brown Company is a larger and longer-term computer user.

TO   Harvey Williamson, Manager of
            Data Processing
FROM   John J. Warren, Director of Marketing
SUBJECT   Viewpoint on Data Processing
DATE   February 12, 1970

At our last executive committee meeting, the
subject of data processing at the Brown
Company was one of the agenda items.
President L. J. Parsons suggested that it
might prove helpful if the department heads
each write you a letter indicating their
feelings and opinions about the progress we
have made with EDP over the past several
years. I do not know how typical my response
will be because I have not discussed the
subject with the other department
directors; however, I have decided to be
extremely frank and candid in giving you my
personal reactions. In so doing, I may
appear to be over-critical, but I hope you
will take my remarks in the constructive way

they are intended. I realize the situation
is a two-sided one and that I have not done
everything I could personally do to take
advantage of EDP. Hopefully, this letter
and the others you receive can lead to the
establishment of meaningful dialogue that
can help resolve some of our existing
problems and help us move ahead to improve
the situation.

I do not think EDP meant too much to me until
three years ago when we installed the third
generation computer that is currently in
operation. Let us discuss the routine
computer applications that were tackled
first, things like processing orders and
analyzing sales history. It appears to me
that we have made some progress; however, I
must state frankly that it has been somewhat
slow and painful. In looking back at the
cutover to our new order processing system,
which occurred two years ago, I know I was
quite upset at the time and lost a great
deal of faith in computer processing. I
know we antagonized several of our key
customers by sending them erroneous
invoices and also by indicating we had
certain items in stock when, in reality, we
did not. I remember the embarrassment, for
example, when the system treated a request
to expedite an order as an order itself. As
a result, the J. L. Craemer Company received
two carloads of its order.

You and your staff had done quite a job in
convincing us that this new system would be
a great success. We believed you because we

really wanted to, and we looked forward to
the new approach with a great deal of
enthusiasm. In retrospect, I think we were
oversold. You should have felt free to tell
us potential problem areas and pitfalls.
Presenting us a more balanced picture would
have prepared us to face the cutover period
with far better perspective. We could have
been in a position to support the system
rather than castigating it. I'm told I still
have an order clerk who uses your inventory
report for posting her manual cardex files.
I don't think that's exactly what you meant
when you said we were going to have a common
data base system. We survived that period
and finally did see the improvements that
you promised us, even though they were from
six to 12 months late in occurring.

Another element that was overlooked (and
this probably is our fault as much as yours)
was that we had very little to do with the
design and development of the system. True,
our people attended a course on EDP, but
I thought the instructors spoke over our
heads and in terminology that was at best
very difficult to understand. I still can't
see what bearing an "octal patch" has to my
operation. This one-shot instruction was
not enough to cover all the things we should
have known about the implementation of a
new system. I probably should have assigned
one of my sales analysts to represent our
interest as the system was developing. Not
having participated in the development, I
naturally tend to resist changes that are
forthcoming. One of the areas in which I

think we should have pressed harder is that
of constructing the system in a manner that
would allow for later additions and
changes. It is true that one of your systems
analysts discussed with me at the very
beginning what type of sales analysis
reports we needed. However, I never saw him
again. The marketing situation is a most
dynamic one as you know, and our needs today
certainly differ from our needs two years
ago. I hate to think that we are locked out
now because we didn't request something
two years ago.

Now, I'd like to turn to the more
sophisticated application areas. I remember
a presentation you made when we started
the conversion to the new system. You spoke
about an integrated data processing system
built around a common data base. You
indicated, at the time, that a complete
sales history file would be maintained and
indexed in such a way that we could obtain
almost any type of analysis required and in
a short response time. Though this can be
done to a limited extent, it hardly
satisfies all our current needs. It seems to
me that we spent a good deal of time working
along with your people in capturing
information that was to become part of this
data base. Other departments also were to
compile information for the data base. For
example, we were told we could get an
up-to-date status of in-process orders
from the factory. In order to do this, we had
to change a number of our existing
procedures and expend a considerable amount
of clerical effort. Very frankly, I have

seen little results from all the work that we put in.

I think the idea of on-line order entry directly to the computer that you spoke about several years ago still presents a great opportunity for us to materially reduce our order cycle time. This would improve customer service in an area that I am sure costs us dearly. Another area I am vitally interested in is an improved sales forecasting system. With our other data processing problems, I wonder if we will ever get to these things before you are ready to change computers again and go through a lengthy conversion process.

In summary, I hope I have not been too critical and I want to state again that I realize I share a good deal of the responsibility for your problems. Maybe the following set of ground rules will help us both:

1. Be frank with the operating departments. We want to work with you, but we need to have a balanced picture.
2. Let's cooperate in determining system specifications. I realize that I need more computer education and I am most certainly willing to get it if I can participate more effectively in EDP operations. This is true of all the people in my department.
3. Let's work together to map out a plan for getting to the real payoff areas that I have mentioned. I realize it

```
      will take time, but I will be satisfied
      if we have long range goals and are
      headed toward those goals.

                          Sincerely,


                          John J. Warren

JJW/rc
```

AN EVALUATION CHECK LIST

Figure 7.1 illustrates an evaluation checklist representative of the type used by consultants and internal audit staffs. This is not as detailed as some, but it does include the salient evaluation areas that distinguish a well-run computer operation from a mediocre one. The first two general categories cover the personnel and organizational aspects of the operation. As indicated in the previous discussion, these areas are quite significant. The next two categories are concerned with the over-all planning and control of operations. The categories proceed from the general to the specific—the following two categories delve into questions pertaining to the quantitative and qualitative aspects of each application under evaluation. The last two categories cover more detailed information concerning specific procedures and documentation. The last three categories can serve as a checklist to evaluate each of the application areas under study. An additional form, listing the applications down the left-hand side of the page with the various checklist items running across the top, can be used for this purpose.

A company must decide on the scope of the evaluation and the time and effort it is able to expend in reviewing its operation. The Boeing Company example, where a 33 man-years' effort was projected, is extreme, and it can be seen that a detailed audit of each application is a time-consuming job. The proper scope might be to perform an over-all evaluation, using the first five categories with a more detailed look, provided by the last three categories, at the major application areas or those not performing up to expectation. A key consideration at the outset of an evaluation effort is that the company recognize that a considerable effort is required to correct serious weaknesses that are uncovered. The

PERSONNEL STRENGTH

No. programmers	_____
No. systems analysts	_____
No. operators	_____
No. O. R. specialists	_____
No. supervisors	_____
Turnover %	_____
Morale	☐
Growth potential	☐
Development plan	☐
Salary levels	☐
Experience level	☐
Personnel back-up	☐
Overall management	☐

EDP—PLACE IN ORGANIZATION

Reporting structure	☐
Contact with operating departments	☐
Contact with top mgt.	☐
Communications within department	☐
EDP steering committee	☐
Job descriptions	☐
Dept. charter	☐

WORK PLAN

Existence of plan	☐
Is it monitored?	☐
Adequacy of plan	☐
Application approval cycle	☐
Cost/benefit analysis	☐
Sign-off procedures	☐
Historical records	☐
Timing estimates	☐
Degree of formality	☐
Reporting cycle	☐
Reports to management	☐

GENERAL PLANNING

1-year plan	☐
3-year plan	☐
5-year plan	☐
Budget—Hardware	☐
—Systems	☐
—Operations	☐
Charge for services	☐
Operate as profit center	☐

Figure 7.1   Evaluation checklist.

evaluation is but one aspect of the maintenance and modification job. The most important aspect is the action taken as a result of the evaluation. If the company does not intend to allocate the resources necessary to remedy the problems, then it may be better not to undertake the evaluation in the first place.

FINE TUNING

The results of the evaluation may show that more than fine tuning is in order—it may well be that major readjustments are necessary. Experience indicates that the maintenance effort, measured in man-months, is about 20 percent of the development effort—that is, if it takes 10 man-

APPLICATIONS (QUANTITATIVE)

No. of applications _____

Basic _____ Advanced _____

Programming languages _____

Operating systems _____

Multiprogramming _____

Tape Systems _____ Disk _____

No. in design _____

No. in programming _____

No. in test _____

Backlog _____

APPLICATIONS (QUALITATIVE)

Degree of integration ☐

Modularity ☐

Ease of maintenance ☐

Timeliness of output ☐

Benefits ☐

Meets objectives ☐

Meets system spec. ☐

Quality of code ☐

Efficiency of code ☐

PROCEDURES

Procedures manual ☐

Operating manual ☐

Standards manual ☐

Operating schedule ☐

Checkout procedures ☐

Difficulty log ☐

Scheduling system ☐

File labels ☐

File maintenance ☐

Audit controls ☐

Backup facilities ☐

DOCUMENTATION

Narrative ☐

Flow chart ☐

File layouts ☐

Input/output forms ☐

Education manuals ☐

Error routines ☐

Special handling ☐

Source listings ☐

Operating instructions ☐

Maintenance procedures ☐

Figure 7.1 Evaluation checklist (cont.)

months to design, program, and test a program, it will take two man-months to maintain the program over its useful life. Regardless of whether the evaluation uncovers major or minor problems, all problems must be corrected in order to create a smooth-running shop and to reestablish confidence in the operation.

After the evaluation, the first order of business is to establish priorities among the problem areas. Errors in applications like payroll or commission payments, which involve monetary payments to employees, represent high priority items. On the other hand, inconsistencies in a quarterly report which does not involve monetary payment is categorized as a low priority item. It is relatively easy to determine priorities in these examples; in practice there will be situations that require considerable judgment before a realistic priority can be established.

It is important to distinguish between two categories of computer problems. The first category represents problems that are definite errors and have to be corrected in time. This class of problems falls under the category of maintenance. The other category is called modification. Modification requests do not represent actual errors but rather alterations or changes that will improve the effectiveness of an application. For example, it might be as simple as a buyer wanting to see the sequence of columns reversed on a particular report for greater clarity, or it may be the addition of a maximum/minimum field to an inventory status report. Although these are desirable changes, they are not errors as such. Most of these modifications are a result of the lack of communications between the systems analyst and the operating department during the design of the application.

Another cause is that the operating personnel begin to see additional benefits once they receive computerized reports on a regular basis. The EDP department should have a procedure for handling the maintenance and modification problems because these can get out of hand easily and cause a great deal of user dissatisfaction. This is evident in the letter from the marketing director of the Brown Company to his EDP director. Figure 7.2 presents a simple procedure for categorizing requests for systems changes and corrections.

The first step is to determine whether a request for change falls in the maintenance (error) category or in the modification category. A rating can then be given for each category for its relative priority and the effort required to make the change. Thus a MAIN-A1 category would indicate that the particular problem is in a maintenance category, has the highest priority, and can be resolved in less than a day.

Another important consideration is the development of the proper organization to routinely handle systems changes. One must recognize that there is a basic conflict in assigning people to the maintenance function. For the most part, systems designers are creative individuals who are looking for increased systems challenges. They are anxious to work on the advanced or more sophisticated application areas. Therefore, they do not look with favor on reworking and refining applications that

		Priority		
Effort		A	B	C
Less than a day	1	√		
Several days	2			
More than a week	3			

Figure 7.2

are already in operation. A paradox exists, for though the maintenance work may not be the most desirable activity, it requires a highly experienced and skilled programmer or systems analyst. This is true because the analyst must be able to interpret and understand a program that he was not involved in and that often is poorly documented. It becomes a demanding logical exercise to trace through the program, find the error, correct it, and test it against a variety of conditions. In addition, it is necessary to ensure that the correction resolves the error but does not cause additional problems in other parts of the program.

For these reasons, many companies establish a separate maintenance section distinct from the new application section. They staff the group with competent junior personnel who can benefit from this experience and can see an opportunity to display abilities in the logic and diagnostic area. It is an excellent training ground for broader systems work. The size of the EDP budget and the scope of the job will determine if a separate maintenance group is required. Whether it be a separate group or the same group that originally designed and programmed the application, the importance of a sound maintenance and modification program to fine tune programs cannot be overstressed. The EDP department must counter the tendency to move on to new application areas prematurely. System errors have a way of proliferating unless they are caught and corrected early.

PLANNING

We now turn to a discussion of the important planning function. Planning more or less completes the cycle and sets the stage for the next round of systems development. Though it is important to evaluate and determine what type of job has been done, it is equally important to determine future direction. The following quotation is from the McKinsey and Company study.

> The computer management problem as it confronts corporate executives today, then, is a matter of future direction rather than current effectiveness. The key question is not "How are we doing?" but "Where are we heading, and why?"

Surveys point out that fewer companies than might be imagined have short- and long-range plans. One survey indicates that only half of the small companies have a plan for the next two years and less than a third have a plan for three or more years. The larger companies show more concern with planning—two-thirds plan for two years and half plan for three or more years. The question of whether a company has a one-year plan was not asked, but I feel strongly that the number of companies who do not also would be surprisingly large.

Although the lack of formal planning can be understood, it cannot be condoned. Planning follows an evolutionary path as an industry matures. This is so because history and past experience are prime indicators of the future. The EDP industry, relatively, is still in its infancy, and changes in hardware, software, and applications are taking place with great rapidity. This situation does not mitigate the need for formalized and detailed EDP planning, but rather increases the necessity.

ORGANIZATIONAL PLANNING

The evaluation checklist, Figure 7.1, presents questions that should be raised concerning the organizational strengths of the EDP operation. It is a cliché that nothing gets done without people, but this is particularly pertinent in an industry where demand far exceeds the supply of competent people. The discussion in the previous chapter and the organization illustrated in Figure 6.10 should be reviewed in light of the company's existing organization, the experience the company has had in installing its computer, and its future plans for application growth. It is not surprising to observe an imbalance between a company's expectations of EDP and the budget it allocates to it. The organizational review may point out the need for additional staff positions devoted to improving the administration, planning, and control of operations. In addition, an expanded systems/programming staff will be required if the company wishes to press ahead with advanced applications. The need for a separate maintenance section has been discussed earlier in the chapter.

This points out the necessity of a realistic appraisal of the EDP budget and organization required and justified in light of future plans. The EDP department has become an important department where it competes with the other line and staff departments for development dollars. If the EDP results have been beneficial to company operations, it probably has become a very solid competitor.

Operating the EDP department as a service or profit center seems to be increasing in popularity. This is particularly appropriate in a company that employs the profit center approach throughout its operation. The EDP department is viewed as a service group providing information to the various using departments. When a job is requested by an operating department, it is costed and a tentative schedule is projected. A monthly charge for the implemented application, based on the development costs plus anticipated operating costs, is quoted to the user. This has the advantage of qualifying application development because the requesting department manager has a basis of determining the value of the application to his area of operation. In a like manner, the EDP department can negotiate with an operating department on a practical dollar and cents basis. This cost consciousness and competitive awareness can be heightened if the operating department is allowed to obtain bids from an outside EDP service center. The company must decide if it wants to go to this extreme in providing a competitive environment for its EDP operation.

The intent of this discussion is to demonstrate that EDP must be looked at as a viable entity within an organization and that its relative newness should not preclude its being organized, budgeted, and controlled according to the same guidelines as other departments. Organizational and budgetary considerations must go hand in hand with the planning of future EDP direction and growth.

APPLICATION APPROVAL CYCLE

The selection and establishment of priorities for new application development is a vital element in the effective operation of EDP. In many companies, the responsibility for this key area has fallen to the EDP manager. It is unfortunate that the EDP manager, in most instances, does not have the over-all business background or perspective to make the proper decisions. Yet the unfulfilled promise of EDP can be traced directly to the fact that the computer has not been put to work in the key money-earning areas of a business where the leverage on profits is high. Management is recognizing the significance of this problem, and its involvement in application selection is definitely on the rise. Many companies have a formal application approval procedure similar to that illustrated in Figure 7.3.

Phase 1 indicates that requests for new applications may originate from a variety of sources; certainly no single department has a monopoly on good ideas. The origin of a new application also may be in sources outside the company; for example, an executive may get a good idea from a conference or seminar he attends and a buyer or salesman may be stimulated by reading an article in a business periodical. The output of this phase is a request for a new application. The feasibility of the request has not been established as yet.

Phase 2 involves reviewing the request by the EDP department in order to prepare a definite statement of need. The statement of need is developed in accordance with a predefined format. A preliminary benefit and cost estimate is made at this time if the nature of the application readily lends itself to it. The significance of this step is to screen out application development that is obviously far beyond the scope or capability of the company and to translate a broad request statement into a more comprehensive and logical statement of need. A review by the EDP steering committee, usually comprised of EDP management and operating management, concludes Phase 2 of the application approval cycle.

Phase 3 commences after the steering committee recommends additional evaluation. It is necessary to screen the requests because Phase 3

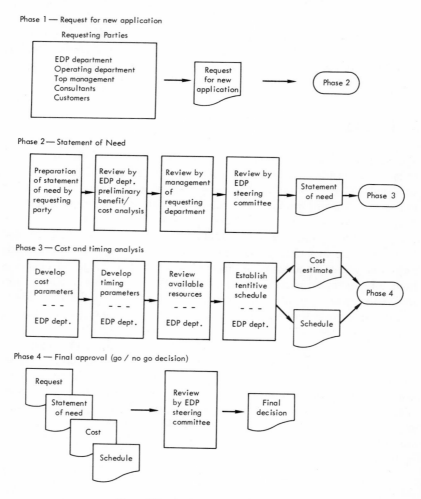

Figure 7.3 Application approval cycle.

involves the detailed evaluation of an application and this takes considerable time and effort. It is the province of the EDP department to establish cost and time parameters, review the available resources, and develop a project schedule. These are accomplished according to a prescribed format. It is important to standardize the evaluation procedures so that each request for a new application receives the same treatment and the evaluations are carried out in a consistent manner.

The outputs of the three phases—request for new application, statement of need and cost, and schedule—enter Phase 4. Here the EDP steering committee, meeting for this purpose on a monthly basis, reviews the application requests on the agenda and decides which ones it will approve for implementation; which it will disapprove; and which it will order to be reworked or tabled for subsequent review or both. This is no mean task, and it is not unusual for these sessions to go well beyond the scheduled time and to involve intense discussion and debate. However, the importance of the selection process warrants the time and effort devoted to it. Evaluation criteria and selection indices are necessary to assist in reaching consistent conclusions; for example return on investment, payback period, or break-even analysis. A well-conceived application approval cycle can ensure that a company is committing its computer dollars to the key operating areas of its business.

THE CHANGING EDP ENVIRONMENT

Planning for the development of new applications and the extended use of data processing is not an easy task. Many of the changes in the EDP industry that compound this problem have been covered in previous chapters. This section will combine these changes in order to give perspective to the planning process.

There are many ways to categorize and view the changes that are occurring. Figure 7.4 gives an outline for discussing these changes under four general headings. The changes are looked at from the computer user's point of view. These headings are: (1) advanced applications, (2) systematic, logical growth, (3) reduced systems implementation cycle, and (4) economical, efficient operation. Each of the four categories covers the user environment that brings on the change and the systems needs that are outgrowths of the environment.

1. Advanced applications. Management is becoming impatient over the lack of solid computer results. It is impatient with promises of good results and it wants immediately forthcoming results. Coupled with this demand is a desire to use the computer in decision making, which distinguishes the computer from predecessors that were primarily directed

1. Advanced applications

   User environment
   * Results-oriented
   * Aid in decision making
   * Integration of functions
   * Geographical diversification

   Systems needs
   * Management information systems
   * Communications
   * Data management
   * Management science

2. Systematic, logical growth

   User environment
   * Business growth (volume & complexity)
   * Rapidly changing technology
   * Fragmented service structure

   Systems needs
   * Hardware modularity
   * Software modularity
   * Standardization
   * Meaningful conversion

3. Reduced systems implementation cycle

   User environment
   * Skills shortage
   * Turnover problem
   * Programmer productivity
   * Application backlog

   Systems needs
   * Application packages
   * Higher level languages
   * Documentation
   * Education

4. Economical, efficient operation

   User environment
   * Rising cost of EDP
   ° Increasing uptime demand
   * Throughput and turn-around
     time requirements

   Systems needs
   * Reliability
   * Simpler operating systems
   * Multiprogramming/multiprocessing

Figure 7.4 Changes in data processing.

at producing the same kind of reports and analyses in a faster and cheaper manner. This point warrants emphasis.

A brief discussion of the various types of information required to effectively plan and control operations will shed light on the use of a computer in decision making. Information is becoming an increasingly valuable commodity in the increasingly complex world of business. It is considered by many to be as significant a resource as the traditional four m's of men, machines, material, and money. Information has many shapes and forms, but for purposes of this discussion, it can be characterized by the matrix shown in Figure 7.5.

Internal information is a by-product of the normal operations of a business. For example, a recording of inventory usage for the past week is typical internal information. Internal information usually is historical

Type of information	Reported	Processed
Internal	A	B
External	C	D

Figure 7.5 Information matrix.

or static; it is after-the-fact data. This is true at least in Category A when the information is reported but not statistically processed. In the case of inventory usage, if the information is limited to prior history and no attempt is made to statistically sample or draw meaningful correlations from the data, it represents internal reported data. However, if inventory usage is statistically plotted to project future usage patterns that are used to set optimum inventory levels, it represents an example of Category B, or statistically processed internal information.

External information is data whose source is outside the operations of the company. An example is population growth in the market served by a company or the changes in ethnic makeup of the market. Category C reports the data, but makes no attempt to statistically analyze it and Category D uses various mathematical techniques to analyze and correlate the data. A sales forecast that projects the future based on historical sales movement would be Category B information whereas a sales forecast that also includes external market statistics and trends would be a combination of B and D. The relative use of the various forms of information by a computer system is consistent with the alphabetical sequence; that is, A is found in a computer system more often than B, and so on. In order for the computer to have a direct influence on top management decision making, applications must be developed utilizing processed external information.

Another part of the user environment is functions integration that is required in business operation. The emergence of the top computer executive indicates management's desire to bring together the coordination and control of EDP systems. It is a recognition that a good deal of duplication and redundancy exist under a split-control arrangement. Furthermore, it indicates management awareness that information subsystems cannot be built in isolation of other subsystems. This was brought out in the discussion of the integrated systems concept, where it was seen, for example, that the order processing system affects the inventory, productive control, and purchasing subsystems.

Geographical diversification has become a way of life even to small companies. Mergers, establishment of new branches and divisions, and other forms of national and international growth place considerable demand on systems design and development. The source of data is remote from the processing of the data and the results of the processing must be distributed to remote spots. This must be considered carefully in systems planning.

The systems needs that are an outgrowth of this user environment include first the concept of the management information system or integrated system. If properly conceived, this approach can satisfy the results orientation and the development of a system to aid management decision making. It is a fact of business life that very few top or middle managers within an organization actually see computer output. Their subordinates receive computer printout and make additional manual interpretations and analyses before the information is passed upstairs for decision making. A management information system should be broad enough to incorporate management's needs into the basic design, thus establishing the relevance of direct computer output. Whether a manager receives and utilizes output directly from a computer is a lead indicator of the effectiveness of a management information system.

Communication systems are direct outgrowths of the geographical diversification that is taking place. Systems must be able to incorporate a variety of remote devices on-line to a central computer. In addition, systems must ensure that the response time is consistent with user requirements.

Data management techniques provide the foundation upon which management information systems are built. These techniques facilitate the gathering, updating, organization, and retrieval of an information data base, a necessary prerequisite to the development of the MIS concept.

Management science techniques blend the processing of external as well as internal information to facilitate computer-aided decision making. Management science, or operations research as it is sometimes called, can be defined as the application of mathematical methods to the solution of business problems. A management science technique can range from a simple use of regression analysis for plotting a sales trend line to a complex simulation model of the entire operation of a business or a particular segment of it. Return on investment analysis, linear programming and queueing theory are other techniques utilized in management science applications.

2. Systematic, logical growth. It is a business fact that most companies are expanding and growing with the increase in gross national product and the population expansion. Keeping pace with the growth in volume is the increasing complexity of a company's products and services. There exists within a company a phenomenon that might be called the geometric growth syndrome. It can be applied·equally to people or products. In the case of people, the interaction pathways of four people are more than double that of two people. The progression is one of a geometric nature rather than an arithmetic nature. Thus, there is one communication path with two people, three with three people, six with four people, ten with five people, and so on. Adding a fifth communication party increases the communication pathways not by 25 percent, but by 67 percent. Thus, as a company adds products and people, the information flow between them is greatly increased and the need for application growth is accentuated.

Businesses are facing a rapidly changing technology particularly with the growing application of automation to manual tasks. This has occurred in both the factory and the office. It is probably most evident in the computer field where three generations of hardware (each one making the previous one completely obsolete) have appeared in less than 20 years. Many companies have passed through the three generations in a time span of less than ten years, though not without serious repercussions.

Another complication is the fact that the computer user is operating within a fragmented service structure. The IBM separate pricing policy added new impetus to the already expanding EDP service field. As a result, the EDP user now faces a more difficult job in selecting the right combination of products and services to accomplish his data processing job. If he is successful, he will obtain more beneficial results, quite possibly at a lower over-all price; however, there is greater risk that parts of the total offering may not dovetail with other parts.

Systems needs to satisfy the environment are first hardware and software modularity. The EDP user does not want to be forced into purchasing hardware or software that is not consistent with his growth plans. This emphasizes the value of the family concept within a computer manufacturer's line. The user wants to add computing power with minimum inconvenience and with little, if any, rework of existing programs.

Standardization also is significant as a requirement for logical and systematic growth. A company may have more than one computer, necessitating the interchange of program and data. Program and data compatibility do not occur by chance. They must be planned and the planning requires some form of standardization. The media on which data is stored as well as the device that reads the data are considerations in a standardization program. Internal work standards such as tape labelling and programming conventions also must be observed by the EDP user.

Conversion is defined as replacing a computer system, either with one of another manufacturer's line or of a new line offered by the user's current vendor. The natural growth in business activity and the development of advanced applications can cause a company to reach a stage where a change to a new line of computers becomes increasingly attractive. The constantly improving performance/price ratio and the advanced features of newer equipment add further impetus for change. A negative influence is the bad experience that many users have had in converting. This is a result of a combination of inadequate conversion aids on the part of the vendor and unpreparedness on the part of the user because of ineffective or nonexistent internal standards.

3. Reduced systems implementation cycle. An often heard complaint in the EDP business (probably the most common of all) is: "Why does it take so long to get an application up and running?" The user environment causing such a statement is the severe skills shortage that exists in the industry. The turnover rate accentuates the seriousness of the situation. The current education and training facilities do not ensure that there will be an adequate number of systems analysts and programmers to satisfy the increasing business demands. Many in the industry feel the gap is widening. As has been stated, the implementation cycle for a computer application lengthens without competent personnel.

Another factor affecting the systems implementation cycle is programmer productivity. It is tempting to hide below par productivity and weak supervision behind the personnel shortage. Programmer productivity is an area that must be recognized and improved.

The result of the three conditions listed is a sizable application backlog experienced by most users. Various surveys estimate this backlog to be between 15 and 20% of operating programs. It is obvious that the saturation of computer applications still is a long way off.

Systems needs as a result of this user environment include application packages, higher level languages, documentation, and education. Although an application package to produce a complete turn-key solution to a payroll job or an inventory control application has yet to be developed, pieces of the application (subroutines) are available and further improvements will make it possible to approach the turn-key solution. The use of these packages can assist a company in obtaining more mileage from its own systems and programming staff.

Higher level languages or enhancements to existing languages like COBOL and Fortran can move the computer programmer still further away from the painstaking and tedious job of computer programming and thus reduce the systems implementation cycle. It may even be feasible for managers to write their own instructions, which can be interpreted directly by the computer. According to one line of thinking, this will be the wave of the future. I feel that there still will be the need for information middlemen between management and the computer, although the development of higher level languages will help reduce the communications barrier between management and the systems analyst.

Improved documentation and educational techniques also play a part in enabling systems analysts and programmers to be more productive in a shorter time period. Advances in automated documentation methods—for example, where the computer actually produces a flow chart—permit the programmer to concentrate on the main-line job of getting the program in operation while the necessary documentation is produced automatically as a by-product. Improved educational methods, such as programmed instruction texts and improved audio/visual facilities, will greatly improve the educational process and accelerate the learning curve.

4. Economical, efficient operation. Computer users spend more for EDP each passing year. This is a statistical fact of life. Figures show that the average hardware upgrade for a company is between 12 and 15 percent per year whereas nonhardware costs are rising at a slightly higher rate. A key consideration, in light of this rising cost curve, is that the EDP staff make the most efficient use of the computer facility.

Another environmental element is the increasing demand for uptime. Communications and real time information needs emphasize the fail safe concept. A batch operation in which reports are produced and distributed at the end of each day can tolerate downtime to a greater extent than a system that processes an inquiry from a sales office and returns the status of an inventory item within seconds.

Coupled with the uptime demand are the requirements for throughput and turn-around time. These two concepts have been described earlier—throughput is the measure of the total output of a system and turn-around time is the interval between the initiation of a particular job and the completion of it. The two concepts usually conflict so that efficiency and economical operation are reached where throughput and turn-around time requirements are placed in proper balance.

One of the systems needs brought on by the environment is reliability of operation. Mechanical or electromechanical devices, because of the number of moving parts, are not as reliable as electronic devices. Therefore, there is more concern with peripheral devices than with central processors. Systems planning should take this into account and provide suitable back-up facilities for those devices that have the highest downtime expectation and/or operate in a fast turn-around mode.

Today's computer users require operating systems for advanced multiprogramming and communication processing. Operating systems have tended to be complex, difficult to understand and execute, and often inefficient as well. Users facetiously refer to operating systems as "egotistical" software systems—that is, software that is so complicated that it pays more attention to its own needs than it does to the user's needs. Users seek improvement that they reason may emanate from incorporating functions currently performed by the software into the hardware. The hope is that this firmware concept will produce easier to use and more efficient operating systems.

Multiprogramming and multiprocessing are the significant elements in achieving a higher performance-to-price ratio. As has been stated earlier, there is a considerable imbalance between the slow peripheral devices and the high-speed memory and arithmetic units of a computer. Multiprogramming and multiprocessing enable jobs to run concurrently, thus reducing this imbalance and achieving the most efficient use of the total facilities.

The performance-to-price ratio has been increasing notably in each succeeding generation of equipment. Mass-produced electronic components and batch fabrication methods have enabled the manufacturer to offer greater power per dollar of cost. The key measurement of performance to price has been the number of instructions that can be executed in a specified time period. However, because of the firmware concept and the power of multiprogramming and multiprocessing, instruction execution time is no longer a meaningful performance indicator. The overall execution time of the total application library of a user becomes the significant measurement.

Four major changes in EDP usage have been explored to emphasize the need for a comprehensive short- and long-range plan that puts these changes in proper perspective. Because of the dynamic technology and the burgeoning list of EDP products and services, the planning job is a formidable one. The EDP director must stay abreast of the developments that promise potential for his operation. However, he must not react to the product offerings by seeking change for change's sake or desiring the latest gadget only so that he may appear progressive. The planning process should be based on a careful cost/benefit analysis, the background of the company's over-all goals and objectives, and the information systems that are required to reach them. As one EDP spokesman has stated with considerable insight: "The computer affords us a device to take us where we don't want to be faster than any other device in history." Sound EDP planning must be employed to prevent this possibility.

SUMMARY

The maintenance and modification subphase completes the computer system selection and installation cycle. The important follow-on areas of evaluation, fine tuning, and planning have been explored. The relative pros and cons of outside versus inside evaluation and the key performance and problem areas in an evaluation were listed. An important indicator of the success of an EDP operation is management's evaluation of it—and this was emphasized by referring to various survey reports on the subject. An evaluation checklist of areas requiring improvement and alterations was described. The establishment of a separate maintenance section was explored as well as other methods to enable a computer shop to remain in good working operation.

A discussion of the planning function concluded the chapter. Organizational planning was stressed as well as the development of an application approval cycle. Finally, major EDP changes were categorized under four headings, serving to summarize the user environment and systems needs that must be considered in the plan.

THREE B'S, INC.

Dexter Johnson reflects on the first anniversary of the computer installation. Although it took extra time and expense, the full audit of his operation by a consulting firm proved invaluable, he believed. He considered that the turning point occurred after the consultant's report was submitted. Previously, he was discouraged with the over-all operation and his ability to organize the plan. Management, particularly sales director Paul Peters, production vice president Warren Coolidge, and plant manager Burt Harrison besieged Johnson with complaints and criticisms. The EDP director had president Barrett's support from the beginning, but he thought this was beginning to wane because of the constant harassment he was receiving from the other members of management. Although Johnson realized that there was considerable room for improvement, he knew that he and his group had worked long and hard and he thought it more a case of underestimated resources than of lack of effort or ability.

The consultant's study confirmed Johnson's feelings and served to put the EDP operation back in perspective. The recommendation was for a moratorium on new application development while the operating applications were altered and modified to correct the discrepancies listed on the program difficulty report. It was recommended further that the EDP staff be augmented by at least two people, one assigned permanently to handle maintenance and the other to improve Three B's' capacity to move forward on the planned new applications after the moratorium period.

In two months, the programs were running smoothly and the difficulty report was reduced to one or two small errors. The maintenance experience had enabled most program corrections to be made in a day or two. Previously, corrections had taken up to two weeks. With the addition of a programmer and a competent systems analyst, Johnson was able to show significant progress. He now was devoting full time to managing and directing the department and had time to conduct fre-

quent meetings with the operating managers to ensure that they were satisfied with the computer results. These sessions proved very helpful in gaining management's cooperation and participation in systems development.

The inventory system was up and running and a sales forecasting system had just been put into operation. Furthermore, a good start was made on a production scheduling system and though it was a rather basic approach, it was a major improvement over the previous system. Johnson could see where added features would tighten up the system and make it even more useful. The important thing was that the production people had grown less impatient and were now optimistic about the future. This attitude was becoming infectious.

Surveying the entire picture, Johnson felt that the single most significant accomplishment was the establishment of a company environment in which operating personnel viewed the introduction of the computer with the proper perspective. They were not balking at it any more. Typical of the change in attitude was that displayed by sales administration clerk, Mabel Smith, who had been with Three B's since the company first opened its doors and was responsible for auditing and spot-checking orders and invoice extensions for accuracy and reasonableness. Because of her efficiency she had saved the company a good deal of money in her lengthy tenure. This is the way she spoke of the computer installation to Johnson.

> You know, I'm always one to call a spade, a spade; and I've been skeptical of the computer since you first started talking about it. But I've learned that it really can add just as well as I can. I've been checking its work for the past six months, and it doesn't do half bad. I don't know what I'd do now with the assistant my boss was going to get for me to handle the increasing sales work load. The computer has made life a lot more pleasant for me, as it handles the routine orders, giving me time to focus on the more complicated larger ones—and that's where an error can really cost us.

Dexter Johnson reflected that Mabel in her simple way had stated the real purpose and potential of electronic data processing.

SOURCE MATERIAL AND SUPPLEMENTARY READING

Adams, D. L., "Planning Check List for a Computer Installation," *Datamation* (June, 1967).

Blanchard, B. and E. Lowery, *Maintainability Principles and Practices.* New York: McGraw-Hill, 1969.

Datamation. The June 1969 issue is devoted to the subject of business data processing.

Goldman, A. S. and T. B. Slattery, *Maintainability—A Major Element of System Effectiveness.* New York: John Wiley & Sons, 1964.

McCollum, P., "Computer System Audit," *Marketing Accounting* (May 1969).

McKinsey & Company, Inc., *Unlocking the Computer's Profit Potential.* Research Report for Management, New York, N. Y., 1968.

Pinkney, A., "The Audit Approach to Computers," The Accountant, London, England, (May, 1969).

Research Institute of America, Computers in Business. An RIA survey of users and nonusers. New York, April, 1968.

INDEX